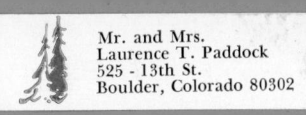

COLORADO RAILROADS

The Alamosa Depot about 1885—Courtesy, Littleton Area Historical Museum

COLORADO RAILROADS

CHRONOLOGICAL DEVELOPMENT

Compiled by Tivis E. (Tiv) Wilkins

PRUETT PUBLISHING COMPANY
BOULDER, COLORADO 80302

© Copyright 1974 Tivis Wilkins

All rights reserved, including those to reproduce this book, or parts thereof, in any form, without permission in writing from the Publisher.

Library of Congress Catalog Card Number: 72-95495
ISBN: 0-87108-073-7

First Edition
1 2 3 4 5 6 7 8 9
Printed in the United States of America

ACKNOWLEDGMENTS

In any work of this kind one must rely on the generosity of many people. One problem in attempting to name every person who contributed in one way or another is the possibility of overlooking someone. Nevertheless my deep appreciation is extended to all who helped, whether named or not.

Special thanks go to the personnel of the following institutions who so cheerfully provided access to their files and who, in some instances, assisted in the search for material: the Colorado State Archives and Records Service, Denver; the Western History Department and the Business Department of the Denver City Library; the Library of the State Historical Society of Colorado; Denver; the Business Library, the Government Documents Library, the Engineering Library, the Law Library, the Geography Department Map Library and the Department of Western Historical Collections, all at the University of Colorado; the Golden Branch of the Jefferson County Library; the Charles Leaming Tutt Library; the Library of the State Historical Society of Colorado, at Colorado Springs; the Greeley Public Library; the Newspaper Department of the Kansas State Historical Society, Topeka; the Longmont Public Library; the Carnegie Library, Trinidad; the Western History Research Center, University of Wyoming, Laramie and the Colorado Railroad Museum and the Pioneer Museum, both at Golden.

I am deeply indebted to the following individuals who generously responded to my requests for specific information and who, in several instances, offered valuable suggestions for content and format: P. A. Briggs, Burlington Northern, Inc. (formerly CB&Q et al), St. Paul, Minn.; Robert W. Richardson and Gordon S. Chappell, Colorado Railroad Museum, Golden; Lloyd J. Hendricks, Boulder; James W. Kelley, Great Western Railway, Denver; Gil Sweet, Santa Fe Railway, Topeka, Kan.; Jackson C. Thode, Rio Grande Railroad, Denver; F. Hol Wagner, Jr., Denver; Patrick Walsh, C&S Railway, Denver; Edward J. Wojtas, Rock Island Railroad, Chicago; and Rich Yates, CF&I Steel Corporation (parent company of C&W Railway), Pueblo.

Others who deserve special thanks are James Kifer who drew many of the maps, Norm Metcalf who assisted with the proof reading, Mrs. Ann Underwood who typed the preliminary and final drafts of the manuscript and especially my wife, Arlie, for her patience during the many years of research and preparation.

Finally, a word of gratitude to Gerald Keenan, Editor, Western and Regional History of Pruett Publishing Company, and his capable staff for their cooperation in the completion of the manuscript and the splendid work in the production of the final product.

CONTENTS

	PREFACE	vii
PART I	EARLY CONSTRUCTION	1
PART II	EXPANSION AND CONSOLIDATION	29
PART III	CHANGE OF PACE	93
PART IV	ABANDONMENTS AND JOINT LINES	195
	NOTES	276
	BIBLIOGRAPHY	285
	INDEX	295

PREFACE

This chronological account of the development of Colorado's railroad system was compiled to provide a unified source of information and to furnish a nucleus for more comprehensive research into the State's railroad history. The primary objective is to show the physical development of the system, although for explanatory purposes occasional reference is made to corporate actions, court decisions and intercompany relationships. The chronological format was adopted to enable the reader to systematically trace the over-all development through the first hundred years and at the same time observe concurrent developments in the construction and abandonments of the different lines. Factual information rather than entertainment is the underlying theme, with a degree of brevity consistent with adequate communication.

The information is presented in a modified outline form showing the name of the railroad, the section of track constructed or abandoned, the gauge and the mileage. This is usually followed by a brief statement of related information. Gauge changes are shown in the construction sections in the years in which they occurred. When the name of a railroad appears for the first time, succeeding names, if any, immediately follow in parentheses. Only major name changes are shown; slight modifications in corporate titles, such as from "Railroad" to "Railway," are considered irrelevant to the purpose of the report. Where a line of road was built under the charter of a subsidiary company but upon completion was leased and operated by the parent company, construction is shown under the name of the parent railroad with appropriate notation in the text. This procedure is also applied where the original construction was financed by a non-railroad company with a lease or title transfer provision. Initials of railroads, or bynames like "Santa Fe," "Rock Island," and "Rio Grande," are frequently used in the explanatory text. Identifying symbols for individual railroads are shown with their names in the index.

Sidings, yard tracks and industrial spurs within terminal or station switching limits are omitted except where they were used at some time as part of a main track. Although stretches of double track existed on main lines at various times, only single track mileage is shown except where the two tracks are separately owned. Government-owned lines are included only when operated under lease or other agreement by a common carrier railroad, in which case the trackage is listed under the specific railroad with an explanatory note. Street railway systems within towns and cities and their immediate environs, including several short steam tramways which ran between Denver and what were then outlying areas, are not reported. However, electric interurban lines are included even though they might have been physically connected and under common ownership with urban lines. Logging railroads are omitted unless operated as a common carrier, primarily because adequate data on their frequently altered routes was not found. This is not to infer that the information does not exist; perhaps through more diligent research it will be uncovered at some future time, either in total or in part.

Specific dates shown for track completions and initial operations might in some instances differ from those given by the railroad company. This can partially be attributed to the company's practice of reporting such dates. A section of road might have been reported complete either on the date the track was ready for traffic, the date on which scheduled operations began or some other date selected by the railroad company, such as the date of an excursion or other event. Railroad companies frequently contracted with construction companies for the building of lines and in some instances the announced completion date was that on which the line was formally accepted from the construction company. Occasionally accommodation trains were operated by the construction company prior to the initiation of service by the railroad company itself.

An explanation of abandonment dates is appropriate also. Prior to 1907 a line of railroad within Colorado could be abandoned simply by decision of the ralroad company, without interference from any state or federal agency. In March 1907 the Colorado State Railroad Commission was created with certain powers over abandonments. However, the authority of that commission was ineffective and in August 1914 it was succeeded by the Public Utilities Commission of Colorado. The PUC was empowered with more authority than its predecessor in the control of abandonments and was the sole regulatory body in Colorado railroad affairs until Congress passed The Transportation Act of 1920. That regulation gave the United States Interstate Commerce Commission control over the abandonment of most lines of railroads engaged in interstate commerce. The authority of ICC has been broadly interpreted to include nearly all abandonments, regardless of whether the lines crossed state borders. This has somewhat abrogated the PUC authority in that function. As a general rule the effective dates given in PUC and ICC decisions are used in the report for abandonments which occurred after the regulatory laws became effective. For prior years reference was made to company records, reports of public agencies or contemporary news items. Occasionally there was a rather long interval between the actual discontinuance of service and the official abandonment date and in a few rare instances revenue trains were operated over a line after it was declared abandoned.

Distances shown in the report might not in all instances be in exact agreement with those in subsequent track records. Changes in station locations, corrected surveys, alignment changes or the omission of fractional track extensions or reductions could account for differences.

The material was compiled from numerous sources, including railroad company reports and records, reports and files of federal and state agencies, books, newspapers, trade publications and unpublished manuscripts. The elusive nature of some of the material and occasional conflicting information were among the difficulties encountered. Every reasonable effort has been made to provide an accurate account but no matter how diligent the research nor how careful the editing, the possibility of error or omission is ever present in any work of this scope. Then, too, there is the danger of taking the wrong track where conflicts in source material occur. Any documented information in regard to inaccurate or incomplete data will be gratefully received.

Boulder, Colorado   Tiv Wilkins
October 1974

EARLY CONSTRUCTION

PART I

Although railway construction had previously gotten underway in Colorado, 1870 was a particularly significant year in the State's railroad history. In that year two railroads were completed to Denver—the Denver Pacific, which connected with Union Pacific's transcontinental railroad at Cheyenne, Wyoming Territory, and the Kansas Pacific which entered Colorado Territory from the east. The year also marked the beginning of the first two railroads to originate in Colorado. The Colorado Central laid a track from Denver as far as Golden and the Denver & Boulder Valley built a line from the present location of Brighton westward toward the Erie coal fields.

Succeeding years of the 1870's witnessed the spread of other railroads within Colorado, although progress was occasionally interrupted by adverse economic factors or competitive frictions. The more accessible coal fields and metal mining areas were usually the immediate goals but more remote destinations were frequently specified in the charters and plans of individual roads. Prominent among the early railroads was the Denver & Rio Grande which was destined to become the most extensive system within Colorado's boundaries. Its 3-foot gauge tracks were an innovation for North American public railroads. Because of the realtive ease and economy of construction the same gauge was adopted for other roads which extended westward into the mountains. The Atchison, Topeka and Santa Fe, the first railroad to connect Southern Colorado with the East, was completed to Pueblo in 1876, several months prior to the admission of Colorado into the Union. Like many other railroads to be built within the State, construction was under the charter of a subsidiary company.

Before the end of the decade two railroads had crossed front ranges of the Rocky Mountains, a second connection with the main line of the Union Pacific was established a short distance west of Cheyenne and the southern boundary of Colorado was crossed by a railroad for the first time. The first major abandonment also occurred during these early years when the operation of an entire railroad was discontinued less than three years after reaching a terminus somewhat short of its original goal.

More than a thousand people assembled near the fairgrounds northeast of Denver on May 18, 1868 to witness the breaking of ground for the *Denver Pacific railroad.* Following an auspicious ceremony the first mile of grade was completed that day. (State Historical Society of Colorado)

Denver Pacific locomotive No. 24, named "Walter Cheesman" for one of the founders of company, was typical of the early motive power used between Denver and Cheyenne.—(State Historical Society of Colorado)

1867

CONSTRUCTION | Miles

UNION PACIFIC

As the Union Pacific was building its transcontinental railroad westward, the tracks crossed the northern boundary of Colorado in the vicinity of present-day Julesburg and continued within the Territory for a distance of nearly nine miles. That short section of track, built in June 1867, was the first railroad construction in Colorado. (sg)[1]

8.9

1868

No track was laid in Colorado during the year although grading got underway for two railroads. The Colorado Central graded about six miles of roadbed from Golden eastward toward Denver, and the Denver Pacific, which was to link Denver with Cheyenne, Wyoming, completed a large part of its grade between those two points.

1869

CONSTRUCTION

DENVER PACIFIC (Union Pacific, 1880)

Colorado-Wyoming boundary to Evans (sg) *48.0*
   This was the first railroad to enter Colorado for the express purpose of serving the Territory. The laying of track began at a connection with the Union Pacific railroad at Cheyenne on September 15. The tracklayers crossed the northern boundary of Colorado about October 4 and reached Evans just north of the South Platte River on December 13. With the completion of additional tracks and a wye on December 17 the line was officially opened for business.

1870

CONSTRUCTION

DENVER PACIFIC

Evans to Denver (sg) *48.2*
   The laying of iron began at the South Platte River bridge at Evans on May 8 and the main track was completed to Denver on June 22. Regular freight and passenger service between Denver and Cheyenne began the following day.

1870 (Cont'd)

KANSAS PACIFIC (Union Pacific, 1880) — *Miles*

Colorado-Kansas boundary westward to a point near present-day Strasburg. (sg) — *155.8*

From a junction with the Denver Pacific tracks north of the Denver city limits as then defined, eastward to a point near Strasburg (sg) — *36.4*

    The Kansas Pacific crossed the boundary of Colorado 17 miles east of Cheyenne Wells early in the year. The track reached Kit Carson in March and after a short pause continued toward Denver. Another construction crew commenced laying track from the junction with the Denver Pacific in early July. The two crews met August 15 at Comanche Crossing, a short distance east of the present location of Strasburg, thus completing a continuous chain of railroads across the United States.[2] A train from the east entered Denver the day the track was completed and on September 1 through service was inaugurated between Denver and Kansas City, Missouri.

From the junction with the Denver Pacific north of Denver to the Denver station. (sg) — *2.0*

    This section of track was completed on October 3.

COLORADO CENTRAL (Union Pacific Denver & Gulf, 1890; Colorado & Southern, 1899)

From a connection with the Denver Pacific at Jersey Junction, westerly to Golden. (sg) — *14.7*

    Jersey Junction was opposite the Denver Pacific-Kansas Pacific junction north of Denver, known as Kansas Pacific (or KP) Junction, later named Pullman. The rails reached Golden September 22 and completion ceremonies were held four days later.

DENVER & BOULDER VALLEY (Union Pacific, 1898)

From the Denver Pacific tracks at Hughes (now Brighton) to the present location of Dick. (sg) — *7.2*

    This was the beginning of a line extending west from the Denver Pacific tracks to the Erie coal fields and later to Boulder. It was operated under its own corporate name by the DP until September 1879, by the KP to February 1880 and thereafter by the UP.

Total — *264.3*

1871

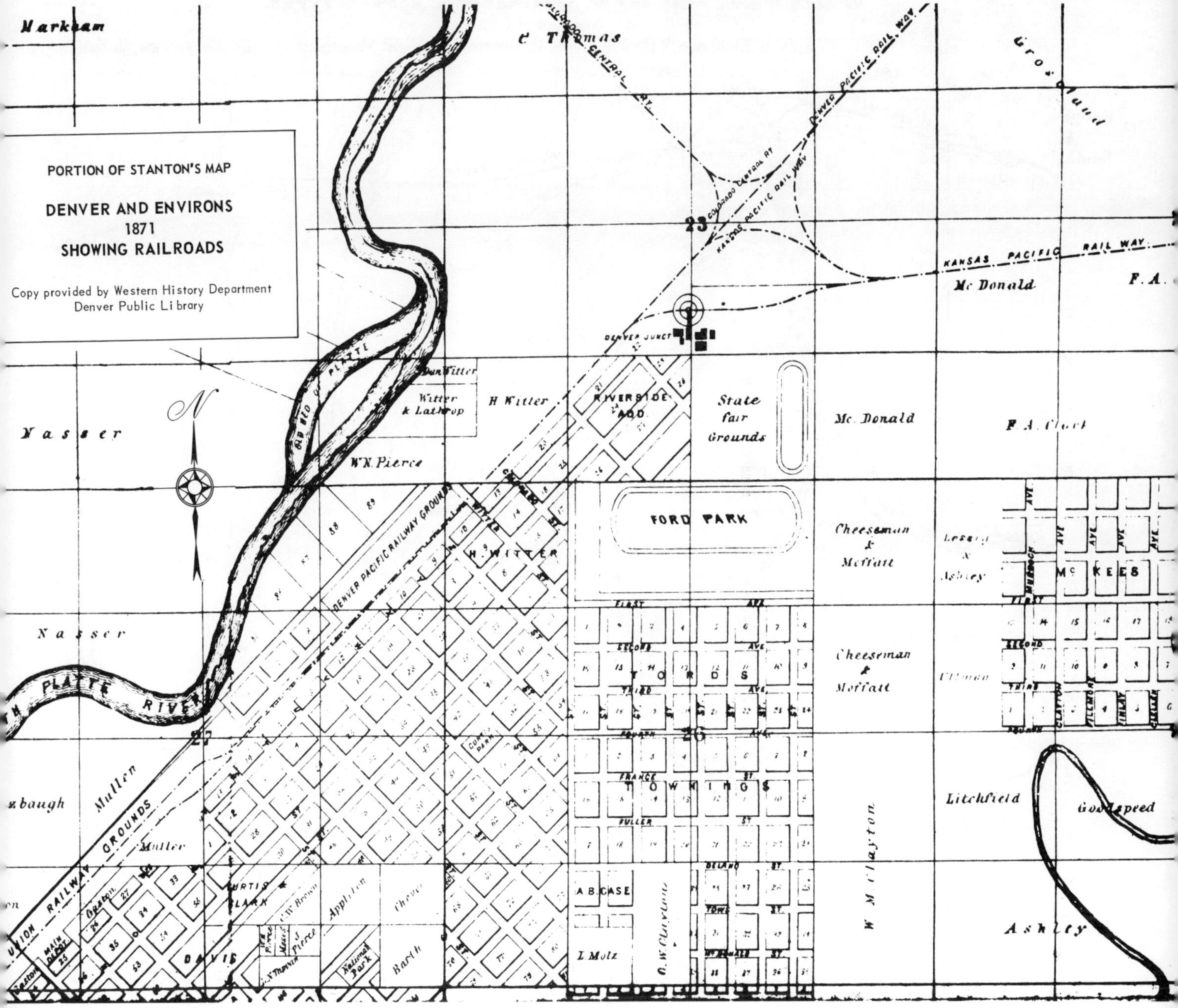
PORTION OF STANTON'S MAP
DENVER AND ENVIRONS
1871
SHOWING RAILROADS
Copy provided by Western History Department
Denver Public Library
KANSAS PACIFIC RAIL WAY
DENVER PACIFIC RAILWAY GROUNDS
UNION RAILWAY GROUNDS
RIVERSIDE ADD.
State fair Grounds
FORD PARK
Mc Donald
Cheeseman & Moffatt
Litchfield
Ashley
W. M. Clayton
A.B. CASE
Nasser
Markham
Mullen
DENVER JUNCT.
DAVIS
CURTIS & CLARK
Appleton
Barth
I. Molz
G.W. Clayton
Goodspeed
FIRST AVE
SECOND AVE
THIRD AVE
FOURTH AVE
FRANCE ST
FULLER ST
W.N. Pierce
H Witter
H. WITTER
Witter & Lathrop
Mc KEES

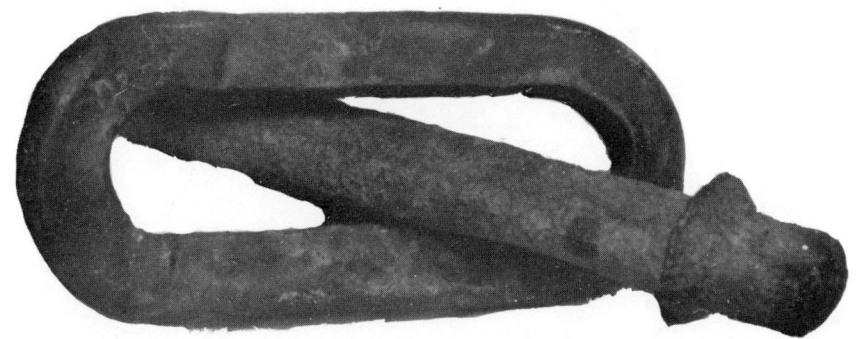

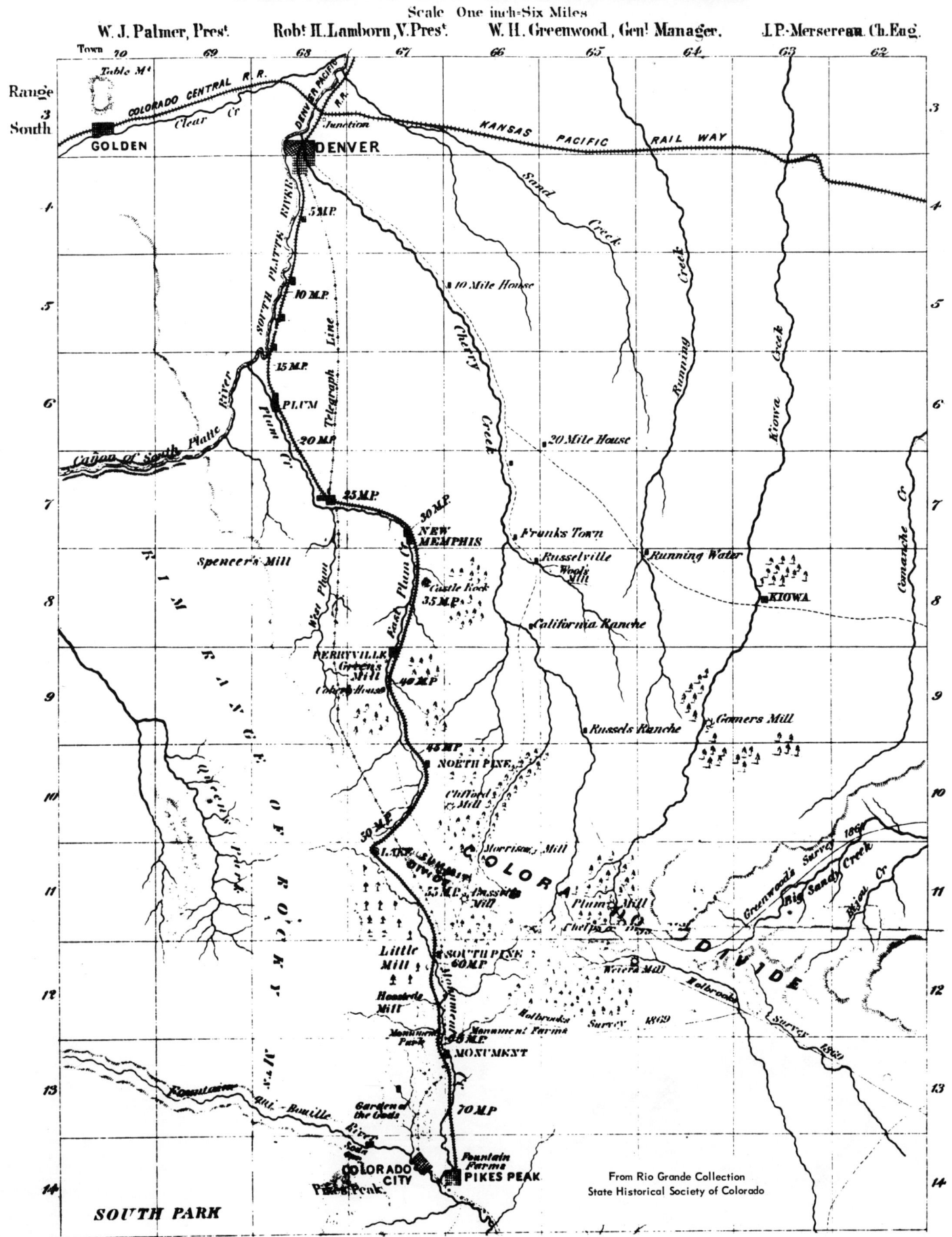

1871

CONSTRUCTION | Miles

DENVER & BOULDER VALLEY

Dick to Erie (sg) | 7.2
   On January 14 the rails reached Erie, which was the western terminus for more than two years.

DENVER & RIO GRANDE (Denver & Rio Grande Western, 1921)

Denver south to Colorado Springs (ng)[3] | 75.5
   The track was completed to the new town of Colorado Springs on October 21 and a special train for newsmen on October 26-27 marked the official opening. Regular service began on January 1, 1872, the date of acceptance from the construction company. The D&RG was the first railroad in Colorado to adopt narrow gauge trackage and its 3-foot gauge was among the very first of that measurement in North America. It was to become the most extensive railroad system in the state.

Total | 82.7

1872

CONSTRUCTION

DENVER & RIO GRANDE

Colorado Springs to South Pueblo (ng) | 44.1
   The track layers reached Pueblo June 15 and the line was extended to South Pueblo on August 1.
South Pueblo west to Labran (later Florence) (ng) | 32.8
   Following the Arkansas River west from Pueblo, the track was completed to Labran on October 15.
Labran south to coal banks (Coal Creek) (ng) | 2.6
   This short segment was completed to the coal banks on October 27. It was built under the charter of a subsidiary, the Canon Coal Railway Company, which was merged with D&RG in 1878.

COLORADO CENTRAL

From Golden west up Clear Creek Canon to Forks Creek (ng) | 13.2
   This initial section of the first railroad to penetrate the mountains of Colorado was completed to Forks Creek on August 31 and on the following day an excursion train passed over the road.

Building south toward Colorado Springs the rails of the *Denver & Rio Grande* reached the divide between drainage areas of the South Platte and Arkansas Rivers in mid-September 1871. A station established there was originally named Divide but later changed to Palmer Lake.—(State Historical Society of Colorado)

1872 (Cont'd)

	Miles
From Forks Creek northwesterly to the end of track at Black Hawk (ng)	7.2

On December 11 the track was completed to the eastern edge of Black Hawk where a temporary station was established. Train operations to that point began on December 15.

Standard gauge to dual gauge[4]—Golden east to Arapahoe (later Golden Junction)

A third rail was added to the standard gauge track east from Golden to Arapahoe, a distance of two miles. From that point a roadbed was being graded northward for a standard gauge railroad which was to connect with the Union Pacific at Julesburg.[5] According to contemporary news reports[6] it was planned to extend the narrow gauge rails from Arapahoe northward on that roadbed to a point opposite the Murphy Coal Mine, located on Ralston Creek three miles west of the grade. A search of available railroad records and newspapers failed to reveal that any narrow gauge rails were laid north of Arapahoe.

	Miles
Total	99.9

Compliments of C.W. Tenney Jan 9th, 1928.
Div 161 B. of L.E. San Francisco

Denver and Rio Grande Railway.

TIME TABLE, No. 7,

To take effect Monday, July 15, 1872, at 6 o'clock A. M.

For the Government and Information of Employees only.

GOING SOUTH.			Telegraph Calls	NAMES OF Stations.	Distance from Denver	No. of Stations	GOING NORTH.		
Way Freight No. 5	Thro. Freight No. 3	Express No. 1					Express No. 2	Thro. Freight No. 4	Way Freight No. 6
Le. 3.45 P.M.	Le. 6.15 A.M.	Le. 8.15 A.M.	Bo.	.0....DENVER....	.0	0	Ar. 5.30 P.M.	Ar. 6.00 P.M.	Ar 12.45 P.M.
4.00 "	6.30 "	8.35 "	Ms.	2.2...M'C'E SHOPS..	2.2		5.20 "	5.45 "	12.30 P.M.
4.50 "	7.20 "	8.55 "	X.	8.4..LITTLETON..	10.6	4	*4.50* "	*4.50* "	11.45 A.M.
5.30 "	8.05 "	9.20 "	2.	6.9....ACEQUIA...	17.5	6	4.25 "	4.05 "	11.10 "
6.10 "	8.48 "	9.45 "	U.	7.2.....PLUM.....	24.7	8	3.57 "	3.18 "	10.30 "
6.29 "	8.55 "	9.50 "		1.2..MILL No. 1..	25.9		3.52 "	3.10 "	10.22 "
6.45 "	9.15 "	*10.02* "		3.2..MILL No. 2..	29.1	9	3.41 "	2.45 "	*10.02* "
6.55 "	*9.25* "	10.08 "	C.	1.7...CITADEL...	30.8	10	3.35 "	2.30 "	*9.25* "
7.22 "	9.53 "	10.24 "	K.	4.6...DOUGLASS..	35.4	11	3.18 "	2.07 "	8.55 "
7.53 "	10.24 "	10.42 "		5.1 ROCK SWITCH	40.5	12	3.00 "	1.40 "	8.20 "
8.10 "	*10.55* "	*10.55* "	Z.	2.8..LARKSPUR..	43.3	13	2.50 "	1.25 "	8.00 "
8.20 "	11.05 "	11.00 "		1.5..PINELAND..	44.8	14	2.40 "	1.05 "	7.40 "
8.34 "	11.22 "	11.08 "		2.3.GREENLAND.	47.1	15	2.32 "	12.52 "	7.28 "
Ar. 9.05 "	Ar. *12.02* P.M.*	11.27 "	Di	5.3.....DIVIDE.....	52.4	16	2.13 "	Le. 12.25 "	Le. 7.00 A.M.
	Le. 12.30 "							Ar. *12.02* "	
	12.50 "	*11.40* "	H.	3.6...HENRY'S...	56.	17	2.00 "	*11.20* A.M.	
	1.02 "	11.48 "		2. ...BORST'S...	58.	18	1.52 "	11.20 "	
	1.14 "	11.55 "		1.9 SOUTHWATER	59.9		1.45 "	11.08 "	
	1.37 "	12.03 "		2.1..HUSTED'S..	62.	20	*1.37* "	10.55 "	
	2.07 "	12.20 "	Mn	5. .MONUMENT..	67.	21	1.20 "	10.23 "	
	2.55 "	Ar. 12.50 "	Cs	8.2 COL. SPRINGS	75.2	22	Le. 12.50 "	9.38 "	
		Le. 1.40 "					Ar. 12.00 M.*		
	3.40 "	2.11 "	W.	8.8..WIDEFIELD..	84.	23	11.30 A.M.	8.54 "	
	4.04 "	2.28 "	Fn.	4.7..FOUNTAIN..	88.7	24	11.13 "	8.30 "	
	4.37 "	2.48 "	Bu.	5.6 LITTLE BUTES	94.3	25	10.53 "	7.57 "	
	4.51 "	2.58 "	G.	2.7...WIGWAM...	97.	26	10.43 "	7.43 "	
	5.35 "	3.30 "	On	8.8....PIÑON....	105.8	27	10.12 "	6.59 "	
	Ar. 6.35 "	Ar. 4.15 "	J.	11.5...PUEBLO...	117.5	30	Le. 9.30 A.M.	Le. 6.00 A.M.	

*Figures in heavy type denote meeting and passing points. *Stop for Dinner.*
The time on this Card, at all Stations, except at terminus of Train run, is leaving time, unless arriving and leaving time are both given.
The clock in the Office of Division Superintendent, in Denver will be the standard time. All Engineers and Train Men must compare their watches before starting. Trains Nos. 1 and 2 will run daily. Trains Nos. 3, 4, and 5 will run daily, except Sunday. Train No. 6 will run daily, except Monday.

W H GREENWOOD,
General Manager and Superintendent.

W. W. BORST,
Division Superintendent.

In this early photo of Forks Creek Colorado Central engine No. 2 is at the head of a train arriving from Floyd Hill. The track on the right follows the north fork of Clear Creek to Black Hawk.— (Denver Public Library, Western History Department)

1873

CONSTRUCTION | Miles

ATCHISON TOPEKA & SANTA FE

From the eastern boundary of Colorado to Granada[7] (sg) | 10.8
    This was an extension of the main line of the Santa Fe which reached the Colorado state line early in the year. Construction in Colorado was under the charter of a subsidiary, the Colorado & New Mexico Railroad Company. After completing the first railroad bridge across the Arkansas River in Colorado in late June, the last rail was spiked down at Granada on July 4. The end of the track remained there until May 1875.

ARKANSAS VALLEY

From the Kansas Pacific tracks at Kit Carson, south to West Las Animas[8] (later Las Animas) (sg) | 56.0
    This was a KP controlled railroad with Pueblo as its objective and a later projection to Trinidad and beyond. It never reached either of those proposed destinations. The rails reached the site of West Las Animas around the middle of October.

COLORADO CENTRAL

From Forks Creek westerly up Clear Creek Canon to Floyd Hill (ng) | 3.3
    The track was completed about March 1 and placed in operation March 19. The end of track remained there for more than four years.

From a connection with the Denver-Golden line at Arapahoe, northerly to Longmont (sg) | 39.2
    The track followed a rather circuitous route via Boulder, reaching Longmont on April 17. Upon completion the connection point at Arapahoe was renamed Golden Junction.

Longmont eastward to the Weld County line (sg) | 2.5
    This extension was in the direction of Greeley on the route projected to Julesburg. Although a large part of the line had been graded,[9] no rails were laid beyond that point. Instead, a connection was later made with the UP a short distance west of Cheyenne (see 1877).

DENVER & BOULDER VALLEY

Extended west from Erie to Boulder (sg) | 11.6
    The extension was completed during the second week of Sep-

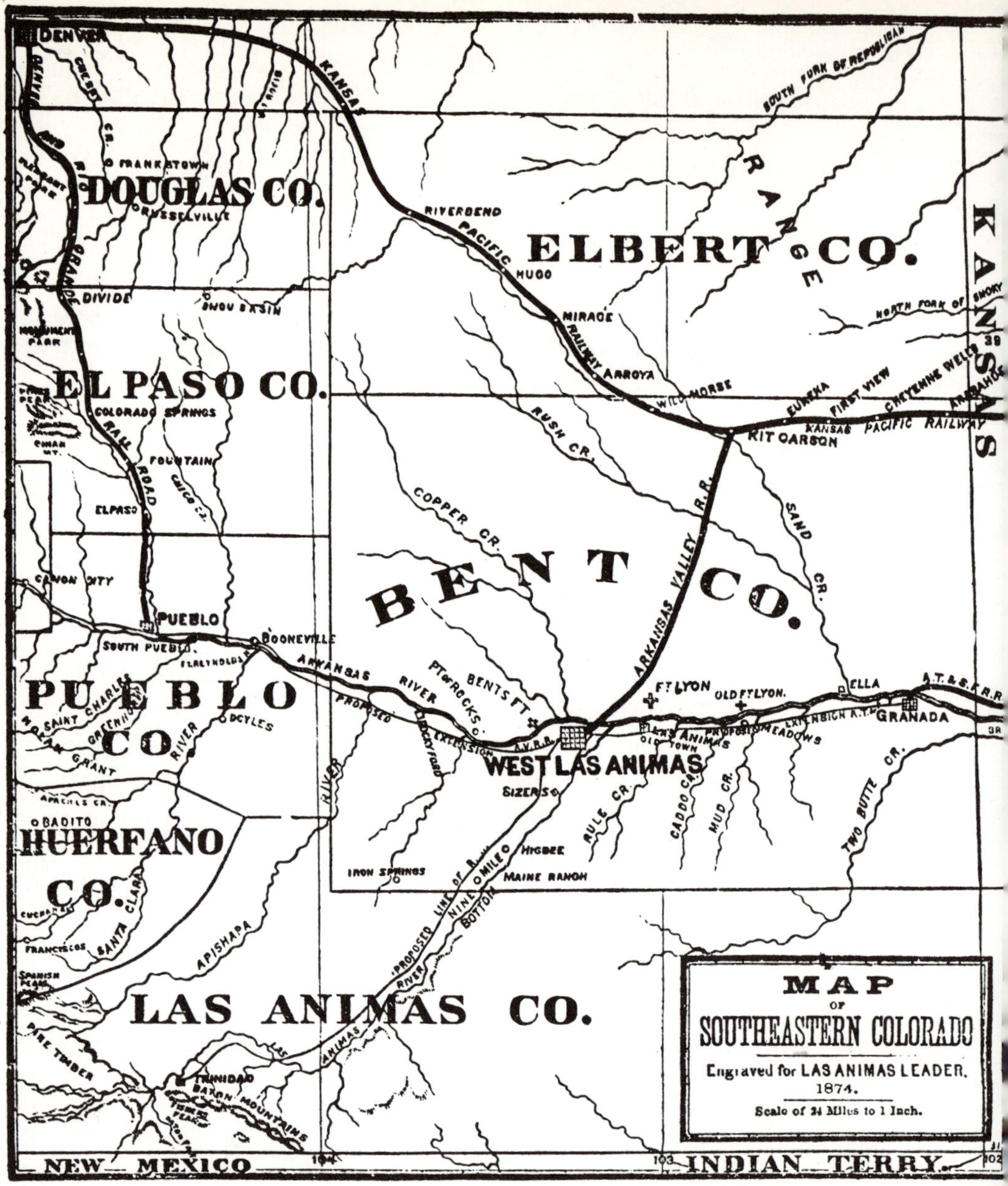

Existing railroads and proposed extensions in Southeastern Colorado are shown on this map which appeared on the front page of the Las Animas Leader on April 24, 1874.—(State Historical Society of Colorado)

1873 (Cont'd)

tember and regular trains commenced running on the line on the 17th day of the month.

	Miles
Total	123.4

1874

CONSTRUCTION — Miles

DENVER & RIO GRANDE

Extended from Labran to Canon City (ng) — 8.4
The completion date for this extension was July 6.

DENVER SOUTH PARK & PACIFIC (Denver, Leadville & Gunnison, 1889; Colorado & Southern, 1899)

Denver south to Bear Creek Junction (later Sheridan Junction) (ng) — 6.7
Bear Creek Junction west to Morrison (ng) — 9.7
  This was the beginning of a narrow gauge railroad which would later cross five mountain passes to reach the South Park, Gunnison and Leadville mining areas. The line was completed to Morrison with the installation of the last switches on June 23. An excursion from Denver ran to Morrison June 26 and the line was officially placed in operation July 1.

COLORADO CENTRAL

From Cut-Off Junction on the Denver-Golden line, south to a new Denver terminal near 16th and Delgany Streets. (sg) — 3.4
  Colorado Central previously used DP tracks between Jersey Junction and Denver. After completion of the new route in early November the section between Cut-Off Junction and Jersey Junction became known as Jersey Cut-Off.

	Miles
Total	28.2

ABANDONMENT

COLORADO CENTRAL

Longmont to Weld County line (sg) — 2.5
  This was the extension constructed the previous year in the direction of Greeley. It was the first main line track abandonment in Colorado.

1875

CONSTRUCTION | Miles

ATCHISON TOPEKA & SANTA FE

From the end of track at Granada, west to a point near the present town of Rocky Ford[10] (sg) — 84.2

> Built by another subsidiary of the Santa Fe, the Pueblo & Arkansas Valley Railroad Company which absorbed the Colorado & New Mexico Railroad Company shortly before construction of this section was started.

ARKANSAS VALLEY

From West Las Animas to Timpas Creek, a short distance west of present-day Swink (sg) — 24.0

> The last 19 miles followed close alongside the Santa Fe tracks. It was completed in December but trains were operated only as far as La Junta, 5 to 6 miles east of the end of the track.

Total — 108.2

1876

CONSTRUCTION

ATCHISON TOPEKA & SANTA FE

Rocky Ford to Pueblo (sg) — 55.7

> The track was completed to the depot grounds at Second and Court Streets in Pueblo on February 29. The first passenger train arrived on the same date and its departure the following morning marked the beginning of regular service between Pueblo and eastern points.

DENVER & RIO GRANDE

From Pueblo south to Cucharas (Cuchara Junction) (ng) — 49.8
> On February 22 the tracklayers reached Cucharas. There the line branched into two sections.

Cucharas southeasterly to El Moro (ng) — 37.0
> The immediate goal of this section was the coal fields in the Trinidad area but the basic plan of the company called for a line across Raton Pass into New Mexico and beyond. The rails reached the railroad company's new town of El Moro on April 6 and passenger service between that point and Denver was inaugurated April 22.

1876 (Cont'd)

Unballasted D&RG track at Francisco Plaza at La Veta, probably on or soon after August 1, 1876. The two poles were used for flags of opposing political parties on the day Colorado was admitted to the Union.
—(State Historical Society of Colorado)

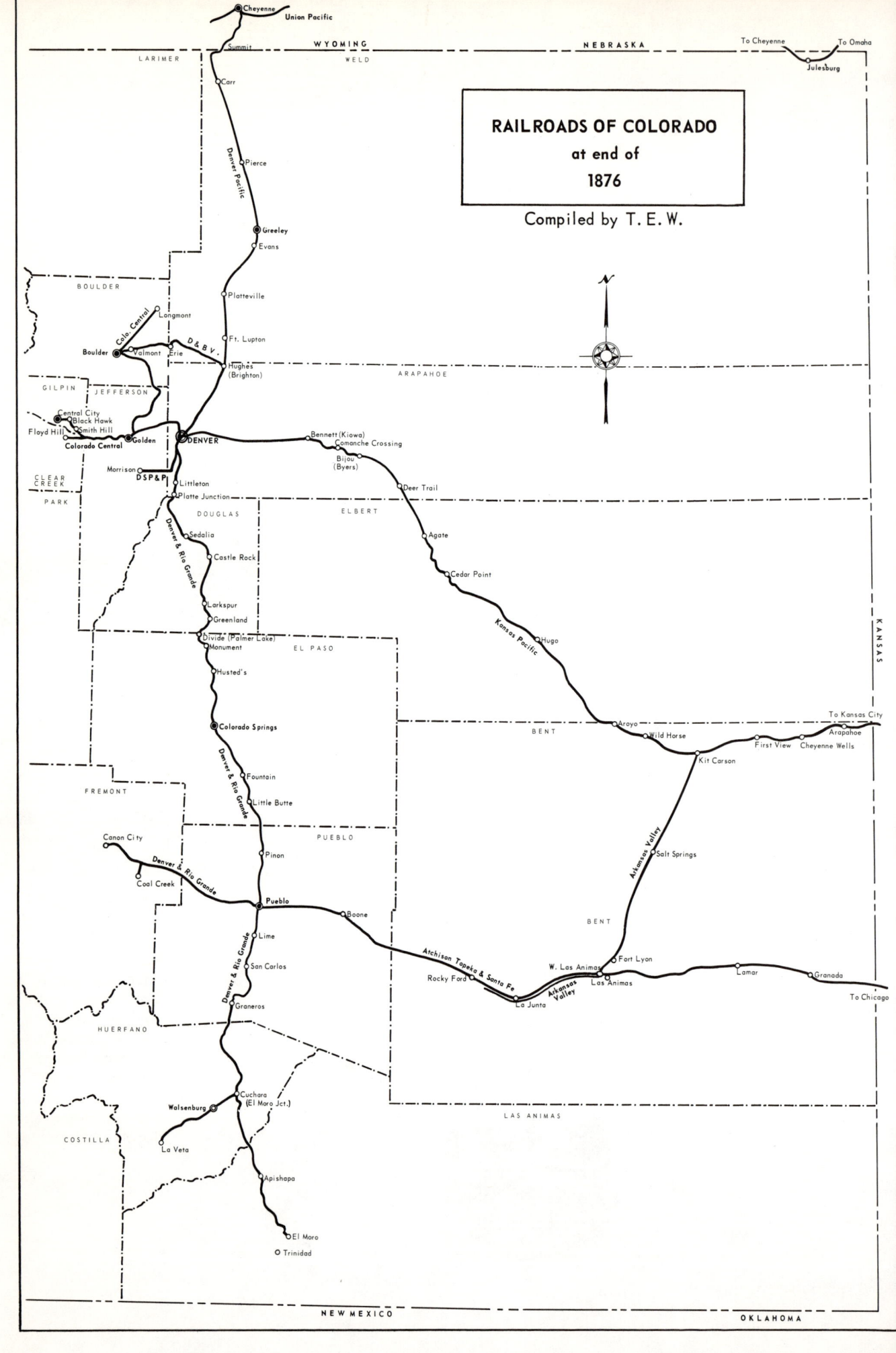

☛ DESTROY PREVIOUS SCHEDULES ☚

Colorado Central Rail Road!

TIME SCHEDULE NO. 25,

To take effect **Monday, October, 26th, 1874**, at 6 o'clock, A. M.

For the Government and Information of Employes only. The Company reserves the right to vary therefrom at pleasure.

DENVER BRANCH.

BOUND WEST.						BOUND EAST.		
No. 7. GOLDEN Accommodat'n Daily.	**No. 3.** EXPRESS. Daily.	**No. 1.** EXPRESS AND MAIL. Daily.	Distance from Denver.	Names OF Stations.	Distance from Golden.	**No. 2.** EXPRESS. Daily.	**No. 4.** EXPRESS AND MAIL. Daily.	**No. 8.** GOLDEN Accommodation Daily.
5:05 p. m. lv.	3:05 p. m. lv.	9:20 a. m. lv.	0	DENVER.	17	11:00 ar.	4:45 ar.	9:09 ar.
5:15	3:15	9:30	2	DENVER JUNCTION.	15	10:50	4:35	8:50
5:43	3:43	9:55	9	ARVADA.	8	10:30	4:15	8:25
6:05	**4:00 Mt L.**	**10:15 Mt L.**	15	GOLDEN JUNCTION.	2	**10:15 Mt L.**	**4:00 Mt L.**	8:10
6:15 ar.	4:20 ar.	10:25 ar.	17	GOLDEN.	0	10:00 a. m. lv.	3:50 p. m. lv.	8:00 a. m. lv.

MOUNTAIN DIVISION.

BOUND WEST.						BOUND EAST.		
No. 5. MIXED. Daily.	**No. 3.** EXPRESS. Daily.	**No. 1.** EXPRESS AND MAIL. Daily.	Distance from Golden.	Stations.	Distance from Black Hawk.	**No. 2.** EXPRESS. Daily.	**No. 4.** EXPRESS AND MAIL. Daily.	**No. 6.** MIXED. Daily.
10:40 a. m. lv.	4:25 p. m. lv.	10:30 a. m. lv.	0	GOLDEN.	21	9:55 ar.	3:45 ar.	3:35 ar.
11:05	4:45	10:50	3-2	CHIMNEY GULCH.	17-8	9:37	3:27	3:17
11:27	5:04	11:10	6-2	GUY GULCH.	14-8	9:19	3:09	2:59
11:39	5:17	11:23	8	BEAVER BROOK.	13	9:06	2:56	2:48
11:49	5:28	11:34	9	ELK CREEK.	12	8:55	2:45	2:37
12:14 p. m.	5:48	11:54	12-5	BIG HILL.	8-5	8:35	2:25	2:17
12:21	5:55	12:01 p. m.	13-5	FORKS CREEK. (Junc.)	7-5	8:28	2:18	2:10
12:50 ar.			17-5	FLOYD HILL. *Georgetown Branch*	11-5			1:45 p. m. lv.
	6:13	12:19	16	COTTONWOOD.	5	8:11	2:01	
	6:31	12:39	18	SMITH HILL.	3	7:53	1:43	
	6:50 ar.	1:00 ar.	21	BLACK HAWK.	0	7:35 a. m. lv.	1:25 p. m. lv.	

EASTERN DIVISION.

BOUND EAST					BOUND WEST.
No. 10. EXPRESS AND MAIL. Daily. Except Sunday.	Distance from Golden.	Stations.	Distance from Longmont.	**No. 9.** EXPRESS AND MAIL. Daily. Except Sunday.	
3:50 p. m. lv.	0	GOLDEN.	41-2	10:25 ar.	
4:05	2	GOLDEN JUNCTION.	39-2	10:15	
4:20	5	RALSTON.	36-2	9:55	
4:45	11-6	CHURCHS.	29-6	9:25	
5:07	20-1	COAL CREEK.	21-1	9:00	
5:17	22	DAVIDSON.	19-2	8:50	
5:30	26	LAKE SIDE.	15-2	8:30	
5:45	28-5	BOULDER.	12-7	8:20	
6:05	35-4	NI-WOT.	5-8	7:55	
6:20 ar.	41-2	LONGMONT.	0	7:40 a. m. lv.	

SPECIAL RULE No. 1.—Full faced figures indicate the meeting and passing points.
SPECIAL RULE No. 2.—Study Rules well, and know that you understand them. Important changes have been made.
SPECIAL RULE 3.—The habitual use of intoxicating liquors will be considered just cause of dismissal from the service of the Company.
☛ All Trains or Locomotives must come to a **Full Stop** before crossing the Denver and Boulder Valley Rail Road at Boulder, and Enginemen must know that the Track is clear before proceeding.

D. F. CARMICHAEL, G. T. A.   **I. L. OVERTON, Supt.**

(Opposite page) Colorado was admitted to statehood August 1, 1876. At the end of that year there were 930 miles of main line railroad in the state, consisting of 671 miles of standard gauge track, 257 miles of narrow gauge and 2 miles of dual gauge.

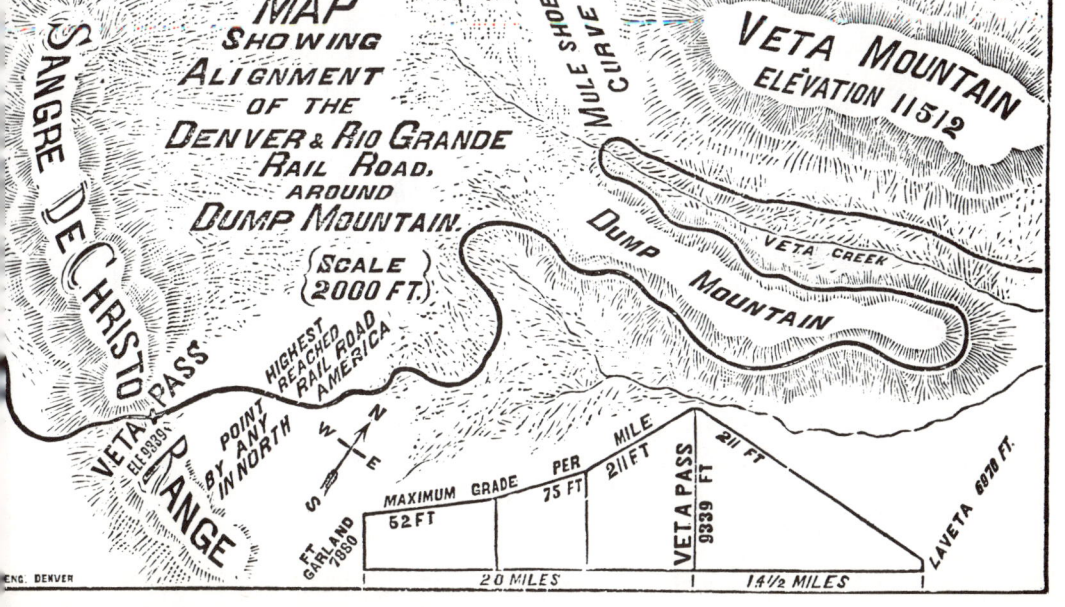

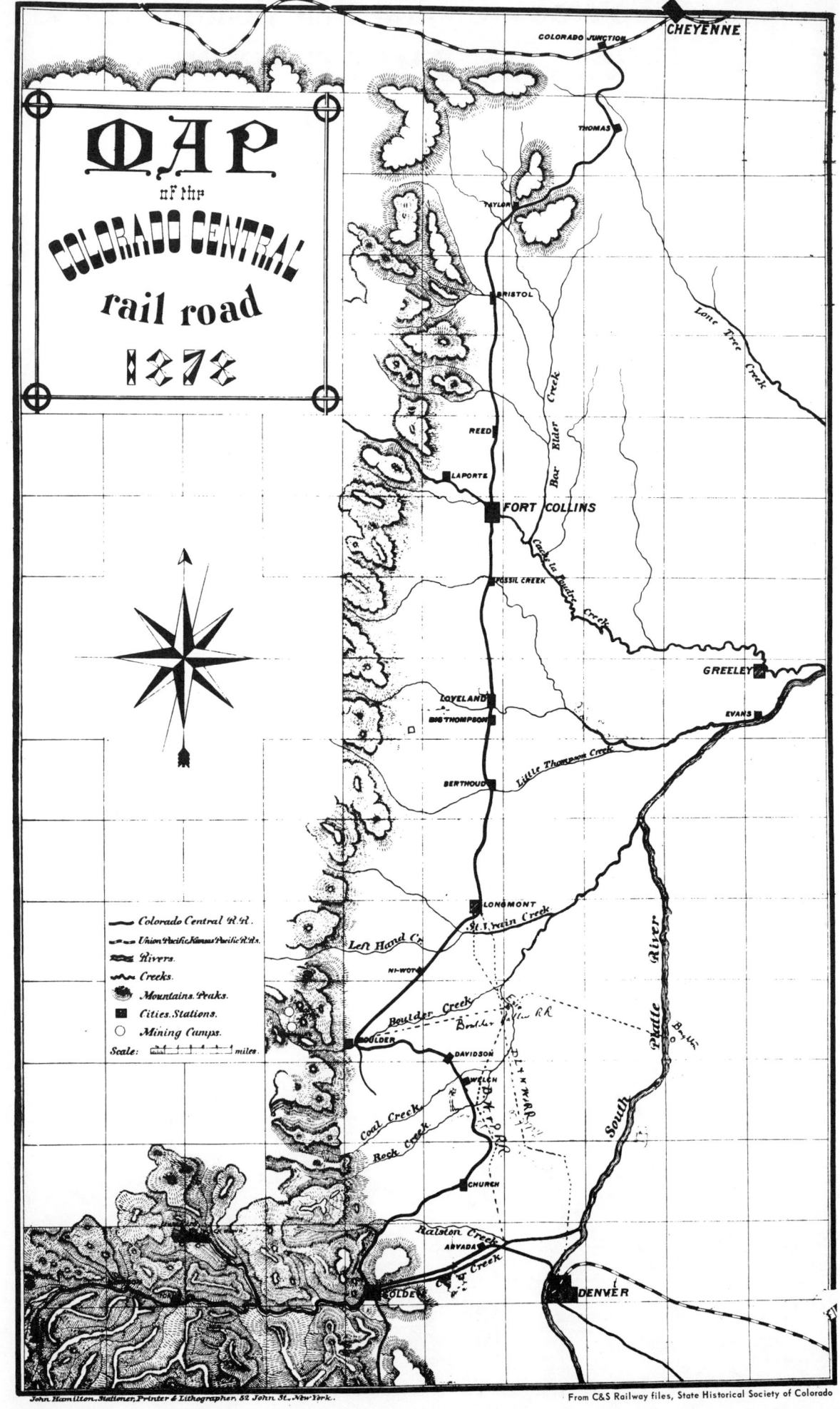

1876 (Cont'd)

Miles

El Moro to Coal Junction, thence to Anderson's Mine (ng) — 4.8
This extension was completed and open for business on June 15.

Cucharas southwest to La Veta (ng) — 21.6
This was the beginning of a D&RG line which would extend into the San Luis Valley and across the Continental Divide to the San Juan mining region. The laying of track was discontinued at La Veta on July 1 and was not resumed until May of the following year.

Total — 168.9

1877

CONSTRUCTION

COLORADO CENTRAL

From the Colorado-Wyoming boundary southward via Fort Collins to Longmont (sg) — 64.5

This was a continuation of a line which connected with the UP at Hazard, Wyoming, six miles west of Cheyenne. The Wyoming segment was incorporated under the name Colorado Central Rail Road (Wyoming). Grading began from both ends of the extension but the rails were laid from the north, crossing the Poudre River into Fort Collins September 26 and reaching Longmont November 4.

Clear Creek line extended from Floyd Hill to Georgetown (ng) — 18.0
The first train reached the northern outskirt of Georgetown on August 1 but because of uncompleted bridges it was August 13 before the first train ran to the depot. The terminus remained at Georegtown for six and a half years.

DENVER & RIO GRANDE

From the end of the track at La Veta, across the Sangre de Cristo range of the Rocky Mountains to Garland City.[11] (ng) — 28.6

The mountains were crossed via Veta Pass at 9,390 ft. altitude, which at the time was the highest point reached by any railroad in the United States but only the first of several altitude records to be established in the development of Colorado's railroad system. The tracklaying gang completed the line to Garland City July 1.

Coal Junction to El Moro Mines (Engleville) (ng) — 2.7
This extension to the mines was completed July 10. Engleville station was later established at that point.

This depot at Fort Collins was built by the *Colorado Central* in 1877. The photograph was taken in 1892 at which time the railroad was operated by the *Union Pacific, Denver & Gulf.*—(State Historical Society of Colorado)

Unloading rock from a D&RG work train on Muleshoe Curve, east of the summit of Veta Pass. This famous curve was an interesting engineering achievement on the line between La Veta and Fort Garland.—(W. H. Jackson Photo—State Historical Society of Colorado)

A D&RG track crew at the summit of Veta Pass.—(State Historical Society of Colorado)

1877 (Cont'd)

GOLDEN BOULDER & CARIBOU

	Miles
From a point near the Colorado Central depot at Boulder, southward toward the Marshall coal banks (sg)	2.0
Total	115.8

ABANDONMENTS

ARKANSAS VALLEY

	Miles
Entire line from Kit Carson to end of track at Timpas Creek (sg)	80.0

Dismantling was started by the Kansas Pacific, the parent company, the following year. It was the first major railroad abandonment in Colorado and remained the State's largest single abandonment for more than 40 years.

DENVER & RIO GRANDE

Coal Junction to Anderson's Mine (ng)	0.7
Total	80.7

1878

CONSTRUCTION

ATCHISON TOPEKA & SANTA FE

From La Junta southwest to Trinidad, thence to the Colorado state line at Raton Pass (sg)	96.2

The track reached the summit of Raton Pass December 7 and continued into New Mexico. Control of the pass was gained by locating the route and initiating preliminary construction a few hours ahead of the arrival of a D&RG construction crew.[12] The pass was first crossed via a series of switchbacks near the summit but these were eliminated after the completion of a tunnel the following year.

COLORADO CENTRAL

From Golden around the west side of north Table Mountain, thence north and east to a connection with the Golden-Cheyenne line at Leyden Gulch north of Ralston Creek (sg)	7.8

The rails of the main line between Golden Junction and Leyden Gulch on the east side of North Table Mountain were taken up

An excursion train for newspaper and magazine editors stopped in the AT&SF yards at Trinidad for water on October 27, 1882 before starting its climb over Raton Pass.—(State Historical Society of Colorado)

This early AT&SF depot at Trinidad collapsed during a 1904 flood when the Purgatoire River (foreground) cut through the bank and undermined the structure. (Aultman Collection, State Hist. Society of Colo.)

The present Santa Fe depot at Trinidad was built in 1960 a short distance west of its predecessor. The older facilities were then demolished.—(Author's Collection)

1878 (Cont'd)

Miles

and immediately placed on the roadbed of this new line. The transfer began February 23 and was completed two days later. All traffic between Golden and Cheyenne was discontinued while the work was in progress.[13]

Clear Creek line extended through Black Hawk (ng) — *0.5*

Black Hawk to Central City (ng) — *3.7*

Completion of the extension was celebrated at Central City on May 22, the date of arrival of the first train. The air line distance between the two stations was slightly over one mile but the difference in altitude was nearly 500 feet. A long switchback was employed to overcome the steep grade.

Standard gauge to dual gauge—From Golden to a point near Dry Creek (now Van Bibber Creek), a small stream north of Golden. The third rail was added after the standard gauge track was laid to accommodate traffic originating on a narrow gauge line to the Murphy coal mines. (See Golden & Ralston below.)

GOLDEN & RALSTON

From a connection with the Colorado Central near Dry Creek to Murphy Coal Mine (ng) — *2.0*

Trains used the dual gauge track of the Colorado Central between Dry Creek and Golden. This railroad, sometimes referred to as the "Knox Railroad," was opened for traffic about the third week of March.

DENVER & RIO GRANDE

Garland City west to Alamosa (ng) — *30.6*

The tracklayers reached the depot site of the newly established town of Alamosa on June 26 and the first passenger train arrived the following day. The completion of the line was celebrated with an excursion from Colorado Springs on July 4.

DENVER SOUTH PARK & PACIFIC

From the original depot at Denver to the Denver Union Terminal (ng) — *0.9*

Garfield Quarry Spur—from Morrison north to Garfield Quarry (ng) — *2.8*

Soda Lakes Spur—from a point one-half mile east of Morrison, south to Soda Lakes (ng) — *0.3*

Bear Creek Junction to Webster (ng) — *62.0*

This was the first segment of what was to become the main line to South Park and beyond. The tracklayers reached Webster

A view of Morrison around 1890. Railroad facilities and equipment are seen in the center of the photo.—(State Historical Society of Colorado)

This structure has been identified as an early D&RG depot at Alamosa, evidently built about 1885. It is known that there was a one-story frame depot there as late as 1884. No photographs are known to exist for the earlier structure unless it is the single-story section in this photograph. The two-story section was gutted by fire on December 17, 1887.—(State Historical Society of Colorado)

A new depot was built at Alamosa in 1888. It too was destroyed by fire, on Christmas Day 1907. (See title page). The original section of the present depot was built in 1909. A two-story addition was completed at the rear (north) of the head house in March 1945.—(O. T. Davis Photo, State Hist. Society of Colo.)

The Alamosa depot as it appeared in 1966.—(Lloyd Hendricks photo)

1878 (Cont'd)

near the end of the year and the line was placed in operation to that place in January 1879.

GOLDEN BOULDER & CARIBOU

From the railhead south of Boulder to the Marshall coal banks (sg) — 3.4
  The last rail was spiked down at Marshall about January 10 but the line was not placed in service until a month later.

Total — 210.2

ABANDONMENT

COLORADO CENTRAL

Golden Junction to Leyden Gulch via the east side of North Table Mountain (sg) — 4.7
  Operations had been transferred to the new line around the west side of the mountain.

1879

CONSTRUCTION

ATCHISON TOPEKA & SANTA FE

From Canon City through Royal Gorge to a point near Texas Creek (ng) — 22.3
  Construction was by two subsidiary companies, the Canon City & San Juan, which started the construction work, and the Pueblo & Arkansas Valley, which absorbed the former company and completed the line on June 16. The trackage was later conveyed to the D&RG in settlement of a dispute over the route through the Royal Gorge.[14]

COLORADO CENTRAL

Standard gauge to dual gauge—Denver to Golden Junction
  The completion of this conversion to the Denver passenger depot on December 4 provided a continuous route for narrow gauge trains between Denver and the Clear Creek mining district.

This photo of a Santa Fe work train near the west end of Royal Gorge in 1879 appeared in a book entitled "Our Indian Summer in the Far West" by S. Nugent Townshend, printed in London in 1880.—(Denver Public Library, Western History Department)

An 1879 photo showing parts of Pueblo and South Pueblo which appeared in the April 30, 1904 issue of "Camp and Plant," a Colorado Fuel and Iron Company publication. The view is toward the north. The white building in the center of the picture directly across the track from the round house is the Union Station for *Rio Grande* and *Santa Fe* trains.—(State Historical Society of Colorado)

An early view of Golden looking southwest. The *Colorado Central* track to Black Hawk followed the stream flowing from the mouth of Clear Creek Canon. The *Golden City & South Platte* trestle over Clear Creek is at right center.—(State Historical Society of Colorado)

1879 (Cont'd)

Miles

DENVER SOUTH PARK & PACIFIC

From Webster west over Kenosha Pass (altitude 9,991 feet) to Como, thence southwesterly through South Park to a point near the summit of Trout Creek Pass.[15] (ng)

46.6

GOLDEN BOULDER & CARIBOU

Marshall to Fox Mine (sg)

0.6

GOLDEN CITY & SOUTH PLATTE

From the Colorado Central depot at Golden south to clay beds (ng)

1.7 [16]

> This company, a CC satellite, was chartered in 1872 as the Golden City & South Platte Railroad & Telegraph Company to build from Golden southeasterly to Acequia, a point on the D&RG south of Denver. A major part of the route was graded but construction was discontinued in 1873 without any rails having been laid. A part of that grade was used for this short section of track.

Total 71.2

EXPANSION AND CONSOLIDATION

PART II

Railroad construction in Colorado reached its greatest heights during the 1880's and early 1890's. Previously established roads were extended into the more remote areas of the State, three additional trunk lines entered the State from the East and a number of new local railroads emerged. Total mileage more than tripled during the period, although the pattern of activity was quite erratic.

The mileage added during the three years beginning with 1880 exceeded that of all previous years combined, with the D&RG contributing about half of the increase. This flurry of activity was followed by an abrupt decline in 1883 and by 1885 new construction was almost at a standstill. But this interlude ended as suddenly as it had developed and in 1887 expansion reached a yearly record which was never again equaled. New construction in the four succeeding years was at an uneven pace somewhat below the 1887 peak but still at a relatively high level. By the close of 1891 Colorado's greatest railroad boom had ended. A greatly expanded network of railroads had developed on both sides of the Continental Divide, an entry had been opened into Utah and a new southern outlet provided a direct route to Texas.

The Denver and Rio Grande, originally narrow gauge throughout its route, launched an extensive gauge conversion program during this period of expansion. Provision for accommodating standard gauge equipment was made by either adding a third rail to existing trackage or by broadening the track to standard gauge. By 1891 standard gauge equipment could pass over DR&G main lines and most of its branches from Denver via Tennessee Pass into Utah and from Pueblo south to both La Veta and Trinidad.

The first of two major consolidations during the period occurred in January 1880 when the Denver Pacific and the Kansas Pacific railroads were merged into the Union Pacific system. The other took place ten years later when twelve Union Pacific controlled roads were combined to form a new company—the Union Pacific, Denver & Gulf. This consolidated system was initially operated as a division of the Union Pacific but was divorced from the influence of that company in 1893 when the two railroads were placed under separate receiverships.

By the fall of 1880 extensive railroad yards had been laid out by the D&RG at Salida, a bridge had been constructed across the Arkansas River for the Gunnison Extension and a stone depot had been completed.—(State Historical Society of Colorado)

An early W. H. Jackson photograph of Manitou with Pikes Peak in the distance. The D&RG Manitou branch ended at the freight house, only a few car-lengths west of the stone depot at lower left.—(State Historical Society of Colorado)

1880

| CONSTRUCTION | Miles |

ATCHISON TOPEKA & SANTA FE

Pueblo northwest to Clelland (sg) — 33.4
Clelland to Rockvale (sg) — 2.8

> The line from Pueblo paralleled the D&RG track up the Arkansas River Valley to coal fields near Canon City. Construction of both segments was under the charter of the Pueblo & Arkansas Valley Railroad Company. The road was opened to Rockvale in November.

COLORADO CENTRAL

Julesburg Branch—from a connection with the UP main line at Denver Junction (later Julesburg), southwest to a point near the present location of Union (sg) — 80.0[1]

> This was the beginning of a cutoff between the UP main line and the Denver-Cheyenne Division. It was constructed by and for the UP which controlled Colorado Central at the time. The track was opened for traffic as far as Iliff, 43.8 miles from Denver Junction, early the following year.

DENVER SOUTH PARK & PACIFIC

From the railhead near the summit of Trout Creek Pass to the Arkansas River (ng) — 14.8

> Arkansas Station (later Macune) was established on the east side of the river. Trains between that point and Denver were placed in operation February 11. A bridge was built across the river soon after the track reached the east bank.

From the Arkansas River crossing west to the grade of the D&RG[2] (ng) — 1.0

> This line would permit direct passage to the D&RG line to Nathrop, yet to be constructed, without going into Buena Vista.

From the crossing of the Arkansas River northerly to Buena Vista (ng) — 2.1

> The rails reached Buena Vista March 3 and Denver trains began running to and from the town on that date.

Nathrop west to St. Elmo (ng) — 14.6

> D&RG trackage was used between Buena Vista and Nathrop. The line was opened for traffic as far as Cascade, 18 miles from Buena Vista and 10.5 miles west of Nathrop, on December 11.

Lechner Mine spur—Como north to Lechner Mine (ng) — 1.4

> The first one-half mile of this spur was later used as a part of the main line over Boreas Pass.

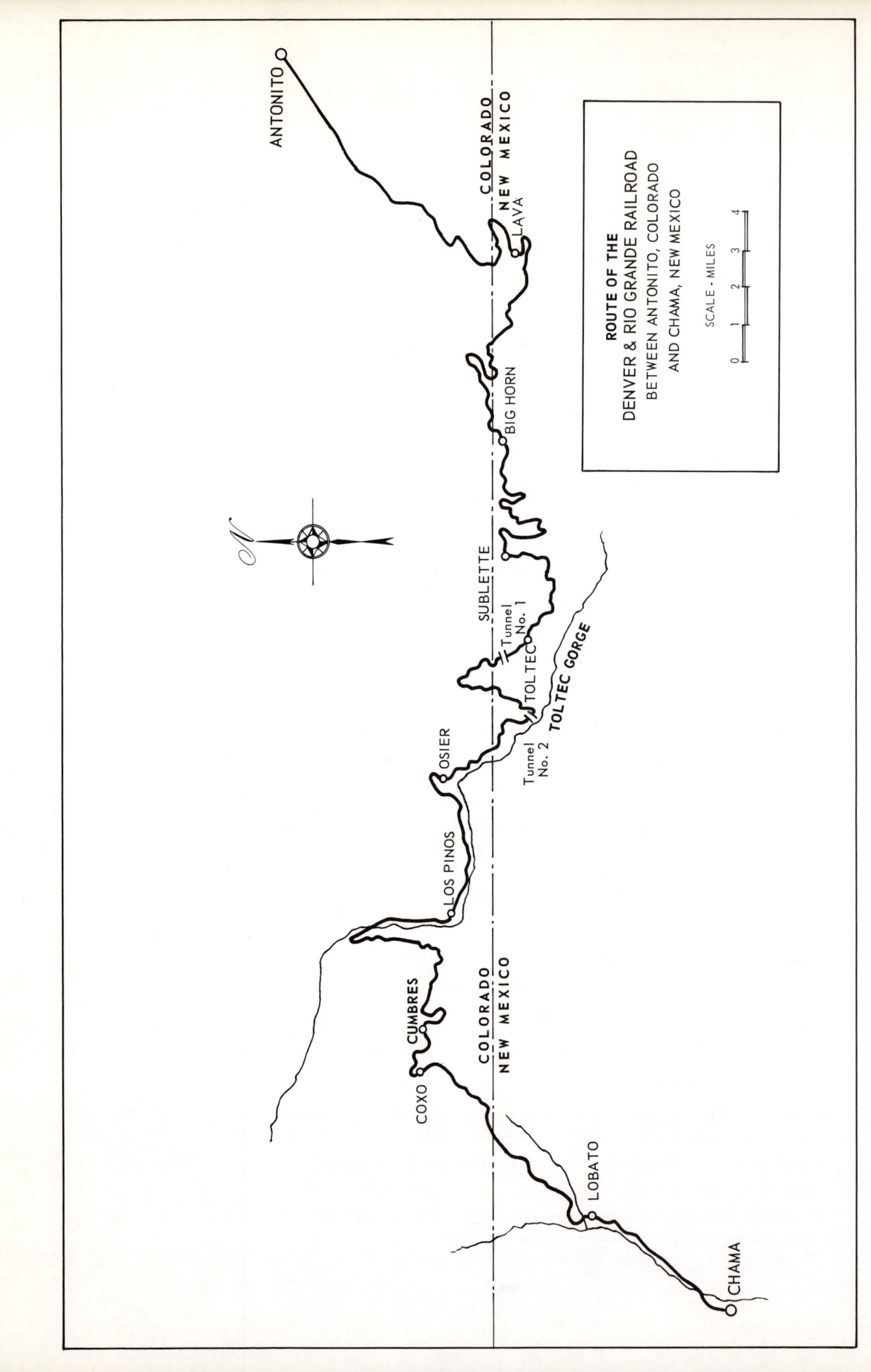

1880 (Cont'd)

	Miles
King Mine spur—from Coal Branch Junction about one mile east of Como, southeast to the King Mine (ng)	3.3

DENVER & RIO GRANDE

From a point near Texas Creek to South Arkansas (later Salida) (ng) — 33.9

    This trackage was built from the end of the line acquired from AT&SF in the settlement of the Royal Gorge dispute.

South Arkansas to Nathrop (ng) — 17.9

Nathrop to Buena Vista (ng) — 7.5

    This section of track was used jointly by the D&RG and the DSP&P until 1884 under an operating agreement which included other trackage.

Buena Vista to Malta (ng) — 30.6

Malta to Leadville (ng) — 5.2

    The Santa Fe had previously graded several sections of roadbed between Texas Creek and Leadville which helped speed the progress of the D&RG track laying crews. The track was completed to South Arkansas May 20, to Nathrop June 1, to Buena Vista June 9, to Malta June 29 and to Leadville July 20. The first D&RG train reached Malta June 30 and by July 6 the DSP&P was running two daily passenger trains between Denver and Malta.[3] On July 22 the first D&RG passenger train arrived at Leadville with General U. S. Grant aboard. However, passenger service did not begin on a regular schedule until about August 2.

Blue River Extension—Leadville to Kokomo (ng) — 18.2

    This was the beginning of a branch projected into the Ten Mile and Blue River mining districts. The tracks crossed the Continental Divide at Fremont Pass (11,328 feet) on November 15 and reached Kokomo December 27.

Eagle River Extension—Malta to Crane's Park (ng) — 9.6

    This by-pass west of Leadville was completed and opened for business on November 22.

Arkansas Valley Smelter Spur—Eilers to the smelter (ng) — 1.8

    The spur left the main line at Eilers, 2.5 miles south of Leadville. There also was an extensive system of switching tracks at this and other adjacent smelters.

Alamosa south to Antonito (ng) — 28.7

    The track was completed to Antonito in early April. There the line branched, one division going westerly toward the San Juan mining district, the other south into New Mexico.

San Juan Extension—Antonito westward to the Colorado state line northeast of Chama, New Mexico (ng) — 33.2

    The Colorado-New Mexico border was crossed eleven times along this serpentine route. After wandering across the plateaus west of Antonito on a rather easy and constant grade, the tracks

1880 (Cont'd)

	Miles
crossed the summit of the Conejos Range at Cumbres Pass (10,015 feet), then descended the west slope of the range on a steep, winding grade to the state line. In the total distance of 54.9 miles, 21.7 miles were in New Mexico. After the last crossing into New Mexico around the end of the year, the track-laying crew continued on to Chama. Regular service to that point was inaugurated in February 1881.	
New Mexico Extension—Antonito south to New Mexico state line (ng)	5.6
This was the Colorado portion of a branch to Espanola, New Mexico. The rails crossed the Colorado line around June 1.	
Manitou Branch—Colorado Springs to Manitou (ng)	5.1
The branch was completed and opened for traffic on July 31.	
Gunnison Extension—South Arkansas (Salida) to Poncha Junction (ng)	5.0
The tracklayers reached Poncha Junction November 14 and the line was opened for business on November 22.	
Silver Cliff Branch—Grape Creek Junction, on the main line 1.8 miles west of Canon City, into Grape Creek Canon (ng)	2.0
This short segment of a branch projected to the Silver Cliff mining district was completed on December 31. Work was discontinued at that time but was resumed the following spring.	
Hathaway Quarry Spur—from the main line at Castle Rock to Hathaway Quarry (ng)	2.3
The tracks reached the quarry June 10 and the line was opened for traffic five days later.	
Coal Creek Branch extended to Coal Creek Mine No. 2 (ng)	0.6
Total	360.6

ABANDONMENT

GOLDEN & RALSTON[4]

Entire line from the Colorado Central connection to the Murphy Coal Mine (ng)	2.0

1881

| CONSTRUCTION | Miles |

CHICAGO BURLINGTON & QUINCY

Colorado-Nebraska state line to Eckley (sg) — 24.8

This was part of a Burlington line projected to Denver. It was built by an affiliated company, the Burlington & Colorado Railroad, organized to construct the portion within Colorado. The rails reached Eckley near the end of the year.

COLORADO CENTRAL

Julesburg Branch—from the railhead near the present location of Union to La Salle (sg) — 71.5

The tracks followed the route surveyed and partially graded by the Colorado Central along the Platte River Valley in the early 1870's, except for two major deviations. On the Julesburg end it ran east of the old grade for several miles and on the west end the line swung southwest at a point about eight miles east of Greeley and joined the Cheyenne Division of the UP at La Salle, 4 miles south of Evans. Tracklaying was completed to La Salle in the latter part of September and a through freight train from Chicago to Denver passed over the line on September 30. Regular passenger service between Denver and Omaha, Nebraska via the cutoff began November 6.[5]

DENVER & NEW ORLEANS (Denver Texas & Gulf, 1886; Union Pacific Denver & Gulf, 1890; Colorado & Southern, 1899)

From Denver southeast to a point near Elizabeth (sg) — 35.0

This was the first leg of a railroad which, after several reorganizations and consolidations, would form a direct line between Denver and Fort Worth, Texas.

DENVER & RIO GRANDE

San Juan Extension—from the Colorado state line northwest of Chama, New Mexico to Durango (ng) — 68.5

After crossing the state line the previous year the track wound through northern New Mexico for nearly 50 miles, crossing the Continental Divide a few miles west of Chama at the relatively low altitude of 7,722 feet. Upon re-entering Colorado it followed the water courses westward for several miles near the southern boundary of the State, then wound across the plateaus from one drainage area to another, finally reaching the Animas River. It then followed that stream the last few miles into Durango where

Passengers and crew of a D&RG mixed train headed by engine 262 pose for the photographer at the Kokomo depot in the early nineties.—(Luke photo, State Hist. Society of Colo.)

A D&RG construction train pauses on the west side of Marshall Pass several track levels below the summit.—(Wm. H. Jackson Collection, State Hist. Society of Colo.)

A view of the summit of Marshall Pass in the early 1880's. In addition to the snow sheds over the winding track, facilities for railroad equipment and personnel were maintained here.—(Wm. H. Jackson Collection, State Hist. Society of Colo.)

1881 (Cont'd)

	Miles
on July 27 a large crowd of townspeople gathered to witness the driving of a silver spike.	
Silverton Extension—Durango to a point near Rockwood (ng)	*19.1*

The track paralleled the Animas River northward from Durango, reaching Rockwood on November 26 and a point about 1.3 miles beyond in early December. The laying of track was then halted until the following spring.

Gunnison Extension—from Poncha Junction, across the Continental Divide via Marshall Pass (altitude 10,845 feet), to Gunnison (ng) — *69.1*

The tracklayers reached Gunnison on August 6 and two work trains entered the town that day. Regular scheduled passenger service began August 8.

Crested Butte Branch—Gunnison north to a point about 1.5 miles north of Crested Butte (ng) — *29.4*

The track was completed November 21 and on that date the first train pulled into Crested Butte. Regular passenger service began November 24.

Silver Cliff Branch—Extended to Westcliffe (ng) — *29.5*

The last rail was spiked in place 0.3 mile south of the depot on April 25.

Eagle River Extension—Crane's Park to Red Cliff (ng) — *21.2*

After crossing the Continental Divide at Tennessee Pass (10,433 feet), the line followed the Eagle River through a deep canyon. On Novmber 20 the track reached a smelter a half-mile beyond Red Cliff.

Del Norte Branch (later Creede Branch)—Alamosa west via Del Norte to South Fork (ng) — *46.5*

The rails followed the Rio Grande to a point near the confluence of the north and south branches of the river, reaching Del Norte on July 13 and South Fork on November 20.

Mears Junction, on Gunnison Extension 6 miles from Poncha Junction, over Poncha Pass (9,060 feet) to Villa Grove, thence to Hot Springs Mines (later Orient) (ng) — *27.8*

The mines were at the foot of the Sangre de Cristo Mountains on the east side of upper San Luis Valley. The track was completed to the mines on October 28 and opened for traffic on the same date.

Blue River Extension—Kokomo to Wheeler (ng) — *6.3*

The laying of iron was completed to Wheeler September 18.

Madge (later Douglas) Quarry Spur—from Douglas, on the main line 2.5 miles south of Castle Rock, northeasterly to Madge Quarry (ng) — *2.6*

The spur was completed and opened for business on November 20.

Chandler Branch—from Chandler Junction on the main line west of Florence, south to the end of track (ng) — *0.4*

This short stub was also opened for traffic on November 20.

The D&RG branch to Villa Grove and Hot Springs Mines branched off the Marshall Pass line and looped over it before beginning its climb to Poncha Pass. In this view looking west a construction train is crossing the main line as it descends toward the junction.—(Wm. H. Jackson Collection, State Hist. Society of Colo. Library)

An early photograph of Durango from the south showing a new 9-stall D&RG round house and the depot in the foreground.—(State Historical Society of Colorado)

A 2-car mixed DSP&P train pauses in Chalk Creek Canon near St. Elmo in the early eighties. The rugged terrain is typical of much of the area through which the line was built.—(Wm. H. Jackson photo, Denver Public Library, Western History Dept.)

1881 (Cont'd)

	Miles
Calumet Branch—Hecla Junction, 9.5 miles north of Salida, east to Calumet (ng)	6.8
The tracklayers reached Calumet on November 28.	
Trinchera Mine Branch—from Placer (later Russell), on the west slope of Veta Pass, to Trinchera Mine (ng)	2.1
The branch was completed to a tramway below the mine and opened for traffic on September 27.	
Oak Creek Branch—Oak Creek Junction, on the main line west of Florence, south to mines (ng)	2.6
The laying of track was completed November 20 and the line was opened for coal trains on December 1.	
Maysville Branch—Poncha Junction to Maysville (ng)	6.9
By March 15 the rails were in place 0.2 mile west of Maysville. The first freight train ran over the branch March 27 and regular passenger service began March 29.	
Fryer Hill Branch—Leadville to mines and smelters (ng)	1.8
This was a series of spurs completed on various dates between January 15 and August 5.	
Durango to San Juan Smelter (ng)	1.0
Narrow gauge to dual gauge:	
Denver to Pueblo	
Pueblo to Minnequa	

DENVER UTAH & PACIFIC (Chicago, Burlington & Quincy, 1908)

From Denver northerly to Mitchell (ng)	22.9
The track was completed to Mitchell and opened for traffic November 24.	

DENVER LONGMONT & NORTHWESTERN (Colorado Northern, 1883; Denver, Utah & Pacific, 1884)

From Longmont south to Mitchell (ng)	9.8
The tracks joined those of the Denver, Utah & Pacific at Mitchell and on November 24 a train operated between Longmont and Denver using the DU&P track south of Mitchell. The entire property of this railroad was sold under foreclosure in May 1883 to the Colorado Northern Railway Company. That company was consolidated with the DU&P in May 1884.	

1881 (Cont'd)

Miles

DENVER SOUTH PARK & PACIFIC

From the railhead near St. Elmo to the west portal of Alpine Tunnel (ng) *10.5*

    Alpine Tunnel was bored through the Continental Divide during 1880-81 at an altitude of 11,612 feet at its apex.[6] The rails reached the east portal on August 11 but the track was not completed through the tunnel until near the end of the year. Meanwhile, scheduled trains were running as far as Alpine, 4.4 miles east of St. Elmo, by May 8 and to Hancock, 3.0 miles east of the tunnel, by July 20.

Fairplay-Alma Branch—From the main line at Garos, in South Park, to Fairplay (ng) *10.0*

    The rails were in place at Fairplay by September 15 but additional ballasting and track repair delayed service over the line until the early part of October. A regular train schedule was put into effect November 13.

Breckenridge Branch (later Leadville Division)—from a point on the Lechner Mine spur one-half mile north of Como to the summit of Boreas Pass.[7] (11,493 ft.) (ng) *10.1*

DENVER WESTERN & PACIFIC (Denver, Marshall & Boulder, 1885)

Longmont south to end of track (sg) *4.4*

Denver north to end of track at the west end of Buffalo Hill, about 2 miles west of the present location of the Broomfield station (sg) *15.7*

    This railroad was to run between Denver and Longmont. Rails were laid from each end of the line with an unfinished gap of some 13 miles between the two segments. There is no evidence that either section was ever used for revenue purposes. In addition to the completed track, this company during 1881 completed 16 miles of grade as follows: Burns Junction to Erie, 11.0 miles; between Longmont and Erie, 2.0 miles; near Longmont and in Left Hand Canon, 1.25 miles; and in St. Vrain Canon, 1.75 miles. Only the grade between Burns Junction and Erie was ever railed.

GREELEY SALT LAKE & PACIFIC (Union Pacific Denver & Gulf, 1890; Colorado & Southern, 1899)

From Fort Collins northwest to a point later named Bellevue Junction, thence south to quarries at Stout (sg) *15.4*

    This line was built primarily to haul stone from quarries southwest of Fort Collins. The rails reached Stout near the end of the year and the first cars of stone were shipped the following February.

1881 (Cont'd)

UNION PACIFIC

	Miles

From the Denver & Boulder Valley track near the eastern edge of Boulder, west through the town to a point near the mouth of Boulder Canon (sg) — 1.8

> The immediate purpose of this trackage was to deliver material for a narrow gauge railroad to be built into the mountains west of Boulder.

Total — 573.5

1882

CONSTRUCTION

CHICAGO BURLINGTON & QUINCY

From the railhead at Eckley, west through Fort Morgan, thence southwesterly to a point 11 miles east of Denver (sg) — 139.1

From Denver east to a connection with the above (sg) — 11.0

> The gap between the two tracklaying crews was closed May 25, thus completing another trunk line between Denver and midwestern points. A train carrying officials of the railroad arrived in Denver the day the track was completed, a freight train arrived on May 29 and regular passenger service began June 26.

DENVER & NEW ORLEANS

From near Elizabeth to Pueblo (Gulf Junction) (sg) — 89.4

> The track continued south across the plains east of Colorado Springs until it reached Fountain Creek a short distance south of the town of Fountain. From there it continued on the east side of the creek to Pueblo. The rails crossed the northern limit of the city on April 29 and were spiked into place at Gulf Junction on May 2. The following day an excursion train from Denver operated over the road and regular service between Denver and Pueblo began May 7.

Branch—From Franceville Junction at M.P. 86.9, northeasterly to coal mines at Franceville (sg) — 4.6

> The branch was opened for the shipment of coal on May 3.

Branch—From Manitou Junction at M.P. 81.6, west to Colorado Springs (sg) — 9.1

> The track was completed to a temporary depot about December 5 and on December 10 a large crowd of Colorado Springs citizens witnessed the arrival of the first passenger train over the branch.

Looking southeast across Silverton with 13,000-ft. Kendall Mountain in the background. The D&RG depot is at extreme right near the foot of the mountain.—(Wm. H. Jackson photo—State Hist. Society of Colo.)

This spectacular location on the D&RG Silverton Branch has been the subject of numerous photographs. The engine and caboose on the shelf above Animas River was posed for W. H. Jackson's camera in the 1880's. Note the antlers on the front of the engine.—(State Historical Society of Colorado)

1882 (Cont'd)

DENVER & RIO GRANDE

Miles

Utah Extension—from Gunnison via Montrose to Grand Junction (ng)   *134.9*

    From Gunnison the track followed a westerly course along the Gunnison River through the valley and into the upper part of Black Canon. It exited from the canyon along Crystal Creek to the townsite of Cimarron, then wound over a steep grade across Cerro Summit (altitude 7,070 feet) and descended to Montrose which was reached by the tracklaying force on September 8. From Montrose the course was northwesterly along the Uncompahgre River to Delta where it again met the Gunnison. It followed that stream to its confluence with the Grand (later Colorado) River. There on November 21 the rails crossed the Grand into Grand Junction on what was described as the longest railroad bridge in Colorado (950 feet).

Grand Junction to Utah state line (ng)   *35.6*

    Northwesterly from Grand Junction the track ran first through the valley of the Grand, then across a barren area reaching the Colorado-Utah border December 19. Construction west of the state line was by the Denver & Rio Grande Western Railway Company[8] which was building east from Salt Lake City, Utah. The completion of the RGW in late March of the following year provided a continuous line between Denver and Salt Lake City.

Silverton Branch—from the end of track near Rockwood to Silverton (ng)   *26.5*

    The track continued to follow the Animas River, first on a shelf above the stream, then along the floor of the canyon. It was completed to Silverton on July 8.[9]

Silverton Smelter Junction to Silverton Smelter (ng)   *1.0*

Blue River Extension—Wheeler to Dillon (ng)   *11.1*

    The laying of track was completed on November 11 and the line was opened for traffic two days later.

Crested Butte Branch—from the end of track north of Crested Butte to Anthracite (ng)   *3.7*

    The track was completed to the Anthracite Coal Mine December 19.

Eagle River Extension—Red Cliff to Rock Creek (ng)   *2.8*

    This short extension in the canyon of the Eagle River was completed in early March. The end of the extension remained there until 1886.

Hathaway Quarry Spur extended to O'Brien's Quarry (ng)   *1.8*

    Stone was being hauled from the quarry by March.

Another example of the mountainous terrain traversed by the DSP&P is shown in this view at the Palisades, west of Alpine Tunnel.—(L. C. McClure Photo—State Hist. Society of Colo.)

A DSP&P mixed train at the London Junction depot about 1886.—(W. H. Jackson photo—State Hist. Society of Colo.)

1882 (Cont'd)

	Miles

DENVER CIRCLE

From its passenger station on the south side of Cherry Creek at 13th and Larimer Streets in Denver, southeast and south on city streets to the site of the Mining Exposition Building at Logan and Exposition Streets (ng) .... 3.8[16]

    The track was opened to the exposition grounds on April 6 although non-revenue trains were operated over short sections of the line as early as January 9.

Branch—from Cherokee Street west on Bayaud Avenue to a connection with the D&RG (ng) 0.3

DENVER SOUTH PARK & PACIFIC

Alpine Tunnel to Gunnison (ng) 40.1

    The line reached the eastern suburbs of Gunnison on September 1 and was extended to a temporary terminus at the track of the D&RG Crested Butte branch the following day. On the morning of September 3 an excursion special departed for Denver, followed by a scheduled passenger train that afternoon. The track was completed to its Gunnison terminal in the western part of town about September 6.

Fairplay-Alma Branch extended to Alma (ng) 5.4

    The specific completion date is rather vague but contemporary news items indicate passenger service was inaugurated in the first half of September.[11]

Breckenridge Branch (later Leadville Division)—Boreas Pass to Dillon (ng) 20.3

    The track was completed to Dillon near the end of the year.

GREELEY SALT LAKE & PACIFIC

Fort Collins to Greeley (sg) 24.5

    The roadbed was graded from Greeley to the eastern edge of Fort Collins but the balance of the grading and the placing of the iron was in the reverse direction. On October 4 the last rail was spiked down at Greeley and four days later an excursion train ran from Greeley to Fort Collins and return. Mixed train service between Greeley and Stout began October 18 and on December 2 a daily train was placed in service between Fort Collins, Greeley and Denver.

From Boulder west through lower Boulder Canon to Four Mile Canon (ng) .... 7.5[12]

On the route westward from Gunnison a section of D&RG track was laid along the floor of Black Canon, pictured above. The sharp pinnacle at left is Curecanti Needle which was for a number of years a part of the road's herald.—(State Historical Society of Colorado)

A W. H. Jackson panorama of the DSP&P winding down the mountain slopes from Boreas Pass. Breckenridge is in the valley at upper left. Note the snow shed on the loop in the middle foreground.— (State Historical Society of Colorado)

This modest stone structure was the South Park depot at Gunnison. The round house is shown in the background at right. (Photo by C.E. Hagie, State Hist. Society of Colo.)

A W. H. Jackson photo of the transfer yards at Buena Vista. Freight was interchanged here between the South Park and Rio Grande lines.—(State Historical Society of Colorado)

The DSP&P depot at Dillon in the early 1880's.—(State Historical Society of Colorado)

The *Greeley, Salt Lake & Pacific* station at Sunset in the middle eighties. The view is toward the west. The line curving toward the left across the bridge is the beginning of a planned extension.—(Photo by Louis St. George Taylor, State Hist. Society of Colo.)

1882 (Cont'd)

LONDON SOUTH PARK & LEADVILLE (South Park & Leadville Short Line, 1885)

Miles

From London Junction, about one mile east of the end of the Fairplay-Alma Branch of the DSP&P, westerly to the London Mine (ng) — 7.4

Elevation at the London Mine was 11,462 feet, more than 1200 feet higher than London Junction. The track was completed in October and ore shipments from the mine commenced about November 9.

Total — 579.9

1883

CONSTRUCTION

DENVER & RIO GRANDE

Del Norte Branch (later Creede Branch)—extended from South Fork to Wagon Wheel Gap (ng) — 14.2

The line was opened for business on July 13.

Maysville Branch (later Monarch Branch)—extended to Monarch (ng) — 9.4

Construction was completed October 18.

Blue River Extension—extended from Dillon down Blue River to end of track (ng) — 1.7

Cannon (later Lehigh) Mine Branch—from Cannon Junction (later Lehigh Junction) on the main line north of Sedalia, southwest to Cannon Mine (later Lehigh Mine) (ng) — 4.6

Iron Silver Mine Branch (later California Gulch Branch)—from Oro Junction on the Leadville Branch southeasterly up California Gulch to mines near Moyer (ng) — 3.4

DENVER CIRCLE

From Mining Exposition Building, south on Logan Street to Evans Avenue (ng) — 1.8

From Logan Street west on Jewell Avenue to Jewell Park (later Overland Park) (ng) — 0.6

Trains were operating to the park by April 5.

Bayaud Avenue line extended west to Raritan Street (ng) — 0.6

1883 (Cont'd)

The South Park station at Dickey where the line branched to Leadville and Dillon.
—(Watley Collection—State Hist. Society of Colo.)

1883 (Cont'd)

	Miles
DENVER SOUTH PARK & PACIFIC	
Gunnison north to old Baldwin Mine (ng)	*17.4*
A station named Baldwin (later Castleton) was established near the confluence of Ohio and Carbon Creeks, 14.7 miles north of Gunnison.	
From Baldwin northwest up Ohio Creek to end of track (ng)	*3.0*
Breckenridge Branch—Dillon to Keystone (ng)	*4.2*
Leadville Division—From Placer (later Dickey) 2.7 miles south of Dillon, to Kokomo (ng)	*16.2*
GREELEY SALT LAKE & PACIFIC	
Narrow gauge line—from end of track in Four Mile Canon to Pennsylvania Gulch (later Sunset) (ng)	*5.7*
By March 12 the tracklayers had reached Pennsylvania Gulch and had begun construction of a wye at that point. On the same day an engine ran to the end of the track and regular passenger service began on the first day of April.	
Total	*82.8*

ABANDONMENT

	Miles
DENVER SOUTH PARK & PACIFIC	
Lechner Mine Spur—from main line one-half mile north of Como to Lechner Mine (ng)	*0.9*

1884

CONSTRUCTION

	Miles
DENVER SOUTH PARK & PACIFIC	
Leadville Division extended from Kokomo to Leadville (ng)	*19.4*
The track was completed to Leadville February 5 but because of weather conditions and other factors regular train service was delayed until October 1.	
Route change between Buena Vista and Nathrop:	
Spur from old line to new Buena Vista station (ng)	*1.6*
From main line, 1.5 mile east of Macune, through Box Canon to Schwanders (a new station) (ng)	*1.1*
From Macune via Schwanders to Nathrop (ng)	*5.4*
The new route was placed in operation in March, giving the DSP&P independent trackage between Buena Vista and Nathrop.	

1884 (Cont'd)

DSP&P trains used this depot at Leadville. At the time this photo was taken in 1892 the South Park lines were operated as the *Denver, Leadville and Gunnison* under control of the Union Pacific.—(State Historical Society of Colorado)

A DL&G freight train at Robinson in the 1890's. The depot at left center is that of the D&RG.—(Buckwalter Collection—State Hist. Society of Colo.)

1884 (Cont'd)

A 5-car freight train on a partially filled trestle on the DSP&P near Leadville in the late 1880's.—(W. H. Jackson Photo—State Hist. Society of Colo.)

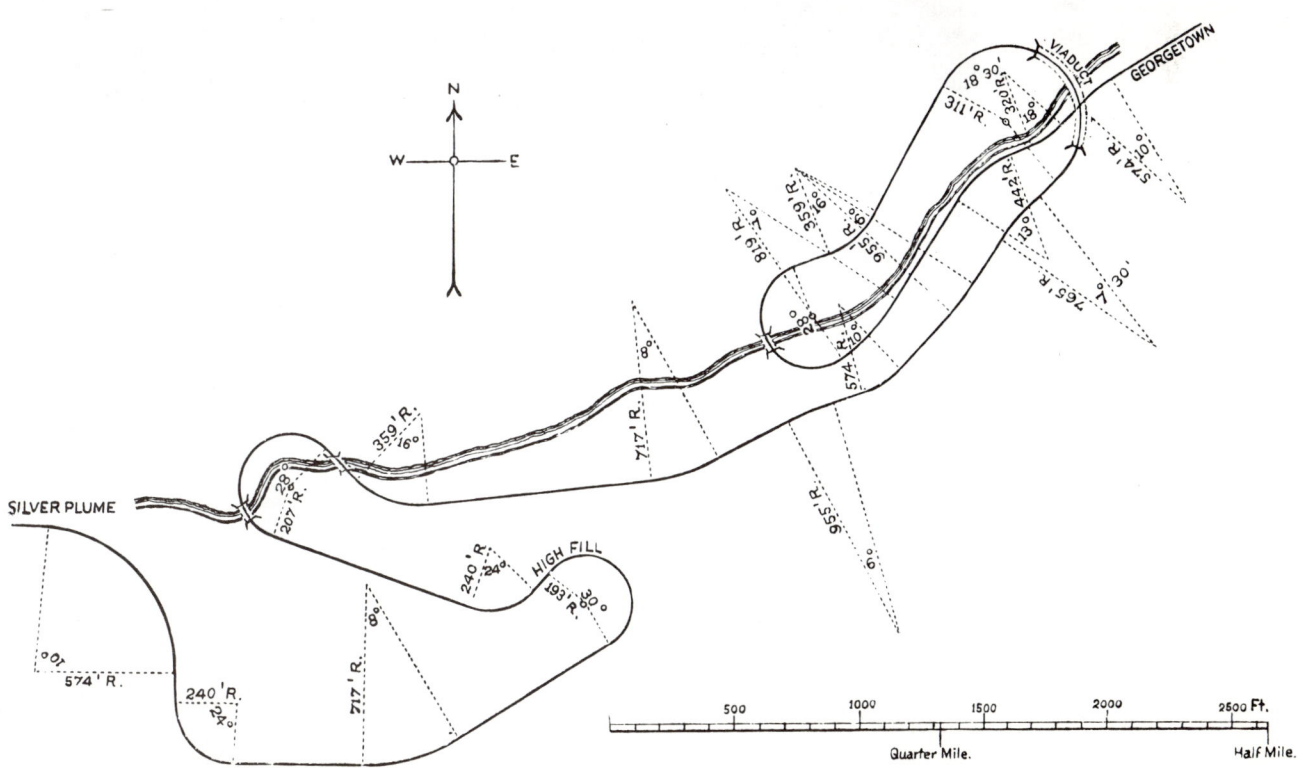

MAP OF ALIGNMENT OF GEORGETOWN, BRECKENRIDGE & LEADVILLE RAILWAY

Silver Plume was just over two miles up Clear Creek from Georgetown but four miles of winding track was required to connect the two towns. In this view looking east from above Silver Plume the famous Georgetown Loop is seen in the center of the picture with Georgetown in the distance.—(Dalgleish Photo—State Hist. Society of Colo.)

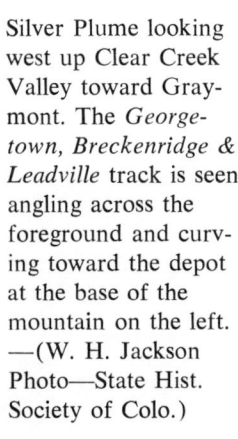

Silver Plume looking west up Clear Creek Valley toward Graymont. The *Georgetown, Breckenridge & Leadville* track is seen angling across the foreground and curving toward the depot at the base of the mountain on the left. —(W. H. Jackson Photo—State Hist. Society of Colo.)

1884 (Cont'd)

	Miles

DENVER & MIDDLE PARK

From Ralston[13] on the Colorado Central north of Golden, northwesterly to Glencoe (ng) — 4.6

  The line was completed and placed in operation in December.

DENVER CIRCLE

Bayaud Avenue line extended from Raritan Street west and north to the intersection of Bryant Street and First Avenue (ng) — 0.7

GEORGETOWN BRECKENRIDGE & LEADVILLE (Union Pacific, Denver & Gulf, 1890; Colorado & Southern, 1899)

From Georgetown west via the Georgetown Loop and Silver Plume to Graymont (Bakerville) (ng) — 8.5

  The line was constructed as an extension of the Colorado Central. Regular traffic to Silver Plume began in April and the line was opened to Graymont in June.

Total — 41.3

ABANDONMENTS

DENVER SOUTH PARK & PACIFIC

	Miles
King Mine Spur reduced (ng)	0.3
Macune to D&RG connection (ng)	1.0
Buena Vista to D&RG connection (ng)	1.1
Trout Creek to Macune (ng)	1.5
Total	3.9

1885

CONSTRUCTION	Miles

DENVER MARSHALL & BOULDER (Union Pacific, Denver & Gulf, 1890; Colorado & Southern, 1899)

From the end of the Denver, Western & Pacific track at Buffalo Hill, westerly to a point 2.0 track miles north of Superior (sg) — 6.1

    The Denver, Marshall & Boulder was organized as a UP subsidiary to acquire the defunct DW&P. The line built from Denver by the latter company in 1881 was used from Argo Junction north to the end of the track. The DW&P tracks between Argo Junction and Denver and the isolated section from Longmont south were abandoned.

DENVER SOUTH PARK & PACIFIC

Connection with new main line at Nathrop (ng) — 0.5

DENVER UTAH & PACIFIC

Longmont northwest to Lyons (ng) — 10.8
    This extension was completed on September 17.

Total — 17.4

ABANDONMENTS

DENVER SOUTH PARK & PACIFIC

Connection with D&RG at Nathrop removed (ng) — 0.8

DENVER MARSHALL & BOULDER

Longmont to end of track (sg) — 4.4
    This was the northern section of track built by DW&P in 1881. It was removed in July or August 1888.[14]

Denver to Argo Junction (sg) — 2.6
    Records indicate that a portion of the track remained in place until the following year.

GOLDEN BOULDER & CARIBOU

Reduced from Fox Mine to Marshall (sg) — 0.9

Total — 8.7

1886

CONSTRUCTION	Miles

COLORADO MIDLAND

From the Denver & Rio Grande interchange at Colorado Springs to a point 1.7 miles west of Colorado City (sg) — *3.0*
    This was the beginning of the first standard gauge railroad to penetrate the mountains of Colorado.

DENVER CIRCLE

From Logan Street east on Evans Avenue to what is now South Adams Street, 7 blocks east of the present campus of Denver University (ng)[15] — *1.8*

DENVER MARSHALL & BOULDER

From the railhead north of Superior via Marshall to Boulder (sg) — *7.7*
    The track was completed to the Marshall mines on March 13 and reached Boulder April 18. The entire line from Denver to Boulder was placed in service about August 1. The section between a junction with the Colorado Central near Buffalo Hill (later named Marshall Junction) and Boulder was initially used for freight only. Passenger service over that section was not inaugurated until September 1890.

DENVER & RIO GRANDE

Eagle River (or Aspen) Branch extended from Rock Creek down Eagle River (ng) — *5.0*
    This was the beginning of an extension to Glenwood Springs and Aspen.

DENVER RAILROAD LAND & COAL COMPANY (Colorado Eastern, 1888)

Denver east to Scranton (ng) — *16.6*
    This railroad, known as the Denver & Scranton, was completed in November. It was the only narrow gauge railroad to be built east from Denver.

    Total — *34.1*

ABANDONMENT

GOLDEN BOULDER & CARIBOU

Entire line—Boulder to Marshall (sg) — *5.1*
    All business of this railroad had been transferred to the DM&B. The tracks were removed in November.[16]

1887

| CONSTRUCTION | Miles |

ATCHISON TOPEKA & SANTA FE

Pueblo to Denver (sg) — 116.4
   The line was constructed under the title of Denver & Santa Fe Railway Company which was leased to the parent company upon its completion and merged into the corporate structure of the AT&SF on January 1, 1900. The track reached the main line of the Denver, Texas & Gulf (formerly D&NO) at what is now South Denver Junction on the last day of September. The company had previously purchased the Denver Circle railroad for terminal facilities at Denver but was denied the right to use it for that purpose. A train schedule was put into effect October 9 with passenger trains using DT&G tracks between South Denver and Union Station. By November 5 the Santa Fe had laid its own track to a new freight house at Fifteenth and Wewatta Streets and independent access to Union Station was accomplished later in the year by an extension from the freight house track.

Clelland to Canon City (sg) — 6.8
   The tracklayers reached Canon City on October 28.

Rockvale Branch extended to Kenwood (sg) — 3.5
   The extension was opened for operation January 1, 1888.

CHICAGO BURLINGTON & QUINCY

From the Colorado-Nebraska state line east of Holyoke, westerly to Sterling, thence west and northwest to the Colorado-Wyoming boundary (sg) — 144.6
   This link in CB&Q's Holdrege, Nebraska-Cheyenne, Wyoming route was built under the name of the Colorado & Wyoming Railroad Company. It connected with two other Burlington subsidiaries, the Colorado & Nebraska Railroad at the Nebraska line and the Cheyenne & Burlington Railroad at the Wyoming line. It was completed and opened for traffic to Sterling on September 27 and to the Wyoming line on December 11.

COLORADO CENTRAL

Dual gauge (3-ft. and 2-ft.). From New York Mill east of Black Hawk to Hidden Treasure mill.
   This conversion was to accommodate equipment of the 2-foot gauge Gilpin Tramway (see Gilpin Tramway below).

1887 (Cont'd)

This was the Santa Fe depot at Colorado Springs from 1889 to 1917.—(W. H. Jackson Photo—State Hist. Society of Colo.)

This panorama showing the ascent of the *Colorado Midland* up the east side of Hagerman Pass was recorded by W. H. Jackson's camera about 1889. The line from Leadville is seen along the mountainside at upper right. Hagerman Tunnel is out of view at upper left.—(State Historical Society of Colorado)

1887 (Cont'd)

These two CM depots offer contrasts in size and design. The above photo shows the small stone station at Manitou facing the track at the south edge of town. The larger, more ornate structure in the picture at right was the Leadville depot.—(Both photos—State Hist. Society of Colo.)

A construction crew has completed the bore for a tunnel in Glenwood Canyon on the D&RG extension to Glenwood Springs in 1887.—(State Historical Society of Colorado)

1887 (Cont'd)

DENVER & RIO GRANDE

Miles

From Engleville Junction, on the El Moro-Engleville Branch, to Trinidad (ng)

4.3

The track was in place to Trinidad by July 26 and regular service began August 2. Construction was under the charter of a satellite, The Trinidad & Denver Railroad Company, which was absorbed outright by D&RG the following year.

Eagle River Extension—from the railhead west of Rock Creek to Glenwood Springs (ng)

58.5

The rails followed Eagle River to its confluence with Grand River (now Colorado River), then down the Grand through Glenwood Canon to Glenwood Springs. The laying of steel was completed to Glenwood Springs on October 5, a special train arrived that evening and scheduled trains commenced operating the following day.

Aspen Branch—Glenwood Springs southeast to Aspen (ng)

41.7

The tracklayers reached the depot site on October 27 and a large crowd of citizens saw the first locomotive enter Aspen as it pushed the work train into town. The first passenger train arrived October 28 and departed the next day for Denver. The official opening of the branch was celebrated on November 1 with the arrival of several excursion trains.

Ryan Cut-Off—from Leadville west to a connection with the Eagle River line at Leadville Junction (ng)

3.2

This line, placed in operation November 27, completed a loop from the main line through Leadville.

Ouray Branch—Ouray Junction, at Montrose, southerly to Ouray (ng)

35.8

The branch was opened for business on December 21.

Narrow gauge to dual gauge:
   Pueblo to Florence
   Coal Creek Branch
   Minnequa to Cuchara Junction

COLORADO MIDLAND

From the railhead 1.7 miles west of Colorado City, via Buena Vista and Leadville to Glenwood Springs (sg)

216.5

Leaving Colorado City the track ran westward up Ute Pass, over Hayden Divide through Eleven Mile Canon to the southern end of South Park, crossed over the tracks of the DSP&P at Trout Creek Pass, wound around the hills to a station at Buena Vista on a hillside above the town, descended to the Arkansas River and paralleled the D&RG northward to Leadville. The rails reached Leadville the last day of August and regular passenger and freight service to that point was inaugurated September 3.

A crowd of citizens was on hand to greet the first locomotive to arrive at Aspen on October 27, 1887.—(State Historical Society of Colorado)

A D&RG locomotive stands at the first depot at Montrose in 1866, the year prior to the completion of the branch to Ouray. —(State Historical Society of Colorado).

1877 (Cont'd)

	Miles
From Leadville the track took a westerly course and crossed the Continental Divide through 2100-foot Hagerman Tunnel (11,528 feet altitude at the west portal). It descended the western slope of the divide on a winding course to the Frying Pan and Roaring Fork Rivers, following the latter into Glenwood Springs. The track reached the Glenwood Springs station on the east side of the river December 12 and regular train service began on December 18.	
Aspen Branch—Aspen Junction (later Basalt) to Maroon Creek (sg)	16.0
The track was completed to the west side of Maroon Creek, December 1 but entry into Aspen was delayed for the construction of a large iron bridge across the creek's ravine. Trains were turned on a wye near the end of the track and regular service between Maroon Creek and Aspen Junction began about December 5. Freight and passengers were transported by horse-drawn vehicles to and from the temporary terminus and the MT office in Aspen.	
Jerome Park Branch—from Cardiff, 3.5 miles south of Glenwood Springs, to Spring Gulch, with a spur to Sunlight Mine (sg)	16.6

DENVER TEXAS & FORT WORTH (Union Pacific, Denver & Gulf, 1890; Colorado & Southern, 1899)

Old Line Junction at Pueblo to Bessemer (sg)	4.8
The Denver & New Orleans, which reached Pueblo in 1882, was reorganized in 1885 as The Denver, Texas & Gulf Railroad Company. In 1887 a companion company, The Denver, Texas and Fort Worth Railroad Company was organized to build south from Pueblo to the Texas-New Mexico border where it would connect with the oncoming Fort Worth & Denver City Railroad. It did not build south of Bessemer but instead entered into an agreement for the use of the D&RG tracks between Pueblo and Trinidad. The extension to Bessemer was officially placed in operation April 1, 1888.	

DENVER UTAH & PACIFIC

From Tower Junction, 1 mile east of Lyons, north to Tower (later Noland) (ng)	3.7
The purpose of this short branch was to haul stone from quarries in the area. It was completed in May.	

1887 (Cont'd)

A more spacious depot was completed at Montrose in 1912. —(State Historical Society of Colorado)

Ouray is nestled among towering mountains and cliffs at the northern edge of the San Juan mountain range. In this photo looking south the D&RG railroad facilities are visible at the base of the cliff at right.—(W. H. Jackson Photo—State Hist. Society of Colo.)

1887 (Cont'd)

	Miles
GILPIN TRAMWAY (Gilpin Railroad, 1906)	
From Black Hawk to Nevada Gulch (2-ft.)	4.5[17]

Commonly known as "The Gilpin Tram," this 2-foot gauge railway connected with the Colorado Central at Black Hawk. A third rail was laid on the Colorado Central 3-foot gauge tracks in Black Hawk, one of the few dual gauge tracks of that combination in Colorado. (See Colorado Central, above.)

Switchback from the main line at Straub, 4.2 track miles from Black Hawk, to Nevadaville (2-ft.) — 0.6[18]

GREELEY SALT LAKE & PACIFIC

Buckhorn Branch (later Arkins Branch)—from the main line of the Colorado Central at Loveland, northwesterly to Buckhorn quarries (Arkins) (sg) — 8.2

The branch was opened for traffic April 17.

MISSOURI PACIFIC

Colorado-Kansas state line to Pueblo (sg) — 152.1

Construction of the Colorado portion of this railroad was under the corporate name of a subsidiary, the Pueblo & State Line Railway. It entered the state about 30 miles north of the Santa Fe main line. After a westerly and southwesterly course across the plains it crossed the mainline of the Santa Fe in the Arkansas River Valley 26 miles east of Pueblo and ran alongside that railroad to its terminus. The track was laid across Fountain Creek on a newly completed bridge into Pueblo on December 1 and crossed the Arkansas River[19] on a temporary structure to a connection with the D&RG the following day. On December 5 the construction company began running trains between Pueblo and Horace, Kansas. The road was turned over to the operating department on December 28 and regularly scheduled trains between Pueblo, Kansas City and St. Louis, Missouri, were placed in service January 1, 1888.

SILVERTON RAILROAD

From Silverton northwest to Burro Bridge (ng) — 5.3

This was the first of three short narrow gauge railroads to originate at Silverton. Work was discontinued for the winter at Burro Bridge in late October or early November.[20]

Total — 843.1

1888

A *Colorado Midland* train crossing the Maroon Creek viaduct into Aspen in the 1890's.—(State Historical Society of Colorado)

(Below) The two railroads serving Aspen entered the town on opposite sides. In this Buckwalter photograph taken from the west the Colorado Midland tracks are seen at the south edge of town.—(State Historical Society of Colorado).

1888

| CONSTRUCTION | Miles |

ASPEN & WESTERN (Crystal River, 1892)

From Carbondale on the Aspen Branch of the D&RG, south up Crystal River to Thompson Creek, thence west up Thompson Creek to Thompson Mine (ng) — 12.9

    The track was completed and opened for business on April 1[21] but little, if any, traffic passed over the road as the mine closed after producing only a small quantity of coal.[22] In 1892 it was sold under foreclosure to the Crystal River Railway Company.

CHICAGO ROCK ISLAND & PACIFIC

From the Colorado-Kansas state line to a connection with the D&RG at Roswell (Colorado Springs) (sg) — 177.0

    The Chicago, Rock Island & Colorado Railway Company was formed in January 1888 to build the Colorado portion of the Rock Island railroad but in June of the same year it was merged with another Rock Island subsidiary, the Chicago, Kansas & Nebraska Railway Company, which built the entire line.

    Upon completion it was leased to the Rock Island and was absorbed by the parent company in 1891. From the Colorado state line the track extended west across the plains to the new town of Limon where it crossed the Kansas Division of the UP. A short distance farther it swung toward the southwest and continued to Roswell, just north of Colorado Springs. There, on October 14, the tracklayers joined the rails with the main line of the D&RG. The construction company began operating a daily mixed train between Colorado Springs and Goodland, Kansas about October 15. The first Rock Island passenger train arrived on November 4 and departed the following morning on an established schedule for midwestern points. Trackage rights to Denver and Pueblo were obtained from the D&RG before the tracks reached Roswell and the following year an agreement was made with UP for the use of its tracks between Limon and Denver.[23]

From Elsmere, 7.5 miles east of Roswell, southeasterly to the McFerran Mine (sg) — 4.7

COLORADO MIDLAND

Aspen Branch extended from Maroon Creek to Aspen (sg) — 2.4
    A depot and much of the track in the corporate limits of Aspen were finished by early January and on February 4 the first train crossed the Maroon Creek bridge into the town.
Aspen to mines located on the south and east sides of the town (sg) — 0.9
Main line extended from Glenwood Springs to New Castle (sg) — 12.6

1888 (Cont'd)

In this view of Aspen from the north the D&RG tracks are shown curving along the north and east sides of the town. The Rio Grande station and yards are barely off the right side of the photo. The MT yards are visible across the town near the base of the mountain with the track extending around the east side of town, paralleling the D&RG to the Mollie Gibson Mine in the foreground.—(L. C. McClure photo—State Hist. Society of Colo.)

In this 1896 scene a track crew has paused for the photographer on the Rock Island line 2.5 miles west of Vona, about midway between the state line and Limon. Evidently the roadbed was being raised at this location.—(Denver City Library, Western History Dept.)

1888 (Cont'd)

The Rio Grande depot in the shadow of Pikes Peak at Colorado Springs was completed in 1887. It was shared with the Rock Island after that railroad reached the city in 1888.—(State Historical Society of Colorado)

The Yankee Girl Mine, one of several mines along the route of the Silverton Railroad. The mine was reached via a switchback from the main line.—(State Historical Society of Colorado)

1888 (Cont'd)

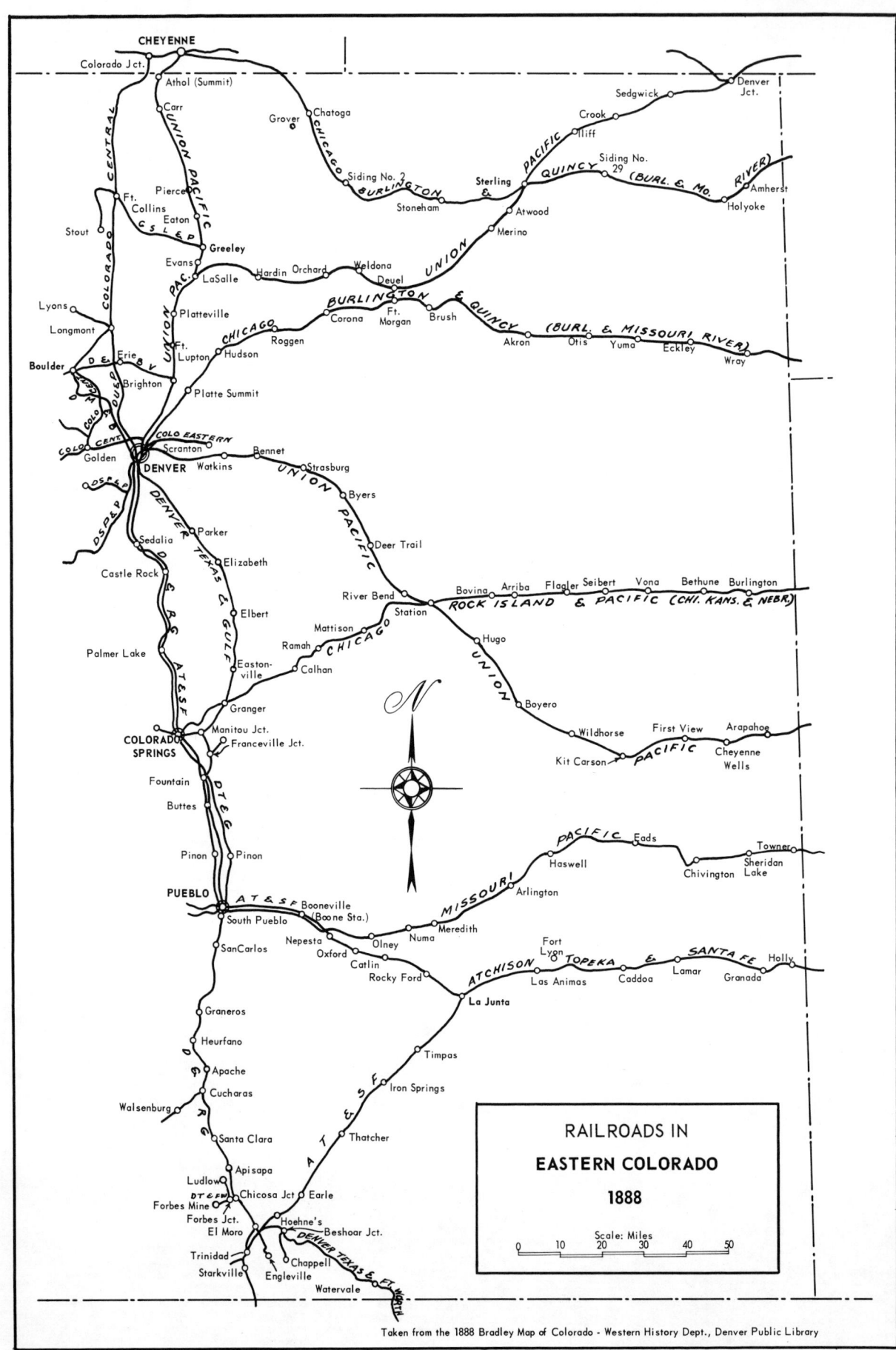

1888 (Cont'd)

	Miles
The track was completed and opened for traffic October 15. That was the end of CM trackage; trains beyond that point were operated over other railroads.	
Main line cutoff—from the main line at Snowden, north to a connection with the main line at Arkansas Junction, 3.8 miles west of Leadville (sg)	6.5
This cutoff was completed near the end of the year and opened for traffic in January 1889. It was built under the name of Aspen Short Line Railroad Company, a subsidiary corporation which was leased by CM immediately upon completion and was later acquired outright by the parent company.	
Moyer Branch—from the main line south of Leadville up California Gulch to end of track near Moyer Mine (sg)	3.3

DENVER & RIO GRANDE

	Miles
Strawberry Branch—Aspen to mines (ng)	1.6
This extension from the Aspen station to mines on the east and south sides of the town was completed in September.	
Rouse Branch—from Rouse Junction, 11 miles south of Cuchara Junction, west to the Rouse Coal Mines (later Old Rouse) (sg)	5.2
The branch was completed to the mines the last day of August.	
Conchita (Santa Clara) Junction, on the Rouse Mine branch, south to Santa Clara (later Rouse) (sg)	5.9
The tracks reached the Colorado Iron and Coal Company mine at Santa Clara about December 28.	
Loma Branch—Loma Junction (at Walsenburg) west to Pictou (sg)	4.6
The last three branches shown above were the first standard gauge lines constructed by D&RG except for an 0.15 mile connecting track built in the Pueblo yards earlier in the year.[24]	

Narrow gauge to dual gauge:
  Florence to Canon City
  Cuchara Junction to Loma Junction
  Cuchara Junction to Trinidad
  Colorado Springs to Manitou
  Leadville to Eilers

DENVER SOUTH PARK & PACIFIC

	Miles
Morrison Branch extended (ng)	0.2

DENVER MARSHALL & BOULDER

	Miles
Louisville to Lafayette (sg)	3.3
This isolated branch which was reached via CC tracks between Marshall Junction and Louisville was completed in September.	

1888 (Cont'd)

DENVER TEXAS & FORT WORTH

Miles

Main line—from Trinidad southeasterly to the New Mexico state line (sg)   *51.6*

> The line continued across the northeast corner of New Mexico to a connection with the Fort Worth & Denver City railroad at the Texas-New Mexico boundary. A portion of the road in New Mexico was built from the Texas state line northwesterly to join the section which began at Trinidad.
>
> On March 14 the two tracklaying crews met at a point about 20 miles south of the Colorado state line. This, with trackage rights over the D&RG between Pueblo and Trinidad and connections with Texas roads, completed a continuous rail line between Denver and the Gulf of Mexico. Intermittent freight service between Trinidad and Fort Worth began on March 15 and regular passenger service between Denver and Fort Worth was inaugurated April 9.

From the main line to the DT&FW freight house at Pueblo (sg)   *0.6*

> This section of track was declared side track in 1913.

Gray Creek Branch—from Beshoar Junction on the main line 7.5 miles east of Trinidad, south to Chappell (sg)   *6.5*

Long Canon Branch[25]—Trinidad west to Long's Junction thence southwest up Long Canon to Martinsen (sg)   *14.2*

Long's Junction to Thompson Mine (sg)   *1.3*

> In 1901 this short spur was sold by a successor company to the Colorado & Wyoming Railway Company.

Sopris Junction on Long Canon Branch west of Trinidad to Sopris Mine (sg)   *0.7*

Chicosa Junction, on the D&RG 12 miles north of Trinidad, southwest to Forbes Mine (sg)   *4.1*

> Construction was under the charter of a subsidiary, The Chicosa Canon Railway Company.

Forbes Junction, on the above line 1.16 miles west of Chicosa Junction, northwesterly to Ludlow (sg)   *4.3*

> This section of track later became part of a main line between Trinidad and Walsenburg.

GILPIN TRAMWAY

Nevada Gulch to Frontenac Mine (2 ft)   *3.5*

SILVERTON RAILROAD

Burro Bridge to Ironton (ng)   *11.2*

> This extension was completed in early November.

Total   *339.1*

1888 (Cont'd)

ABANDONMENT — *Miles*

COLORADO CENTRAL

From a point near Ralston to Colorado Central Junction (sg) — *14.0*
    This section of track had not been used since August 1886 at which time CC trains were rerouted over Denver, Marshall & Boulder tracks between Denver and Colorado Central Junction.

1889

CONSTRUCTION

ATCHISON TOPEKA & SANTA FE

Spur from main line near Castle Rock west to Santa Fe Quarry (sg) — *1.1*

DENVER & RIO GRANDE

Lake Fork Branch—from the main line at Lake Junction, 26 miles west of Gunnison, south to Lake City (ng) — *35.8*
    On June 24 the rails were laid into Lake City and the first locomotive steamed into town that day. The completion of a loop for turning trains and additional ballasting along the line delayed final completion of the branch until July 20. It was officially opened for business on August 15.

Aberdeen Quarry Branch—Aberdeen Junction, on main line 5.8 miles west of Gunnison, south to Aberdeen Quarry (ng) — *4.5*
    The purpose of this branch was to transport stone for the erection of the State Capitol Building at Denver. Tracklaying was completed on July 30 and the line was opened for business on August 15.

Rifle Creek Extension—from Glenwood Springs down Grand River to Rifle Creek (later Rifle) (ng) — *26.6*
    The track was completed and placed in operation in October.

Fort Logan Branch—Military Junction (at Englewood) west to Fort Logan (dg) — *2.5*
    The branch was built under the name of a subsidiary company, the Denver, Clear Creek and Western. The completion date was January 27 and on August 12 it was merged into the D&RG corporate structure.

Dual gauge to standard gauge—Cuchara Junction to Trinidad
Narrow gauge to standard gauge—Engleville Junction to Engleville

DENVER TEXAS & FORT WORTH

Ludlow to Hastings (sg) — *3.3*
    This coal mine branch was constructed under the charter of

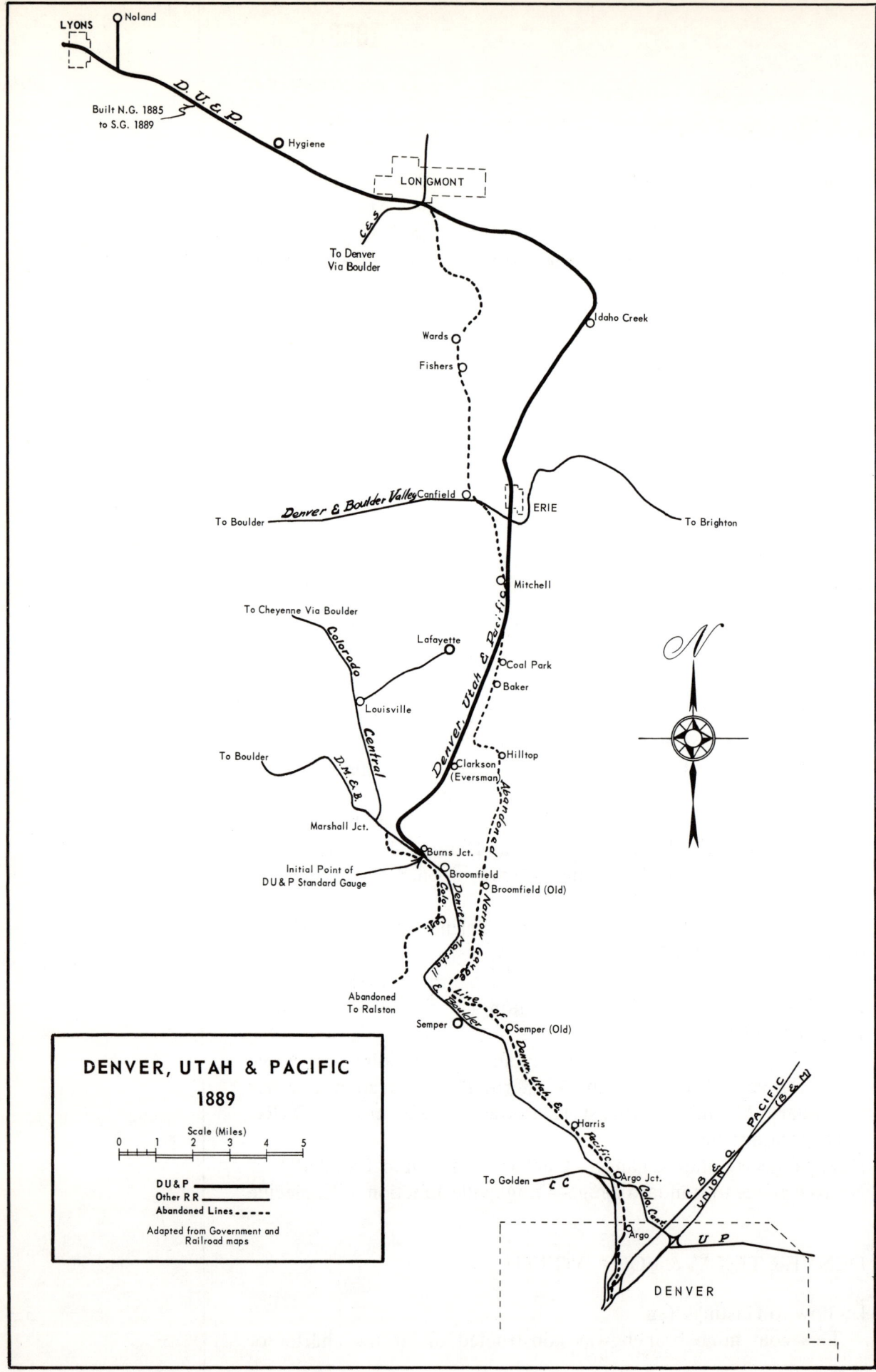

1889 (Cont'd)

another DT&FW subsidiary, the Canon de Agua Railroad Company. It was completed and placed in operation in January.

Miles

DENVER UTAH & PACIFIC

From Burns Junction, on the Denver, Marshall & Boulder main line west of Broomfield, to Longmont (sg) — 21.8

    This standard gauge line was constructed over a different route than the narrow gauge. From Burns Junction to a point about one-half mile south of Erie it was built on a grade previously constructed by the DW&P. From there to Longmont a new line was built a few miles east of the narrow gauge track. At the same time the track between Longmont and Lyons was converted to standard gauge. The new track was reached via DM&B tracks between Utah Junction and Burns Junction. It was completed in late August and leased to CB&Q effective September 1 with scheduled train operations beginning on that date. The line was operated by the Burlington & Missouri Railroad Company, a CB&Q subsidiary, until February 1908 when title was conveyed outright to the CB&Q.

Baker Mine Spur—from the main line about 3 miles south of Erie to the Baker Mine (sg) — 0.6

    From its initial point the line curved sharply to the right, then continued on a short tangent to the mine near the Boulder-Adams County line. The mine had previously been served by a short spur from the narrow gauge line.

Narrow gauge to standard gauge:
  Longmont to Lyons
  Tower Junction to Tower
  Denver to Utah Junction

LITTLE BOOK CLIFF (Colorado, Wyoming & Great Northern, 1894; Book Cliff, 1899)

Trackage at Grand Junction (ng) — 0.5

SILVERTON RAILROAD

Extended from Ironton to Albany (ng) — 1.5[26]

Total — 98.2

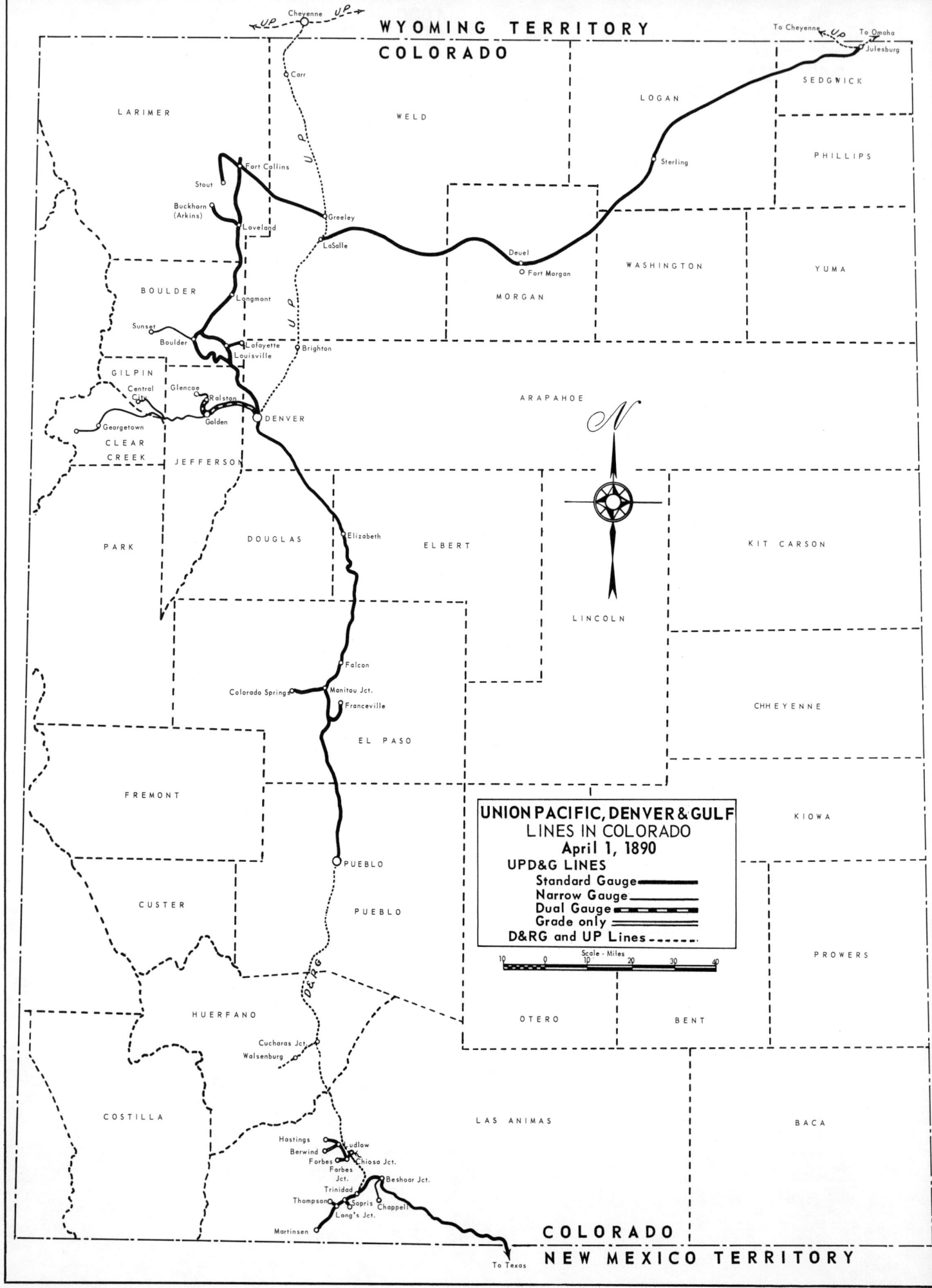

1889 (Cont'd)

| ABANDONMENTS | Miles |

DENVER & RIO GRANDE

Grape Creek Junction to Westcliffe (ng)   *31.5*
  After extensive flood damage restoration did not appear feasible. The rails were taken up the following year.

COLORADO CENTRAL

Fort Collins to Wyoming state line (sg)   *25.3*
  With all through traffic between Denver and Cheyenne moving over the UP, little use was made of the Colorado Central north of Fort Collins after December 1882. The entire track, except a short section from Fort Collins north, was removed in 1890.

DENVER UTAH & PACIFIC

Original line between Utah Junction and Longmont (ng)   *30.4*
  The section between Denver and Utah Junction was widened to standard gauge.

Total   *87.2*

1890

April 1, 1890 twelve railroad companies controlled by the Union Pacific were combined into a single system named the UNION PACIFIC, DENVER & GULF RAILWAY COMPANY. The companies which became a part of the consolidated system were:
  Colorado Central Rail Road Company (of Colorado)
  The Georgetown, Breckenridge & Leadville Railway Company
  The Greeley, Salt Lake & Pacific Railway Company
  The Denver, Marshall & Boulder Railway Company
  The Denver & Middle Park Railroad Company
  The Denver, Texas & Gulf Railroad Company
  The Denver, Texas & Fort Worth Railroad Company
  Three wholly owned subsidiaries of the DT&FW:
    The Canon de Agua Railroad Company
    The Chicosa Canon Railway Company
    The Road Canon Railroad Company (grade only)
  Cheyenne & Northern Railway Company. Its entire line was in Wyoming.
  Colorado Central Rail Road Company (of Wyoming). It was abandoned in 1889 and the only remaining trackage was a short stub off the UP main line west of Cheyenne which was removed soon after the consolidation.

1890(Cont'd)

The first train to the summit of Pikes Peak.—(University of Colorado Museum Collection)

A long stretch of the *Manitou & Pikes Peak Railroad* ascending toward the 10,109 ft. summit of the peak.—(W. H. Jackson Collection—State Hist. Society of Colo.)

1890 (Cont'd)

The disconnected segments were linked by trackage rights over UP and D&RG lines.
The system was operated as a division of the UP until control was vested in a court-appointed receiver in 1893.

CONSTRUCTION

Miles

COLORADO SPRINGS RAPID TRANSIT[27] (Electric) (Colorado Springs & Suburban, 1901; Colorado Springs & Interurban, 1902).

From Tejon Street in Colorado Springs, west on Colorado Avenue through Colorado City, thence over a private right of way to the D&RG Manitou depot. (sg)   5.2

The line was over the route of a 42-inch gauge horse car railway to Colorado City which was completed by the Colorado Springs & Manitou Railway Company in 1888. In early 1890 that company was consolidated with the El Paso Rapid Transit Company to form the Colorado Springs Rapid Transit Company. The new company dismantled the horse car line, replaced it with a standard gauge electric line and extended it to Manitou.

DENVER & RIO GRANDE

Leadville Junction to Pando (ng)   14.8
This new track through a tunnel at Tennessee Pass replaced the original line over the summit. It was converted to standard gauge soon after its completion.
Chandler Creek Branch—extended from end of track to Chandler Mine (sg)   4.2
San Luis Branch—Villa Grove to Alamosa (ng)   54.0
The branch was constructed by separate crews starting at each end. The rails joining the two sections were spiked in place about 17 miles north of Alamosa on October 15, completing a continuous line between Alamosa and Salida. The line was officially opened for business on November 9. Traffic to and from the San Luis Valley and points beyond was shifted to this branch, with stub trains serving Del Norte and Fort Garland. Service over Veta Pass between La Veta and Fort Garland was temporarily discontinued except for occasional local business. A feature of the new line was a 51-mile tangent running north from Alamosa on a nearly level grade.
Narrow gauge to dual gauge:
  Canon City to Salida
  Salida to Malta
  Malta to Eilers
  California Gulch Branch

1890 (Cont'd)

A D&RG passenger train headed south on a high trestle spanning the Lake Fork of the Gunnison River six miles north of Lake City about 1891.— (D&RGW collection —State Hist. Society of Colo.)

1890 (Cont'd)

Miles

Dual gauge to standard gauge:
   Minnequa to Cuchara Junctinon
   Cuchara Junction to Loma Junction
Narrow gauge to standard gauge:
   Leadville to Leadville Junction
   Leadville Junction to Rifle Creek
   Aspen Branch, including extensions to mines
   Grand Junction to Crevasse
   Oak Creek Branch
   Loma Junction to La Veta

LA PLATA

From La Plata Junction on the D&RG main line, 8.5 track miles east of Durango, to the La Plata Mine (ng)   *3.8*
   The track wound over a circuitous route first northeasterly, then northwesterly and finally westerly to the mine.

LITTLE BOOK CLIFF

From end of track at Grand Junction to Little Book Cliff Mines at Carpenter (ng)   *11.5*
   The railroad was built for the express purpose of hauling coal for the Grand Junction and other nearby markets. However, passenger excursions were frequently run during its early days. The track was completed by the end of the year and was in full operation by May 1891.

MANITOU & PIKES PEAK (Cog Road)

Manitou to the summit of Pikes Peak (sg)   *8.9*
   From its depot at Manitou this rack and pinion railroad climbed more than 7,500 feet to reach the 14,109 foot summit of the peak. The last spike was driven October 22 but regularly scheduled trains did not run to the summit until the following spring.

RIO GRANDE WESTERN (Denver & Rio Grande, 1908; Denver & Rio Grande Western, 1921)

From Colorado-Utah state line, northeasterly to a junction with the D&RG tracks at Crevasse (sg)   *13.4*
   This was a successor to the former Denver & Rio Grande Western[28] which had gone through a reorganization and name change. While converting to standard gauge it constructed an entirely new track eastward from Cisco, Utah. After entering Colorado

(above) A train approaches the rocky summit of Pikes Peak at the turn of the century.—(W. H. Jackson Collection, State Hist. Society of Colo.) (left) a M&PP train at the Manitou depot. No. 3 was one of three locomotives acquired by the railroad in 1890, all of which were rebuilt in 1893. Other such units were later added to the roster. Diesel-powered units are used exclusively today.—(Buckwalter Collection—State Hist. Society of Colo.)

A *Rio Grande Southern* train on the Telluride Branch near Anderson. The view is toward the north. The branch left the main line (shown on the mountain slope at left) at Vance Jct. about two miles up track, passed through Illium and Anderson before looping to the opposite side of the small valley and continuing to Telluride.—(W. H. Jackson Collection, State Hist. Society of Colo.)

A new union depot was erected at Pueblo in 1890, a short distance west of the former station. Note the dual gauge tracks and the RGS cars in the yards.—(W. H. Jackson Collection—State Hist. Society of Colo.)

The combined *Little Book Cliff* depot and coal office at Grand Junction as it appeared in the middle nineties.—(Denver Public Library—Western History Dept.)

1890 (Cont'd)

Miles

about seven miles south of the original narrow gauge line of the D&RG it followed the Grand (Colorado) River to the upper end of Ruby Canon, then continued northeasterly to a connection with the D&RG at Crevasse. The company leased the 20-mile section of D&RG trackage between Crevasse and Grand Junction and terminated its trains at the latter point. The first RGW standard gauge train pulled into Grand Junction from the west on June 11 and the same day a westbound train left for Ogden, Utah.

RIO GRANDE JUNCTION (Denver & Rio Grande Western, 1947)

From the end of the D&RG tracks at Rifle Creek to Grand Junction (sg) — 62.1

This railroad served as a connecting link between the D&RG Rifle Creek Extension and the D&RG-RGW tracks at Grand Junction. Its completion, together with gauge conversions of the two other roads, provided a continuous line for standard gauge trains between Denver and Ogden, Utah. The last rail was spiked down at Grand Junction on November 14 and a construction train with a business car attached entered the city the same day. The railroad was jointly owned by the Denver & Rio Grande and the Colorado Midland and a passenger train of each company arrived at Grand Junction on November 16. Midland trains used Rio Grande tracks between New Castle and Rifle under a trackage agreement which in one form or another remained in effect throughout the life of the Midland railroad.

RIO GRANDE SOUTHERN

Ridgway Junction, on the Ouray Branch of the D&RG, to Vance Junction (ng) — 38.8

The rails were in place and scheduled trains were operating over this segment of the line by the middle of November.

Telluride Branch—Vance Junction to Telluride (ng) — 7.3

The track was completed to Telluride on November 21 and scheduled trains were placed in service to that point three days later.

Durango to Porter Coal Mines (ng) — 5.5

Both freight and passenger trains were operating over this segment by December 1.

Construction of the RGS began at Ridgway on the north end and at Durango on the south end almost simultaneously. The character of the land through which it would pass necessitated a rather circuitous route between the two terminals with some engineering problems of major significance.

1890 (Cont'd)

The *Book Cliff* depot and yards at Grand Junction in 1900. The name of the railroad had been changed the previous year.—(Terry Mangan collection)

(D&RG Archives, State Hist. Society of Colo. Library)

THE DENVER AND RIO GRANDE RAILROAD CO.

OFFICE OF GENERAL MANAGER.

Denver, Colorado, Nov 8th, 1890

CIRCULAR No. 98.

The line recently constructed from Villa Grove, mile post 247.2, and extending (southward) westward to Alamosa, mile post 302.2, a distance of 55 miles, will be opened for business on and after the 9th inst and will be designated as the San Luis District of the Third Division.

Stations and sidings on this line are:

Villa Grove,	mile post	247.2	Station No. 247	R.
Hot Springs,	"	252.7	" 253	R.
Mirage,	"	258.8	" 259	R.
Moffat,	"	264.5	" 266	R.
La Garita,	"	270.7	" 271	R.
Dune,	"	276.2	" 276	R.
Garrison,	"	282.0	" 282	R.
Patterson,	"	288.4	" 288	R.
McGinty,	"	295.9	" 296	R.

S. T. Smith
General Manager.

1890 (Cont'd)

	Miles

STONE MOUNTAIN RAILROAD & QUARRY COMPANY
(Noland Land & Transfer Company, 1895)

Tower to Beach Hill (sg) — 4.0
  This railroad was built to deliver stone from several quarries to the CB&Q (DU&P) main line at Tower Junction. It operated over the CB&Q branch between Tower and Tower Junction.

UNION PACIFIC DENVER & GULF

Long Canon Branch extended from Martinsen to New Mexico state line (sg) — 3.9
  This section of track which continued south to Vasquez, New Mexico was placed in service in December.

Ludlow to Berwind (sg) — 2.8
  The track was laid on a grade built the previous year by the Road Canon Railroad Company. It was placed in operation in March.

Denver West Side Line (sg) — 4.8
  This freight by-pass along the west bank of the Platte River in Denver was completed about December 4 but traffic over the line was delayed until February 1891 because of an unsafe bridge.[29]

Total — 245.0

ABANDONMENTS

DENVER & RIO GRANDE

Leadville Junction to Pando (ng) — 17.0
  This was the original narrow gauge line over Tennessee Pass, replaced by the new line through the tunnel.

Lehigh Mine Branch—Lehigh Junction to Lehigh Mine (formerly Cannon Mine) (ng) — 4.6

Crevasse to State Line (ng) — 16.0
  Traffic had been diverted to RGW's new standard gauge line through Ruby Canon.

UNION PACIFIC DENVER & GULF

Short segment between Ludlow and Hastings (sg) — 0.3
Stout Branch reduced (sg) — 0.2
Ralston toward Golden (sg) — 1.9
At Golden (sg) — 0.5
  Part of this short section was removed the following year and the remainder was put into side track.

1890 (Cont'd)

	Miles
At Pueblo—Old Line Junction to Gulf Junction (sg)	1.1
Total	41.6

1891

CONSTRUCTION

CHICAGO BURLINGTON & QUINCY

Canon Mine spur—from a connection with the main line of the Lyons Branch near Mile Post 21, northwesterly to the Canon Mine (later Otis Mine) (sg) — 1.1

  The Canon Mine was in the present corporate limits of the town of Lafayette. Switching and storage tracks at the mine are not included in the mileage of the spur.

From a point 0.43 mile from the end of the Canon Mine spur, north and west to the Simpson mine (sg) — 0.6

DENVER & RIO GRANDE

Creede Branch (formerly Del Norte Branch)—extended from Wagon Wheel Gap to North Creede (ng) — 9.7

  This privately financed extension was built under the title of Rio Grande Gunnison Railway Company. D&RG leased the line upon its completion and acquired title outright in 1908. The last rail was spiked down at North Creede on December 2 and by December 5 ore was being shipped from the Creede mines.

DENVER LAKEWOOD & GOLDEN (Denver & Intermountain, 1904.) The track was electrified in 1909. Part of the line was sold to Associated Railroads in 1953 at which time the overhead electric wires were removed.)

Main line—from the east bank of the Platte River near 14th Street in Denver, west to Golden (sg) — 11.6

  The last spike was driven at Golden on September 7 at the corner of Washington and Third Streets and regular train service began September 20.

Tindale (or Ralston) Branch—from a point near the intersection of Water and Jackson Streets in Golden to end of track (sg) — 1.4

  The line ran between the UPD&G (formerly CC) track and Clear Creek to near the Golden water works, then looped toward the north.

1891 (Cont'd)

A view of Upper Creede in 1896 showing the Rio Grande track running along the street. The depot is barely visible at the upper end of the town.—(State Historical Society of Colorado)

In this turn of the century view looking northeast across Telluride a *Rio Grande Southern* mixed train is ready to depart from the station.—(W. J. Carpenter Photo—State Hist. Society of Colo.)

1891 (Cont'd)

The *Rio Grande Southern* penetrated some of the most rugged terrain in Colorado, necessitating several major engineering tasks. Shown in this photo is a portion of Ophir Loop with its winding track and numerous trestles. The two lower lines are the railroad, the upper grade is a road.—(Photo from Margaret Isabella Tammen Hogan Collection—State Hist. Society of Colo.)

1891 (Cont'd)

RIO GRANDE SOUTHERN

	Miles
Telluride Branch extended to Pandora (ng)	1.6

This extension to the mine at Pandora was completed and in service by July.

North section of main line extended from Vance Junction to Rico (ng)	29.2

The tracklaying crew reached Rico on September 30 and on October 1 the president of the road announced that the line was open for business. The traditional excursion and last spike ceremony was on October 15 and four days later regularly scheduled trains commenced operating between Ridgway and Rico.

North section—from Rico to a point near Muldoon (ng)	17.0
South section—from Porter coal mines via Dolores to a point near Muldoon (sg)	73.1

The joining of the two sections on December 20[30] completed the main line between Ridgway and Durango. A coal train ran from Durango to Rico on the completion date, scheduled trains were running between the two points by late December and through passenger service over the entire road began in January 1892.

Total	145.3

RIO GRANDE SOUTHERN RAILROAD CO.

OFFICE OF PRESIDENT.

Denver, Colorado, October 1st, 1891.

CIRCULAR No. 2.

The line from Illium Junction to Rico will be opened for business on and after this date. Stations and sidings on this line are

Ophir	Distance from Ridgway,	44.9	miles
San Bernardo	"	46.7	"
Trout Lake	"	49.1	"
Lizard Head	"	52.6	"
Coke Oven	"	60.5	"
Rico	"	66.2	"

Otto Mears
President.

(D&RG Archives—State Historical Society of Colorado)

CHANGE OF PACE

PART III

New construction declined sharply from previous levels in 1892 and continued relatively low for the balance of the decade; however, a pickup occurred after the turn of the century with rather substantial activity in some years. Growth of the State's rail system continued until 1913, the peak year of operated mileage.[1]

Activity of the previously established railroads for the balance of the 1890's and during the early 1900's consisted of closing gaps in main lines, building and extending branches and spurs, changing track gauges and retiring trackage which had served its usefulness. The Colorado & Southern Railway Company was incorporated in December 1898 as a successor to the Union Pacific, Denver & Gulf and the Denver, Leadville and Gunnison railroads. It subsequently became the only continuous north-south railroad across the State, but the continuity of trackage existed for only a few years.

A number of new railroads were added to the State's roster during the period, a few of which still exist but not necessarily under the original ownership and name. Probably the best known of these, and certainly the one with the greatest mileage, was the Denver, Northwestern & Pacific, commonly known as the Moffat Road. Its standard gauge track crossed the Continental Divide at the highest point ever reached in the United States by a railroad of its kind and it was the first to penetrate the sparsely settled communities of northwestern Colorado. Others which have survived are the Colorado & Wyoming, built to serve the coal industry west of Trinidad; the Great Western, with a network of tracks in an agricultural area east of Loveland and Longmont, and the Laramie, Hahn's Peak & Pacific which was extended from Wyoming into the North Park area of Colorado.

Other railroads which made their debut on the Colorado scene during the period have since vanished, although a few survived for periods exceeding forty years. Many of these were short mountain roads built to serve remote mining areas. They reached such places at the Cripple Creek gold mining district; mines and mills east and north of Silverton; coal mines and quarries in the Crystal River Valley and adjacent areas; the onetime lumbering center of Pagosa Springs; gilsonite deposits a short distance across the Utah state line and the Ward and Eldora mining areas west of Boulder. One of Colorado's shortest lived railroads, the Denver, Laramie & Northwestern, was completed between Denver and Greeley in 1910. It lasted only seven years.

In addition to the steam railroads which emerged during the period, electric interurbans were built in the Cripple Creek District; between Denver and nearby communities; in the Grand River Valley of western Colorado and from Trinidad to neighboring villages. Today about the only signs of their existence are scattered traces of their abandoned grades.

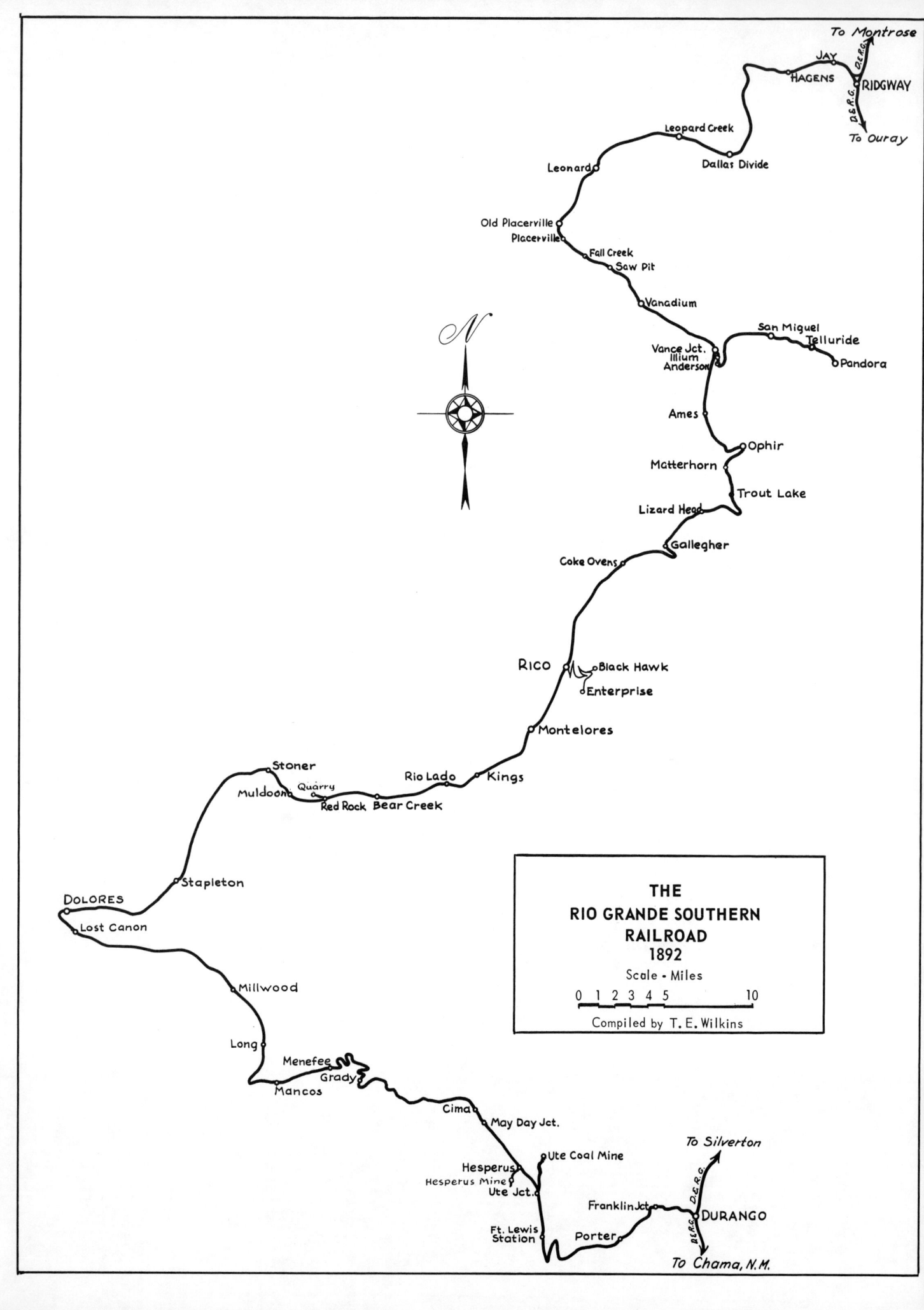

1892

| CONSTRUCTION | Miles |

CHICAGO BURLINGTON & QUINCY

Excelsior Mine Spur—from the main line of the Lyons Branch at Irvington (near MP 22.5) west to Excelsior Mine (sg) — *1.4*
    Two connections were made with the main line, forming a wye. The mileage of the spur includes both legs of the wye but not the side tracks at the mine.

CRYSTAL RIVER

Narrow gauge to standard gauge—from Carbondale south up Crystal River Valley[2]
    This 3.5-mile section was a part of the former Aspen & Western which had been acquired through foreclosure (see 1888).
From the end of the above converted track, south up Crystal River Valley to near Thompson Creek (later Sewell) (sg) — *2.5*
    This section plus the converted trackage on the narrow gauge grade gave 6 miles of standard gauge track up the valley.

DENVER LAKEWOOD & GOLDEN

From the end of the steam line near the Platte River at Denver to Fifteenth and Arapahoe Streets (electric) (sg) — *1.0*
    The track was completed in March but poles and wire were not installed until near the end of the year. The operation of regularly scheduled cars began January 1, 1893. Passengers to downtown Denver were previously transferred from steam trains to the Larimer Street cable car line.

Barnum Line (Electric)—from the steam line at Barnum Junction in Denver, south to and through Barnum (sg) — *3.0*
    The tracks formed a complete loop through Barnum. The first train ran over the line on the last day of the year and the formal opening date was January 1, 1893. The line was later operated by the Denver Tramway system as part of an intra-city route.

RIO GRANDE SOUTHERN

Enterprise Branch—from a point on the main line 1 mile north of Rico to Enterprise Mine (ng) — *4.8*
Ute Spur—Ute Junction, 1.4 miles south of Hesperus, to Ute Mine (ng) — *1.9*
Red Rock Spur—from Red Rock, 2.4 track miles east of Muldoon, to a quarry (ng) — *0.6*

1892 (Cont'd)

What is today the main section of Creede was originally known as Jimtown. In 1892 the D&RG completed a 50-car yard and depot at that point, visible in the center of the photo at right. —(E. E. Pasco Photo—Western History Collection, Univ. of Colo. Libraries)

A special train with Engine No. 1 carried photographer W. H. Jackson over the RGS in 1894. In the photo below the train is seen standing at Lizard Head.—(L. C. McClure photo· Denver Public Library—Western History Dept.)

THE DENVER AND RIO GRANDE RAILROAD CO.

OFFICE OF GENERAL SUPERINTENDENT.

CIRCULAR No. 2.

NOTICE.

Jimtown Station, on the Rio Grande Gunnison Branch, 8.61 miles from Wagon Wheel Gap, is this day opened for Freight, Ticket and Express Business.

W. E. Dingman is appointed Agent. Telegraph call "Ji," Station No. 1661.

N. W. SAMPLE,
General Superintendent.

Denver, Colorado, January 5th, 1892.

THE DENVER AND RIO GRANDE RAILROAD CO.

OFFICE OF GENERAL SUPERINTENDENT.

CIRCULAR No. 6.

South Creede station, on the Garland and Del Norte Branch, Fourth Division, located at mile post 318.7, is this day opened for Freight, Ticket and Express business.

D. O. Heywood is appointed Agent. Telegraph Call "Si." Station No. 1670.

N. W. SAMPLE,
General Superintendent.

Denver, Colorado, March 26th, 1892.

1892 (Cont'd)

	Miles

Hesperus Spur—Hesperus to Hesperus Mine
   The Enterprise branch and the three spurs were ready for service by October 15.³ — 0.7

UNION PACIFIC DENVER & GULF

Ludlow to Acme Junction (sg) — 7.2
   This section of track was completed in August and placed in operation September 1. It later became a part of a main line between Trinidad and Walsenburg.

Acme Junction southwesterly to Aguilar (sg) — 2.5
   The track was completed August 27 and opened for traffic September 1.

Gray Creek Branch extended from Chappell to Gray Creek (sg) — 2.3
   This extension was completed to the mine on December 8 and turned over to the operating department two days later.

Allen Bond Mine Spur—from the main line 1.8 miles north of Louisville, northwesterly to the end of track on the northeast slope of Davidson Mesa (sg) — 0.6

                             Total — 28.5

ABANDONMENTS

CRYSTAL RIVER

From 2.5 miles north of Thompson Creek to Thompson Mine (ng) — 9.4
   This was the remaining part of the former Aspen & Western. Six miles of the track from Thompson Creek west remained in place until 1898.⁴

SILVERTON RAILROAD

Reduced from Albany to near Ironton (ng) — 1.0

                               Total — 10.4

1893

CONSTRUCTION

BUSK TUNNEL RAILWAY (Colorado Midland, 1899)

From Busk on the Colorado Midland, through the Busk-Ivanhoe Tunnel to a connection with the CM near Ivanhoe.
(Tunnel 1.8 mile—approaches 1.1 mile) (sg) — 2.9
   The track was leased by CM which transferred all traffic from

1893 (Cont'd)

the route through Hagerman Tunnel to this lower and shorter route. Operations through the tunnel began on December 17.

Miles

CHICAGO BURLINGTON & QUINCY

From a switch 0.42 mile from the end of the Excelsior Mine spur, northerly to the New Mitchell Mine (sg)   0.6

    The New Mitchell Mine tipple was barely outside the north corporate limits of Lafayette. The main spur extended a short distance north from the tipple.

COLORADO SPRINGS RAPID TRANSIT

Extended from the D&RG Manitou depot west to a new terminus in the Manitou business district (sg)   0.7

CRYSTAL RIVER

From the railhead south of Carbondale to a point near Hot Springs (later Avalanche) (sg)   7.8

DENVER & RIO GRANDE

Floresta Branch—from Floresta Junction, 0.7 miles west of Crested Butte, westward over Kebler Pass (9,957 ft.) to coal mines at Floresta (ng)   10.7

    The track was completed and opened for operations in September.

Fremont Spur—Fremont Junction on Chandler Branch to Fremont Mine (sg)   1.9

MIDLAND TERMINAL

From a connection with the Colorado Midland at Divide, south to Midland (sg)   7.1

    This initial section of a railroad to be built into the Cripple Creek gold mining district was completed to Midland on December 9.

SILVERTON RAILROAD

Silverton east to Waldheim Mine (ng)   2.0

    This section of track later became a part of the Silverton Northern, organized in 1895.

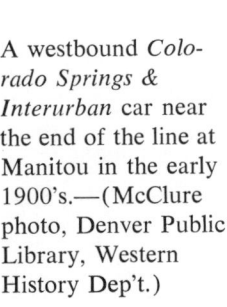

A westbound *Colorado Springs & Interurban* car near the end of the line at Manitou in the early 1900's.—(McClure photo, Denver Public Library, Western History Dep't.)

The four levels of the *Colorado Midland* track on the east side of Hagerman Pass are shown in this L. C. McClure picture. The contractor's plant for Busk-Ivanhoe Tunnel, then under construction, is at the first loop at lower center.—(Denver Public Library, Western History Dep't.)

The Allen Bond coal mine east of Boulder. The slope to the underground workings is at the right of the building. The photo was taken before the UPD&G spur reached the mine in the spring of 1893. —(Denver Public Library, Western History Dep't.)

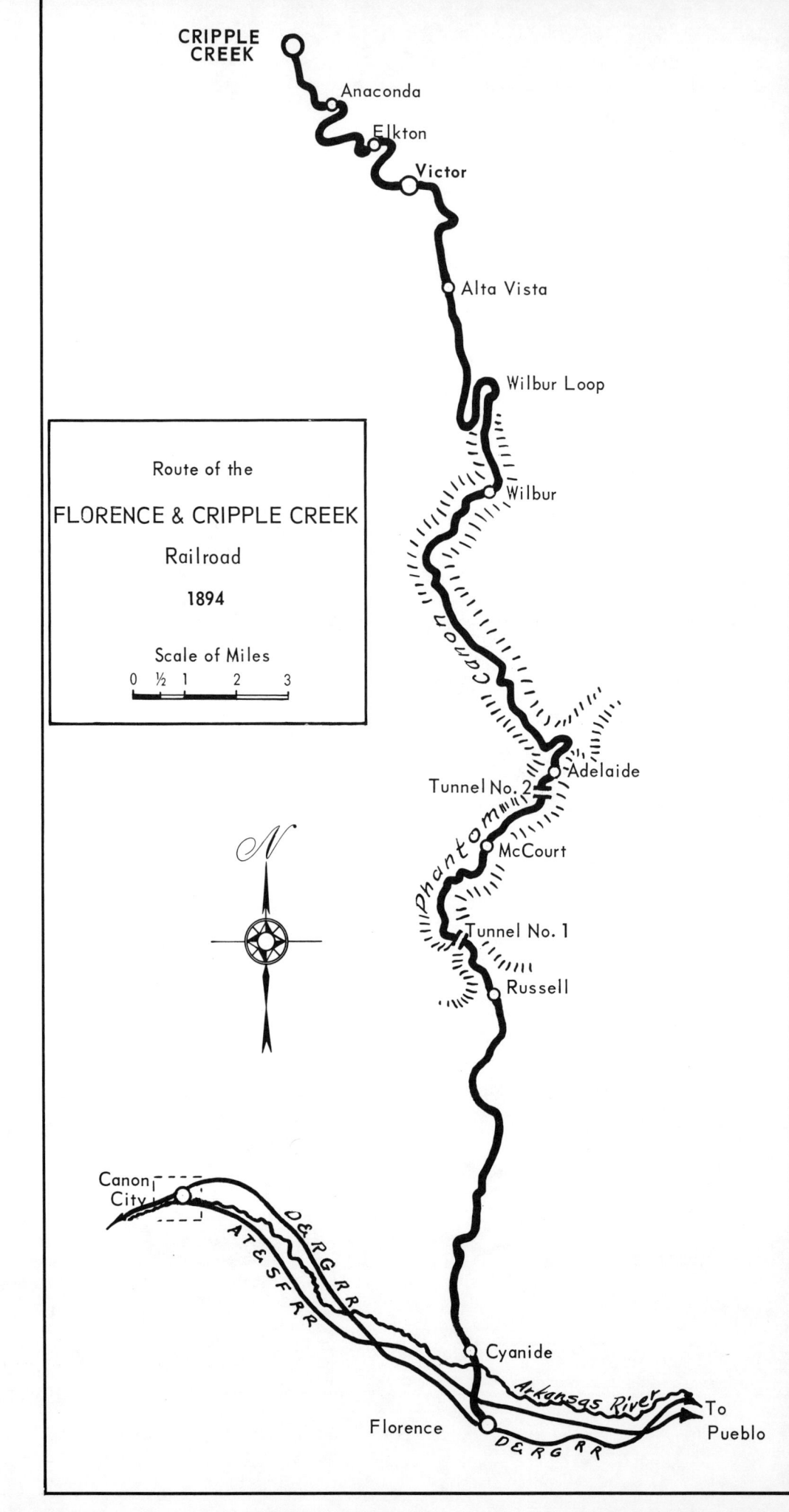

1893 (Cont'd)

UNION PACIFIC DENVER & GULF

Miles

Trinidad to Trinidad Rolling Mill (sg) — 1.9
   The line was opened for traffic in May. It later became a part of the main line between Walsenburg and Trinidad.

Allen Bond Mine Spur—from the end of track, north and west around Davidson Mesa, thence southwesterly to the mine (sg) — 2.6
   The Allen Bond Mine was near the foot of Davidson Mesa east of Boulder, a short distance south of what is now South Boulder Road. Construction of the spur was financed by the Boulder Coal and Fire Clay Company, owner of the mine. It was opened for traffic February 15.

Total — 38.2

1894

CONSTRUCTION

DENVER LAKEWOOD & GOLDEN

Tindale Branch—from the end of track north of Golden, northerly to Tindale (sg) — 5.7
   Tindale was a small coal mining community near Ralston Creek. Coal was being shipped from the mines by October.

FLORENCE & CRIPPLE CREEK (Cripple Creek & Colorado Springs, [part], 1915)

From Florence to Cripple Creek (ng) — 40.3
   This was the first of three railroads to reach the Cripple Creek gold mining district. The rails crossed the Arkansas River a short distance north of Florence, then continued north along an arroyo to the mouth of Phantom Canon. After following the main watercourse through the canyon for some 19 miles, the line looped around an adjacent mountain to the hills south of the mining district, then wound along the mountainsides through Victor and on to Cripple Creek. The track was completed to Cripple Creek on June 30 and on the same date an engine with eight construction cars pulled into town. Passenger service began the following day.

MIDLAND TERMINAL

From the railhead near Midland to Gillette (sg) — 7.3
   The track was completed on July 4 and for the next four and a half months Gillette was the transfer point for Cripple Creek traffic.

(Right) This scene on the *Florence & Cripple Creek* is an example of the rugged terrain encountered in Phantom Canon.—(Denver Public Library, Western History Department)

(Below) The first passenger train to Cripple Creek arrived over the *Florence & Cripple Creek* railroad on July 1, 1894, with the customary turnout of citizens. This was the beginning-of-the-end for the stage coach with the matched six-horse team in the foreground.—(Denver Public Library, Western History Department.)

1894 (Cont'd)

(Above) The F&CC experienced its first serious wreck less than twenty-four hours after beginning operation. At 10 o'clock A.M. on July 2, 1894 the south-bound passenger train left the track on a trestle as it was approaching Anaconda.—(A. S. Harlan Photo—State Hist. Society of Colo.)

(Right) The F&CC depot at Cripple Creek.—(Denver Public Library, Western History Department)

1894 (Cont'd)

Gillette to Portland Mine north of Victor (sg)	8.9
A temporary station was established for the accommodation of Victor passengers and freight just below the Portland Mine shaft house. The first passenger train arrived there December 16.[5] On the same day the transfer point for Cripple Creek passengers and freight was shifted from Gillette to Grassy (later named Cameron).	
Spur from Gillette south to the El Paso Reduction Company plant (sg)	0.7
Total	62.9

ABANDONMENTS

DENVER LEADVILLE & GUNNISON (The former Denver, South Park & Pacific)

Baldwin Branch (Carbon Creek Section) reduced from old Baldwin Mine to a point 1.56 mi. north of Castleton (ng)	0.6
The track was not removed until November 1909.[6] The remaining section along with other trackage was later named Kubler Branch.	

RIO GRANDE SOUTHERN

Red Rock Spur (ng)	0.6

SILVERTON RAILROAD

From near Ironton to Paymaster Mine ore track. (ng)[7]	2.2

UNION PACIFIC DENVER & GULF

Stout Branch reduced (sg)	0.5
Narrow gauge line between Boulder and Penn Gulch (Sunset) (ng)	12.7
This was the former Greeley, Salt Lake & Pacific narrow gauge road. A major portion of the line had been severely damaged by flood.	
Total	16.6

1895

| CONSTRUCTION | Miles |

DENVER LEADVILLE & GUNNISON

Spur—Kokomo to Wilfley's Mill (ng) — 1.1

DURANGO RAILWAY & REALTY COMPANY (Electric)

Durango to Animas City (sg) — 2.0
This electric railway replaced a narrow gauge horse-car railroad which briefly operated in Durango.

MIDLAND TERMINAL

Portland Mine to Victor Junction (sg) — 0.8
The laying of rails to the junction was completed about the middle of January after a delay for the completion of a large cut.

Victor Branch—Victor Junction to Victor (sg) — 0.6
This was a switchback from the main line into Victor proper. A specific date for its completion is not reported, but evidently it was after March 10.[8]

Victor Branch—extended to a point near the Independence Mine (sg) — 0.6

Victor Junction to Anaconda (sg) — 2.8
By October 9 three daily passenger trains were operating in and out of Anaconda. One of the trains was met by a stage from Cripple Creek but Grassy continued to be the transfer point for passengers for the other two trains.

Anaconda to Cripple Creek (sg) — 1.9
The rails reached the corporate limits of Cripple Creek December 19. A temporary station was built and a special passenger train arrived there December 22. Trains began using the permanent depot at the east end of Bennett Avenue early the following year.

RIO GRANDE & PAGOSA SPRINGS[9]

From the Colorado-New Mexico boundary north to Edith (ng) — 0.2
This was the Colorado portion of a railroad which connected with the D&RG main line at Lumberton, New Mexico, 6 miles south of the Colorado state line. The track was completed in late July to a settlement on the Navajo River which was named Edith later in the year.

A view of Victor looking north from Straub Mountain in 1895. The white buildings on Battle Mountain above the town are the Independence Mines with the Portland Mines above. The Strong Mine is left and downhill from the lower Independence. The equipment below the Strong is in the *Florence & Cripple Creek* yards. —(State Historical Society of Colorado)

The poor quality of this early photograph of Cripple Creek is partially atoned for by the unusual view toward the east. The date is probably early fall 1897, after the business section had been rebuilt following a fire which destroyed much of the town the previous year. The Midland Terminal depot is at the end of Bennett Avenue in the center of the picture. The trestles to the right of the depot are across Poverty Gulch at the upper end of Myers Avenue.— (Western History Collection, Univ. of Colo. Libraries.)

Walsenburg in 1895, looking southeast. The UPD&G grade can be seen approaching the town beyond the large trees in the background. The railroad equipment in the center of the scene is on the D&RG tracks.—(Denver Public Library, Western History Dep't)

1895 (Cont'd)

(Above) Anaconda was a thriving mining town when E. H. Yelton pointed his camera toward the southeast across Squaw Gulch in October 1896. The superstructure of the famous Mary McKinney Mine at left center was still under construction. Anaconda was almost totally destroyed by fire in November 1904. Today it is a ghost town.—(Western History Collection, Univ. of Colo. Libraries.)

MIDLAND TERMINAL RAILROAD
1895
Scale - Miles
0 1 2

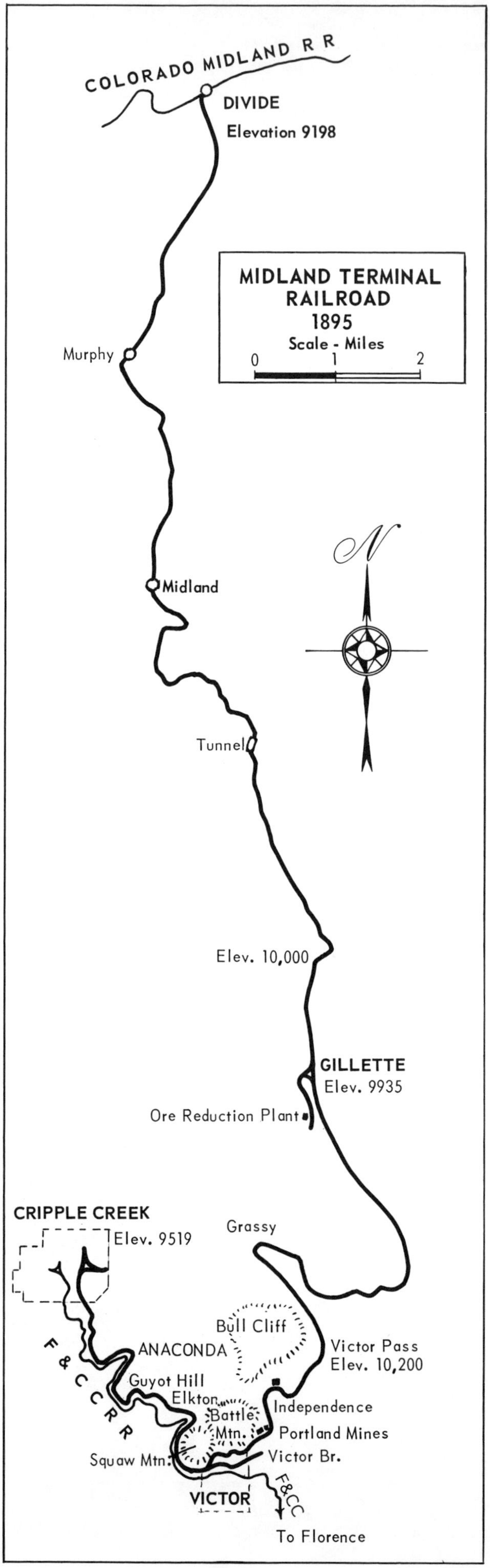

COLORADO MIDLAND R R
DIVIDE
Elevation 9198

Murphy

Midland

Tunnel

Elev. 10,000

GILLETTE
Elev. 9935

Ore Reduction Plant

CRIPPLE CREEK
Elev. 9519

Grassy

Bull Cliff

ANACONDA
Guyot Hill
Elkton
Battle Mtn.
Squaw Mtn.
F & C C R R

Victor Pass
Elev. 10,200

Independence
Portland Mines
Victor Br.
VICTOR
F & C C
To Florence

1895 (Cont'd)

	Miles
UNION PACIFIC DENVER & GULF	
From Trinidad Rolling Mill northeasterly to Forbes Junction (sg)	7.6

A special train ran over this section of track on June 25 on a round trip between Trinidad and Aguilar.

Acme Junction to Walsenburg Junction (sg)	19.9

The laying of the last rail at Walsenburg on July 27 completed a continuous line between that place and Trinidad. On August 1 mixed trains were placed in service between the two towns and on the same date UPD&G trains between Denver and Fort Worth were transferred to the new route. The agreement for the use of D&RG tracks between Walsenburg and Trinidad was terminated.

Total	37.5

ABANDONMENT

GOLDEN CITY & SOUTH PLATTE

Golden to end of track (ng)	1.7

1896

CONSTRUCTION

CHICAGO BURLINGTON & QUINCY

From a point on the track to the Simpson Mine to a junction with the Excelsior Mine spur (sg)	0.7

This closed the gap between the two spurs giving a continuous 2.46-mile loop through Lafayette.

From the New Mitchell Mine spur about 500 feet west of the point of the switch, west to Gladstone Mine (sg)	0.2

DENVER & RIO GRANDE

Loma Branch—Pictou to Maitland (sg)	1.2

DENVER SOUTH PARK & HILL TOP (Colorado & Southern, 1899)

From Hill Top Junction on the Garos-Fairplay-Alma Branch of the DL&G, to mines at Leavick (ng)	11.3

Constructed jointly by the Hill Top Mining Company and the receiver for the Denver, Leadville & Gunnison, the line was completed and opened for business in December. It was operated in

1896 (Cont'd)

The northeastern section of Victor as it appeared in 1896. The buildings in the foreground were on the north side of Victor Avenue and the street at the right is North Second. The railroad equipment below the Strong Mine at center right is in the F&CC yards. The initial point of the *Golden Circle Railroad* is off the picture a short distance to the right of the equipment. The large building at center left is the Public (Victor) Sampling Works. The tops of MT gondolas can be seen to the right of the sampler. Many of the buildings in the photo were destroyed by a fire which swept through the town in August 1899.—(State Historical Society of Colorado)

Three levels of track are seen in this photo taken before 1900 looking northeast across Victor from above Seventh Street. The lower track is the F&CC main line; next above is the MT switchback (Victor Branch) and the rock fill at extreme upper left is on the main line of the MT. Note the equipment on the MT main line just below the Portland Mine at upper right.
—(Denver City Library, Western History Dep't)

112

1896 (Cont'd)

Miles

conjunction with the DL&G. Shortly after its completion title to the mining company's share passed to the DL&G receiver and in 1899 became a part of the Colorado & Southern system.

GOLDEN CIRCLE (Cripple Creek & Colorado Springs, 1915; Midland Terminal, 1921)

From a point near the east end of the Florence and Cripple Creek yards at Victor, northeasterly along the foot of Battle Mountain to Goldfield (ng) — 1.7^{10}

The railroad was organized to serve mines on Battle Mountain and Bull Hill north of Victor. Although a separate corporation, it was controlled by the F&CC. F&CC suburban train service, which had been operating between Cripple Creek and Victor, was extended to Goldfield on November 29, becoming a joint F&CC and GC operation.

RIO GRANDE & PAGOSA SPRINGS

From Edith northeast along the Navajo River to Chromo (ng) — 5.2

ROCKY MOUNTAIN FUEL COMPANY

From the end of the DL&G track 1.56 miles north of Castleton to Kubler Mine (ng) — 1.8

This trackage together with the connecting DL&G track was operated by DL&G and later by D&RG as the Kubler Branch.

SILVERTON NORTHERN

From the Silverton Railroad extension near Waldheim Mine, northeasterly to Eureka (ng) — 6.5

The two-mile track between Silverton and the Waldheim Mine, built by the Silverton Railroad in 1893, was transferred to the Silverton Northern, the two railroads being under common ownership at the time. The last rail was spiked down at Eureka in late June.

UNION PACIFIC DENVER & GULF

Aguilar Branch extended from Brodhead Mine to No. 4 Jct. (sg) — 1.0

This extension was built by the coal company which fact became an issue in abandonment proceedings several years later.

Total — 29.6

1896 (Cont'd)

ABANDONMENTS | Miles

CHICAGO BURLINGTON & QUINCY

Baker Mine Spur (sg) | 0.6

CHICAGO ROCK ISLAND & PACIFIC

Elsmere to McFerran Mine (sg) | 4.7
From 1891 to 1894 UPD&G had trackage rights over 2.5 miles of this track from a connection at Cable Junction, about 0.5 mile south of Manitou Junction, to the mine.

DENVER LAKEWOOD & GOLDEN

Golden to Tindale (sg) | 7.1
The line was declared abandoned by the railroad company after a section was washed out by a June flood. The track was not removed until 1904.[11]

Total | 12.4

1897

CONSTRUCTION

COLORADO & NORTHWESTERN (Denver, Boulder & Western, 1909)

From Boulder westward to end of track in Boulder Canon (sg) | 1.0[12]
This railroad was to follow the general route but not the exact alignment of the abandoned UPD&G (GSL&P) through Boulder and Four Mile Canons.

CRIPPLE CREEK DISTRICT RAILWAY (Electric) (Colorado Springs & Cripple Creek District, 1899)

Cripple Creek to Victor (sg) | 6.4
Starting on Myers Avenue in Cripple Creek the tracks ran east up Poverty Gulch then along a winding route on mountainsides to Midway, elevation 10,480 feet. The gain in altitude was nearly a thousand feet in a little over three miles. From Midway it descended the slopes of Bull Hill and Battle Mountain to Victor, a drop in altitude of around 760 feet. It was said to be the highest electric railway in the world at the time it was built.[13] The grade was completed to Victor November 20 and the rails and

1897 (Cont'd)

Miles

catenary were in place by December 1. Cars for the line were received at Cripple Creek December 13, trial runs were conducted on January 1 and 2, and regular service began January 3, 1898. The Victor terminal was temporarily at Fifth Street and Granite Avenue but a permanent terminal was soon established one block south at Fifth Street and Diamond Avenue. In 1899 the line was purchased by the Colorado Springs & Cripple Creek District Railway Company for use as terminal property and access to mines. After the transfer of title it was named the First Electric Division and later changed to High Line Electric District of the CS&CCD.

GOLDEN CIRCLE

From a point on the loop at Goldfield southerly to the main line of the Midland Terminal (ng)	0.5

The MT track was reached about September but construction was stalled at that point because of refusal of the MT to permit a crossing. A temporary wood trestle over the MT track was completed in the early morning hours of January 1, 1898.[14] It was replaced by a permanent steel structure the following May.

RIO GRANDE & PAGOSA SPRINGS

Extended from Chromo up Little Navajo Creek (ng)	3.0
From Chromo easterly up Navajo River to Howes Springs (ng)	4.0
Total	*14.9*

ABANDONMENTS

DENVER LEADVILLE & GUNNISON

Extension from Castleton up Ohio Creek reduced (ng)	0.5

UNION PACIFIC DENVER & GULF

Forbes Junction to Forbes Mine (sg)	2.6
Total	*3.1*

1898 (Cont'd)

Looking north across Ward the C&NW depot is seen at upper left. The extension to New Market was on the grade along the hill at upper right.—(H. H. Lake photo, State Hist. Society of Colo.)

The Golden Circle was required to build a steel tunnel above ground on the southeast slope of Battle Mountain to permit the Portland Mine to utilize its dumping grounds. It was eventually covered with waste rock from the mine. Construction of the skeleton of the tunnel was under way when this photo was taken in 1898.—(State Historical Society of Colorado)

1898 (Cont'd)

| CONSTRUCTION | Miles |

COLORADO & NORTHWESTERN

From the railhead in Boulder Canon to the mouth of Four Mile Creek, thence through Four Mile Canon to Sunset (ng) — 12.3
    A special train ran as far as Wallstreet (about M.P. 9) on February 13. The rails reached Sunset February 20[15] which was an occasion for an excursion train to that point.

Culbertson Spur—from a connection with the UPD&G at Allison (Culbertson) 4 miles east of Boulder, north to Culbertson (Pennsylvania) Mill (dg) — 1.7
    This isolated spur was reached over UPD&G tracks to which a third rail had been added from Boulder to Allison Station. The first shipment of ore was received at the mill on May 23.

Sunset to Ward (ng) — 12.8
    From Sunset the track climbed northeasterly along the north wall of Four Mile Canon then reversed its route toward the west and passed across a ridge to the upper reaches of Left Hand Canon, thence northward around a series of curves along a mountain slope to Ward. The tracklaying gang reached Ward July 1 and the following day a train arrived at the station.

Extension—Ward to New Market (ng) — 0.5
    Some additional grading was done but no record was found of any steel beyond New Market.

CRYSTAL RIVER

From end of track near Hot Springs to Redstone (sg) — 4.2
    The track was completed to Redstone in December.

DENVER & RIO GRANDE

Ibex Branch—from Ibex Junction (at Leadville) to Ibex (ng) — 7.2
    An extensive mining area east of Leadville was served by this branch. It reached an altitude of 11,550 feet near Ibex, 1,350 feet higher than the Leadville station. The line was completed and opened for traffic on November 24.

Standard gauge to dual gauge—Chandler Junction to Fremont Mine.
    This conversion was to permit F&CC narrow gauge equipment to operate to the mine.

GILPIN TRAMWAY

Pease-Kansas Branch—from main track 4.6 miles from Black

The Gilpin Tram hauled ore from the mines to the mills and delivered coal to the mines. (Above) A train of ore drifting downgrade in Chase Gulch above Black Hawk. (Below) Two Shay engines head a train with four cars of coal and a string of ore cars on Quartz Hill.—(Both photos, Denver Public Library, Western Hist. Dept.)

1898 (Cont'd)

Hawk to Pease-Kansas Mine (2 ft.)	0.7
Spur to Clifton Belle Mine in Russell Gulch (2 ft.)	0.3

GOLDEN CIRCLE

Extended from the MT crossing on the east slope of Battle Mountain to Isabella Mine (ng) — 3.2

   The track followed a circuitous route with maximum grades exceeding 4 percent along the slopes of mountains to the mine on the north slope of Bull Hill.

Bull Hill Branch—Lillie Junction (later Bull Hill Junction) to Lillie Mine between Independence and Goldfield (ng) — 1.0

   Lillie Junction was near the saddle between Battle Mountain and Bull Hill, 3.3 miles from the Victor station.

LEADVILLE MINERAL BELT (Colorado & Southern, 1900)

From a connection with the DL&G at L.M.B. Junction, 1.2 miles north of the Leadville station, southward to mines in the Fryer Hill and Graham Park areas (ng) — 2.3

RIO GRANDE & PAGOSA SPRINGS

Extended from Howes Springs up Navajo River to Price (ng) — 2.0

UNION PACIFIC DENVER & GULF

Berwind Branch extended to Shelbina (sg)	0.4
Lafayette-Louisville Branch extended (sg)	0.5
Standard gauge to dual gauge—Boulder east to Allison Station[16]	
Total	49.1

ABANDONMENTS   Miles

DENVER CIRCLE

Entire system (ng) — 9.7

UNION PACIFIC DENVER & GULF

Track between Silver Plume and Graymont (Bakerville) reduced (ng) — 3.7

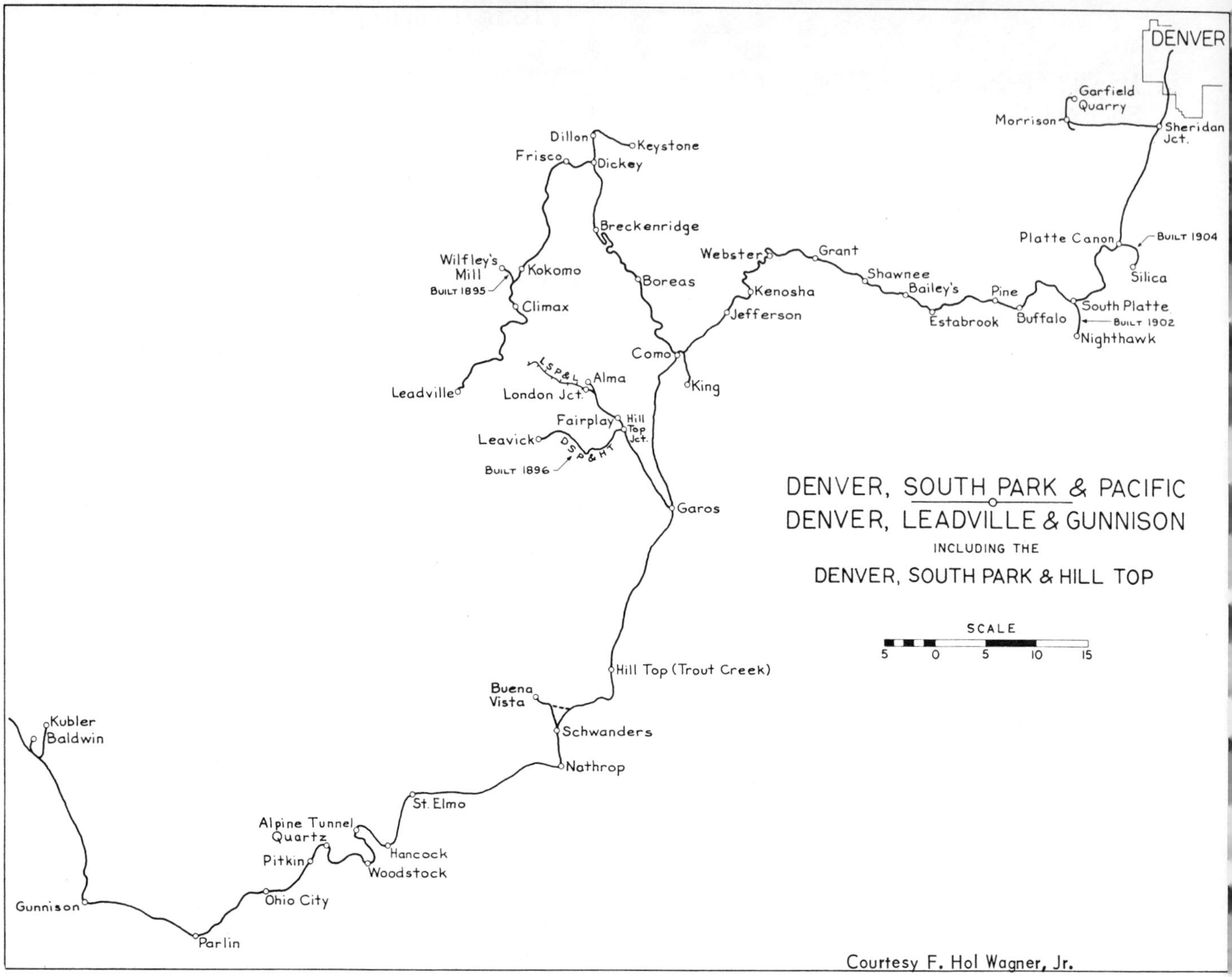

Map of the DSP&P.—
(Courtesy of F. Hol
Wagner, Jr.)

120

1898 (Cont'd)

	Miles
Remaining section of former Colorado Central trackage from Fort Collins north (sg)	0.6
Franceville Branch—Franceville Junction to Franceville (sg)	4.6
Ralston to Glencoe (former D&MP) (ng)	4.6
Total	23.2

1899

On December 18, 1898 the COLORADO & SOUTHERN RAILWAY COMPANY was incorporated for the specific purpose of acquiring by purchase through foreclosure proceedings all properties of

> The Union Pacific Denver & Gulf Railway Company, except the Julesburg-La Salle Branch which by prior agreement was sold to the Union Pacific Railroad Company, and

> The Denver, Leadville & Gunnison Railway Company, including the Denver South Park & Hill Top Railway Company.

The Colorado & Southern commenced operating the system under its corporate name January 11, 1899.

CONSTRUCTION

ATCHISON TOPEKA & SANTA FE

Curtis Mine Spur—from a siding adjacent to the main line about 3.5 miles north of the Colorado Springs station, east to Curtis Coal Mine (sg) — *1.3*

CANON CITY & CRIPPLE CREEK

From Canon City east to a junction with the F&CC at Oro Junta, 6.8 miles north of Florence (ng) — *7.2*

> The last rail was laid on December 18 and the line was immediately leased to the F&CC. The two companies, along with the Golden Circle and the Midland Terminal, were consolidated into a holding company, The Denver & Southwestern Railway Company, although each road retained its corporate identity.

COLORADO & NORTHWESTERN

Spur from Big Five Junction, 2.5 track miles east of Ward, to Dew Drop Tunnel (ng) — *0.7*

This little locomotive was purchased by the *Golden Circle Railroad* in 1898 for use in suburban commuter service.—(Western History Collection, Univ. of Colo. Libraries)

A 2-car F&CC-GC commuter train on the loop at Vista Grande. (From a booklet entitled "A Trip to the Great Gold District.", State Hist. Society of Colo.)

1899 (Cont'd)

	Miles

COLORADO & SOUTHERN

From Rugby, on the main line 4 miles north of Acme Junction, westerly to Primrose Mine (sg) — 1.9

From Forbes southwesterly to Forbes Mine (Cox & Wood) (sg) — 1.7
    This was a different opening than the Forbes Mine served by DT&FW and UPD&G between 1888 and 1897.

CRYSTAL RIVER

Redstone to Placita (sg) — 3.4
    On September 28 the track was completed to Placita, the end of construction for this railroad. An extension was later built by a separate company.

DENVER & RIO GRANDE

From La Veta over La Veta Pass to Wagon Creek Junction (sg) — 26.5
    This was a new standard gauge line to the south of the narrow gauge over Veta Pass. It joined the narrow gauge route at Wagon Creek Junction.

Narrow gauge to standard gauge—Wagon Creek Junction to Alamosa.

FLORENCE & CRIPPLE CREEK

Spur from Vesta Junction, 2.1 miles north of Florence, east and south to ore reduction plants (ng) — 1.9

GOLDEN CIRCLE

From the Isabella Mine to Vista Grande (Midway) (ng) — 0.9
    That was the end of the line. Trains were turned on a balloon loop, the westernmost part of which was only about two hundred feet from the Cripple Creek District Electric line. The last rail was laid on the loop about the middle of March and on April 2 suburban train service was extended from Goldfield to Vista Grande.

Lillie Branch extended to Cripple Creek Sampler at Bull Hill (dg) — 0.5

RIO GRANDE PAGOSA & NORTHERN (Denver & Rio Grande, 1908)

From Pagosa Junction on the main line of the D&RG 61 track miles east of Durango, northerly to end of track (ng) — 14.5
Construction was discontinued in December because of snow.

Engine No. 52 heads a 3-car F&CC-GC commuter train south of Anaconda in the late spring of 1901. The large building in the background is the superstructure of the Mary McKinney Mine.—(State Hist. Society of Colo. Library)

Looking southeast across a section of the Cripple Creek District shortly after the turn of the century, the *Florence & Cripple Creek* track is seen winding along the south slope of Guyot Hill and the upper reaches of Arequa Gulch. Mountain appears at upper right.—(Denver Public Library, Western History Dept.)

1899 (Cont'd)

	Miles

RIO GRANDE WESTERN

Grand Junction to Sugar Factory (sg) 1.2
  This spur was used jointly by RGW, D&RG & CM.

SILVERTON GLADSTONE & NORTHERLY (Silverton Northern, 1915)

From Silverton north to Gladstone (ng) 7.3
  This short railroad which served mines and mills located along Cement Creek was completed on August 1. A time table in a September 2 issue of a local newspaper showed twice-a-day mixed train service over the line.[17]

VICTOR FUEL COMPANY

From a connection with the C&S at Hastings to the Victor Fuel Company mine at Delagua (sg) 2.4
  The track was conveyed in 1903 to the Colorado & Southeastern Railway Company.

Total 71.4

ABANDONMENTS

COLORADO & SOUTHERN

King Mine spur (ng) 2.7
  A 0.29 mile section was left in place for use as one leg of a wye.

COLORADO MIDLAND

Original main line between Busk and Ivanhoe via Hagerman Tunnel (sg) 9.8
  In 1897 the Colorado Midland transferred operations back to its old line through Hagerman Tunnel. However, after a costly experience with snow in the winter of 1899, it permanently abandoned the higher route and again transferred operations through Busk-Ivanhoe Tunnel, acquiring the Busk Tunnel Railway Company outright at the time.

DENVER & RIO GRANDE

Narrow gauge line between La Veta and Wagon Creek Junction (ng) 26.5

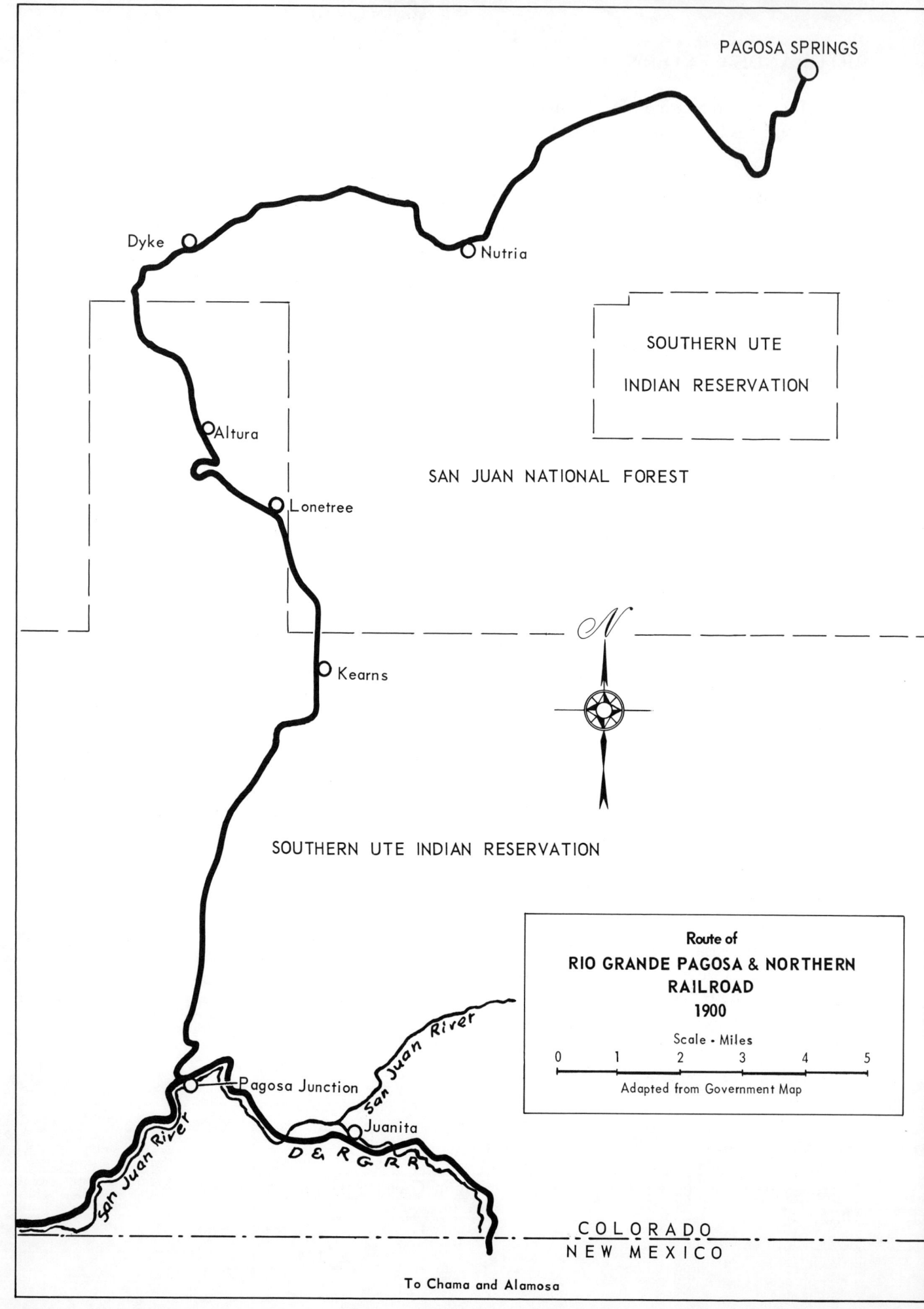

1899 (Cont'd)

With the new standard gauge line over La Veta Pass, this narrow gauge trackage was no longer needed. The track was removed as far as Placer in 1902. The section between Placer and Wagon Creek Junction and the branch to the Trinchera Mine was sold to the Trinchera Estate but evidently was never used. The Trinchera Mine closed about 1883.[18]

	Miles
Total	39.0

1900

CONSTRUCTION

CHICAGO BURLINGTON & QUINCY

From Colorado-Nebraska state line south to a junction with the UP at Sterling (sg) — 27.8

From the main line of the Burlington at Brush, north to a junction with the UP at Pawnee (later Union) (sg) — 11.4

    These two sections were built by another CB&Q subsidiary, the Denver & Montana Railroad Company, as part of a line linking Alliance, Nebraska with the main line to Denver.

    Both sections were opened for traffic on September 16. An agreement was reached to use UP tracks for the 23 miles between Sterling and Pawnee.

COLORADO SPRINGS & CRIPPLE CREEK DISTRICT

Electric line between Cripple Creek & Victor (sg) — 5.1

    This was an addition to the Cripple Creek district electric railway system purchased by the CS&CCD in 1899. Construction began at Fourth Street and Warren Avenue in Cripple Creek and followed a winding course somewhat lower in altitude and shorter in distance than the route via Midway. The rails reached the Victor terminus on Victor Avenue at Fourth Street on September 7 and regular service started two days later. The line was first designated as the Second Electric Division and later became the Low Line Electric District of the CS&CCD.

Main Line—Colorado Springs to a point near Summit (sg) — 20.0[19]

    This was to be the third railroad into the Cripple Creek District originating from the outside. It was built along the sides of mountains and rims of canons through the rugged country east and south of Pikes Peak. The altitude gain in the 20 miles between Colorado Srings and the railhead near Summit was about 3,750 feet. On September 1 an excursion passenger train ran over 7 miles of the new track from Colorado Springs to a point beyond Point Sublime.

The Burlington depot at Brush in 1900.—(Denver Public Library, Western History Dep't.)

Switchbacks on the *Crystal River* narrow gauge between Redstone and Coal Basin.—(State Historical Society of Colorado)

A depot and other railroad facilities were completed at Pagosa Springs shortly after the RGP&N reached the town. In this photo taken from the west some twenty years later we see the well preserved depot and the water tank. An engine with several box cars in tow has pulled forward after spotting a combine at the station. —(Denver Public Library, Western History Dep't.)

1900 (Cont'd)

CRYSTAL RIVER

	Miles
Coal Basin Branch—from a connection with the main line near Redstone, west up Coal Creek to mines at Coal Basin (ng)	11.8

    The extreme curvature and grade of this branch dictated the use of narrow gauge trackage. The completion date was November 22.

DENVER & RIO GRANDE

Graham Park Branch—Graham Park Junction on Chrysolite Branch in Leadville District to Wolftone Mine (ng)	1.6
Westcliffe Branch—from the main line at Texas Creek southward toward Westcliffe (sg)	3.0

    This was the beginning of a standard gauge branch which would follow a different route to Westcliffe than the narrow gauge line abandoned eleven years earlier. Construction was by the Rio Grande Railroad Company, a subsidiary which later built other D&RG extensions.

Narrow gauge to dual gauge—Alamosa to Monte Vista.

LEADVILLE MINERAL BELT

From the end of the C&S main line south of the Leadville station to the Bon Air Mines (dg)	0.7

    Title to the LMB was transferred to C&S on June 26, about two months after completion of this section of track.

COLORADO & SOUTHERN

From Forbes Mine spur 0.10 mile from Forbes, westerly to Majestic Mine (sg)	1.5

Narrow gauge to dual gauge—former LMB line to mines in Graham Park area in Leadville district.

RIO GRANDE PAGOSA & NORTHERN

Extended from the end of track to Pagosa Springs (ng)	16.3

    The track was completed by October 13 and a construction train entered Pagosa Springs on that date. Scheduled trains were operating over the line ten days later. All the capital stock of the railroad was acquired by D&RG in 1902. In 1908 it became a part of the D&RG corporate structure and was thereafter operated as the Pagosa Springs Branch.

Total	99.2

(Right) An 1897 Buckwalter photo of Rico. The Enterprise Mines were on the mountain slopes above the village.—(State Historical Society of Colorado)

(Below) One of the many spectacular views on the route of the CS&CCD showing three levels of track, tunnel and trestle near St. Peters.—(L. C. McClure photo, State Hist. Society of Colo.)

1900 (Cont'd)

ABANDONMENTS

	Miles
LA PLATA	
Entire line—La Plata Junction to La Plata Mine (ng)	3.8
RIO GRANDE & PAGOSA SPRINGS	
Chromo up Little Navajo Creek (sg)	4.0
RIO GRANDE SOUTHERN	
Enterprise Branch—Rico to Enterprise Mine (ng)	4.8
SOUTH PARK & LEADVILLE SHORT LINE	
Entire line—London Junction to London Mine (ng) This was the former London, South Park & Leadville.	7.4
Total	20.0

1901

CONSTRUCTION

ATCHISON TOPEKA & SANTA FE

New line between Pueblo and Bragdon (sg) — 11.6
  This was a main line relocation along the western limits of Pueblo.

BOSTON COAL & FUEL COMPANY (Calumet Fuel Company, 1906)

From Franklin Junction on the RGS 2.8 miles west of Durango, west and north to coal mines at Perrins (ng) — 4.7
  The line was completed in November. In 1906 it was leased by RGS and thereafter operated by that company as the Calumet Branch.

CHICAGO ROCK ISLAND & PACIFIC

From the main line about 1.5 miles east of Roswell, northerly to Rapson No. 2 Mine[20] (sg) — 1.1

"Devils Slide," on the CS& CCD between Duffields and Summit. —(W. H. Jackson photo—State Hist. Society of Colo.)

1901 (Cont'd)

Pikes Peak looms in the distance as two CS&CCD passenger trains meet at the summit of Hoosier Pass, about five miles from the Cripple Creek station.—(A. J. Harlan photo, State Hist. Society of Colo.)

D&RG locomotive No. 527 running special to Westcliffe on June 17, 1901 with a mixed consist for use on the first regular train to depart from the town.—(State Historical Society of Colorado)

A view of Westcliffe shortly after 1900 looking west toward the majestic Sangre de Cristo Mountain Range. The D&RG depot was at the west end of the town's main street, shown in this photo.—(Denver Public Library, Western History Dep't)

A D&RG train at "Inspiration Point" on the Westcliffe Branch. — (State Historical Society of Colorado)

Looking northeast across Edith about 1901. The *Rio Grande & Pagosa Springs* track from Lumberton, N. M. angles across the picture in the foreground. —(State Historical Society of Colorado)

1901 (Cont'd)

Miles

COLORADO & SOUTHERN

From the main line at Loveland east to the site of the Great Western Sugar Factory (sg) — *1.0*

    Building material and supplies were being hauled over the completed line to the factory site by March.

From the main line east of Marshall, west and north to the Fox Mine (Fox Patterson Mine) (sg) — *1.0*

    The opening of this mine was at a different location than that of the earlier Fox Mine served by the GB&C.

COLORADO & WYOMING

From a connection with the AT&SF at Jansen, 2.1 miles west of Trinidad, westerly to Weston (sg) — *19.2*

Branch—Primero Junction to Primero (sg) — *2.6*

    The tracks to Weston and Primero were completed in March and placed in operation in June.

COLORADO SPRINGS & CRIPPLE CREEK DISTRICT

From the railhead near Summit to Cameron (sg) — *19.0*

Cameron via Hoosier Pass to Cripple Creek (sg) — *5.8*[21]

    The completion of the road was celebrated with a last spike ceremony at Cripple Creek on March 23. A special train from Colorado Springs ran over the line the day of the ceremony, another on March 27 and regular passenger service began April 8.

Victor Branch—Cameron to Victor (sg) — *5.1*

    The tracklaying crew reached Victor November 7 and on November 9 a train with railroad officials and invited guests aboard ran to the terminal at Second Street and Diamond Avenue. A regular schedule went into effect November 10 with stub passenger trains connecting with Cripple Creek sections at Cameron.

Portland Branch—from Lillie Junction[22] (later Vindicator Junction) on the Victor Branch, northwesterly through Independence, thence southwesterly via the Portland Mines to the Ajax Mine (sg) — *2.0*

    This steam branch crossed the First Electric Division line near Dyer station.

Colorado City Branch—Colorado City Junction to ore reduction plants (sg) — *2.0*

DENVER & NORTHWESTERN (Electric)

From the end of the Berkley Park street car line in Northwest

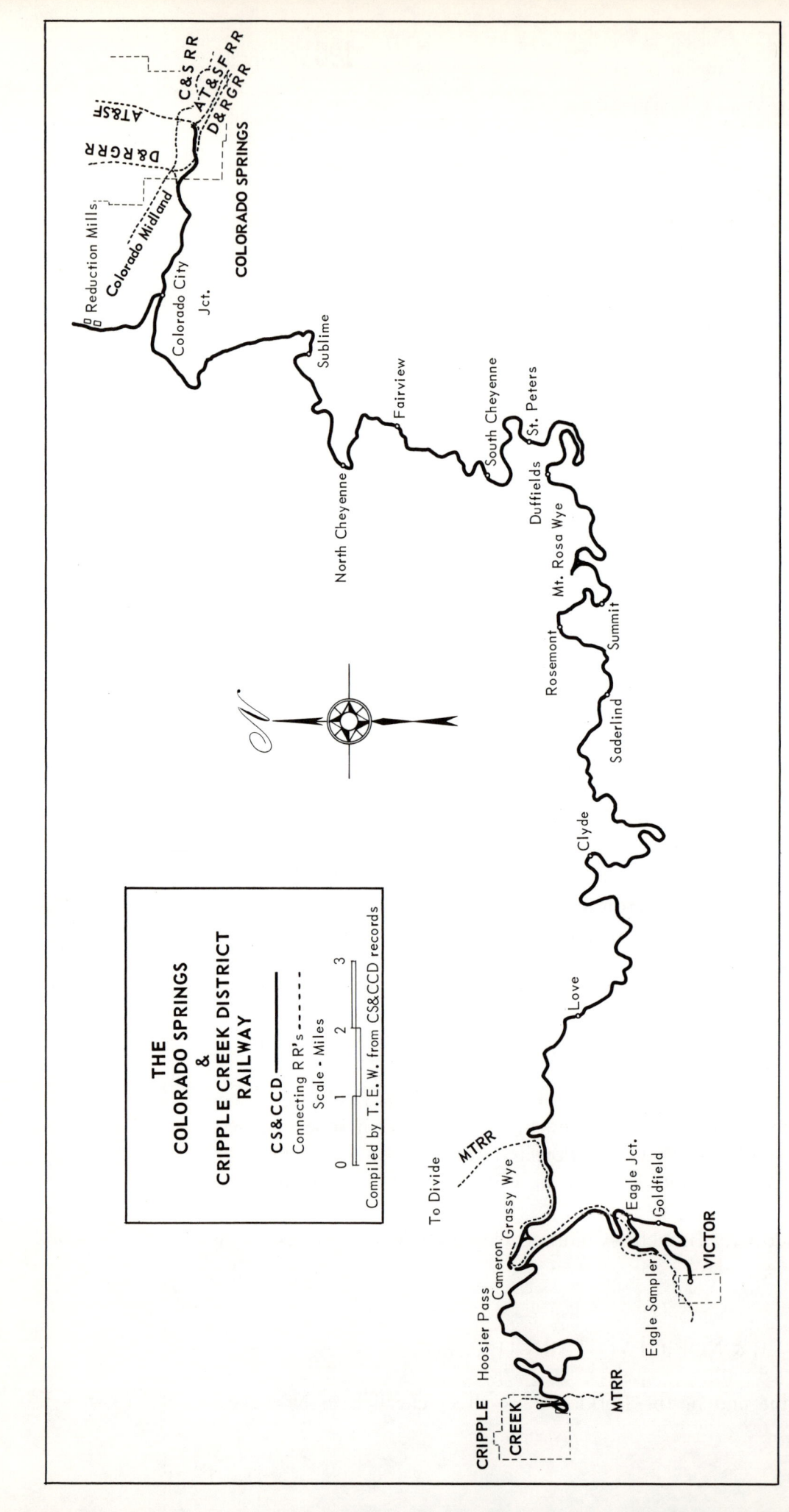

1901 (Cont'd)

	Miles
Denver (later Lakeside), west and north to Arvada (3 ft.-6 in.)	
This initial section of a line to the Leyden Mines was placed in service in November.	3.0

DENVER & RIO GRANDE

Westcliffe Branch—extended from end of track to Westcliffe (sg)	22.5
The branch was completed and opened for business on June 18.	
Crestone Branch—Moffat to Cottonwood (ng)	17.0
This branch, built under the name of the Rio Grande Sangre de Cristo Railroad Company, was completed August 22.	
Narrow gauge to dual gauge:	
Alamosa to Antonito	
Monte Vista to Del Norte	

RIO GRANDE & PAGOSA SPRINGS

From Edith north to Boone on Coyote Creek (ng)	6.0
This was the beginning of a new line in the direction of Pagosa Springs.	
Total	123.6

ABANDONMENT

ATCHISON TOPEKA & SANTA FE

A section of the original main line between Pueblo and Bragdon (sg)	10.6
This was the original main line between the two points.	

1902

CONSTRUCTION

ATCHISON TOPEKA & SANTA FE

From the Curtis Mine spur about one-half mile east of its initial point north to Danville Coal Mine (sg)	0.4

COLORADO & SOUTHERN

Minnequa Junction to Southern Junction (sg)	2.0
The track was placed in operation early the following year.	
South Platte (Watertown) on old DL&G line to Night Hawk (ng)	4.1
Aguilar Branch extended from No. 4 Jct. to Beacon Mine (sg)	0.8

The CS&CCD electric cars made frequent runs through the Cripple Creek gold mining district. A high line car passes the Portland No. 1 Mine on the southeast slope of Battle Mountain above Victor prior to 1903.

This 1904 view of the CS&CCD electric line is on the south slope of Bull Hill just below the Blue Bird Mine.
—(Both photos—State Historical Society of Colorado)

1902 (Cont'd)

COLORADO & WYOMING

	Miles
From end of track at Weston southwest to Tercio (sg)	10.2

The track was completed in February.

Piedmont Branch—Sopris east to Piedmont Mine (sg)	0.8

The specific completion date for this branch is not recorded.

Primero Branch extended (sg)	0.4

COLORADO SPRINGS & CRIPPLE CREEK DISTRICT

Colorado Springs yard to a connection with the AT&SF (sg)	1.1
Eagle Sampler Spur—from the main line at Eagle Junction, 0.3 mile north of the Goldfield station, to the Eagle Sampler on the east slope of Battle Mountain (sg)	1.1
Economic Mill Spur—from Economic Junction on the Second Electric Division (Low Line), 0.8 mile west of the Victor Terminal, to the Economic Mill (sg)	0.5

The spur was not electrified.

Altman (Midway) Branch—from the main line at Hoosier Pass south and southeasterly to Midway (sg)	1.2

This branch became a part of the electric car route in 1905.

First Electric Division (High Line)—from Dyer Station near the saddle between Bull Hill and Battle Mountain to a connection with the Portland Branch at a point thereafter known as Portland Junction (sg)	0.1

The connection was completed near the end of the year. The purpose was to provide a connection for a new route for electric cars over the steam lines between Portland Junction and the Victor terminal at Second Street and Diamond Avenue. Electrification of the steam lines was completed about the middle of the following February and electric car service over the new route began March 1, 1903.[23]

DENVER & NORTHWESTERN (Electric)

From the end of track at Arvada, northwesterly to Leyden Junction (3 ft-6 in.)	5.2

DENVER & RIO GRANDE

North Fork Branch—from Delta northeasterly up the valley of the North Fork of the Gunnison River to Somerset (ng)	43.1

This coal branch, built under the charter of the Rio Grande Railroad Company, was completed to a coal mine at Somerset on December 21.

1902 (Cont'd)

	Miles
Blende (Zinc Smelter) Spur—Zinc Junction, south of Minnequa, to Blende (sg)	3.4

    Completed in August under the name of Rio Grande, Pueblo & Southern Railroad Company, this branch served a zinc smelter at Blende, southeast of Pueblo.

Overland Junction (at Denver) to Overland Park (sg)	0.7

Dual gauge to standard gauge:
    Denver to Pueblo
    Manitou Branch
    Fort Logan Branch
    Alamosa to Del Norte
    Eilers to Oro Junction
    California Gulch Branch

Narrow gauge to standard gauge:
    Castle Rock to O'Brien's Quarry
    Del Norte to North Creede

FLORENCE & CRIPPLE CREEK

Beacon Hill Branch—from the main line about 0.7 track mile south of Anaconda, southwesterly to El Paso Mine on the northwest slope of Beacon Hill (ng)	0.8

GREAT WESTERN

From Loveland easterly and southeasterly to Johnstown, thence west to Buda (sg)	15.7

    This was the first segment of a railroad owned by the Great Western Sugar Company, built primarily to haul sugar beets to the company's plants.

RIO GRANDE & PAGOSA SPRINGS

From Boone north to Blanco (ng)	7.0
Total	98.6

ABANDONMENTS

COLORADO & SOUTHERN

Allen Bond Mine Spur (sg)	3.2
Jersey Cutoff reduced (sg)	0.5
Former Colorado Central transfer track at Fort Collins (sg)	0.2
Aguilar Branch—a section of track between Acme Junction and Brodhead Junction (sg)	0.4

1902 (Cont'd)

This was replaced by another track the following year.

Miles

DENVER & RIO GRANDE

Douglas to Madge Quarry (ng) — 2.6

NOLAND LAND & TRANSFER COMPANY

Trackage reduced (sg)[24] — 0.5

RIO GRANDE & PAGOSA SPRINGS

Edith to Price (ng)[25] — 11.0

Total — 18.4

1903

CONSTRUCTION

COLORADO & SOUTHERN

Fort Collins to Wellington (sg) — 10.8
    This segment was built under the name of Fort Collins Development Railway Company which was controlled and operated by C&S. It later became a part of the Colorado Railroad Company, another C&S subsidiary organized in 1906. The laying of the track was completed about October 18 and the first sugar beet train operated over the road on October 23. It was a freight-only line until passenger service was inaugurated in August 1905.

From the main line 1.7 miles north of Acme Junction, westerly to end of track at Southwestern Mine (sg) — 1.0

Aguilar Branch—No. 4 Junction to Beacon Mine (sg) — 0.5
    This relocation of a section of the original line was completed in November.

COLORADO & WYOMING

Tercio to end of track at Cuatro (sg) — 2.3
    The track was completed in March and coal shipments from the Cuatro Mine began in June.

Hezron Branch—Hezron Junction, on the Santa Clara Mine Spur of the D&RG, westerly to Hezron (sg) — 1.7
    This short spur, 35 miles from other C&W trackage, was operated by D&RG.

1903 (Cont'd)

Two shafts of the Leyden mines as they appeared in 1914.—(Denver Public Library, Western History Dept.)

Primero became an important C&W shipping point for coal after a nearby Colorado Fuel and Iron Company mine was opened in 1902.—(State Historical Society of Colorado)

1903 (Cont'd)

COLORADO SPRINGS & CRIPPLE CREEK DISTRICT

	Miles

Joe Dandy Spur—Raven Hill Station on the electric High Line to Joe Dandy Mine (sg) — 0.5
   October 18 was the completion date for this spur, the first of three mine spurs built from the High Line route on Bull Hill. None of the spurs was electrified.

Blue Bird Spur—Blue Bird Station on High Line to Blue Bird Mine (sg) — 0.3

Electric Lines—from the Low Line terminal at Fourth Street and Warren Avenue, north to the track of the High Line on Myers Avenue (sg) — 0.1

From the High Line track on Myers, north on Second Street to Bennett Avenue (sg) — 0.1
   This was the beginning of a loop through the central business district of Cripple Creek. After two restraining orders and a change in the proposed route, the tracks and overhead wire were in place by late May. On June 3 all cars of both the High Line and Low Line began using the new terminal at Second and Bennett.

Electric Lines—High Line route extended from the joint steam and electric terminal at Victor, west along Diamond Avenue to Third Street, south on Third one block to Victor Avenue, thence west one block to a connection with the Low Line at Fourth Street (sg) — 0.3
   The last rail was spiked in place July 10, thus closing the final gap between the two electric lines. The junction became the Victor terminal for both routes.

Electric Lines—route on Cripple Creek streets extended east on Bennett Avenue to Third Street, thence south on Third to the track on Myers Avenue (sg) — 0.2
   This section of the loop was completed in late July. Thereafter cars were routed via Third Street and Bennett Avenue to the terminal at Second Street, thence via Second back to Myers Avenue.

DENVER & NORTHWESTERN

Leyden Junction to end of line at Leyden (3 ft.-6 in.) — 2.7
   The line was completed to the Leyden Mines about July 1.

Narrow gauge (3 ft.-6 in.) to dual gauge—from an interchange with the C&S at Arvada to Leyden.
   A standard gauge rail was added to permit the shipment of coal from the Leyden Mines to off-line points.

DENVER & RIO GRANDE

Calcite (Howard) Branch—from main line at Howard, westerly to Howard's Quarry (Calcite) (sg) — 5.8

1903 (Cont'd)

By the end of 1903 Segundo was an important point on the *Colorado and Wyoming* railroad. Located seven miles east of Weston, it was the site of two large coal washers and eight hundred bee-hive coke ovens. The C&W yards and round house are in the foreground of this photograph which appeared in the January 1904 issue of "Camp and Plant."—(State Hist. Society of Colo. Library)

Mine and railroad facilities at Tercio were still in the process of development in 1903.—(from "Camp and Plant," June 20, 1903, Western History Collection, Univ. of Colo. Libraries)

1903 (Cont'd)

Construction was finished and the branch was put in operation in October.

Miles

DENVER NORTHWESTERN & PACIFIC (Denver & Salt Lake, 1913; Denver & Rio Grande Western, 1947)

Utah Junction to Coal Creek (sg)   18.0
This was the beginning of David Moffat's railroad projected through the mountains to Salt Lake City. It ascended the mesas west of Denver over a nearly continuous 2 percent grade, around a big S-curve to the base of the foothills, thence northwesterly to Coal Creek, reaching that point on October 18.

GREAT WESTERN

From Buda west to the end of the track at Welty (sg)   2.0

RIO GRANDE & PAGOSA SPRINGS

Blanco to Chambers (Gladwin) (ng)   4.0

UNION PACIFIC

From Erie south to Lehigh Mine (sg)   1.3

Total   *51.6*

ABANDONMENTS

COLORADO & SOUTHERN

Silver Plume to end of track (ng)   0.5
Jersey Cut-Off reduced (sg)   0.1
Aguilar Branch—part of the original line between No. 4 Jct. and Beacon Mine (sg)   0.5
A section of the track was left in place for use as a sidetrack.

COLORADO SPRINGS & CRIPPLE CREEK DISTRICT

Electric line between Dyer Station and Victor (sg)   1.4
The new route over the steam line tracks via Independence and Goldfield eliminated the need for this steep grade along the east and south slopes of Battle Mountain.

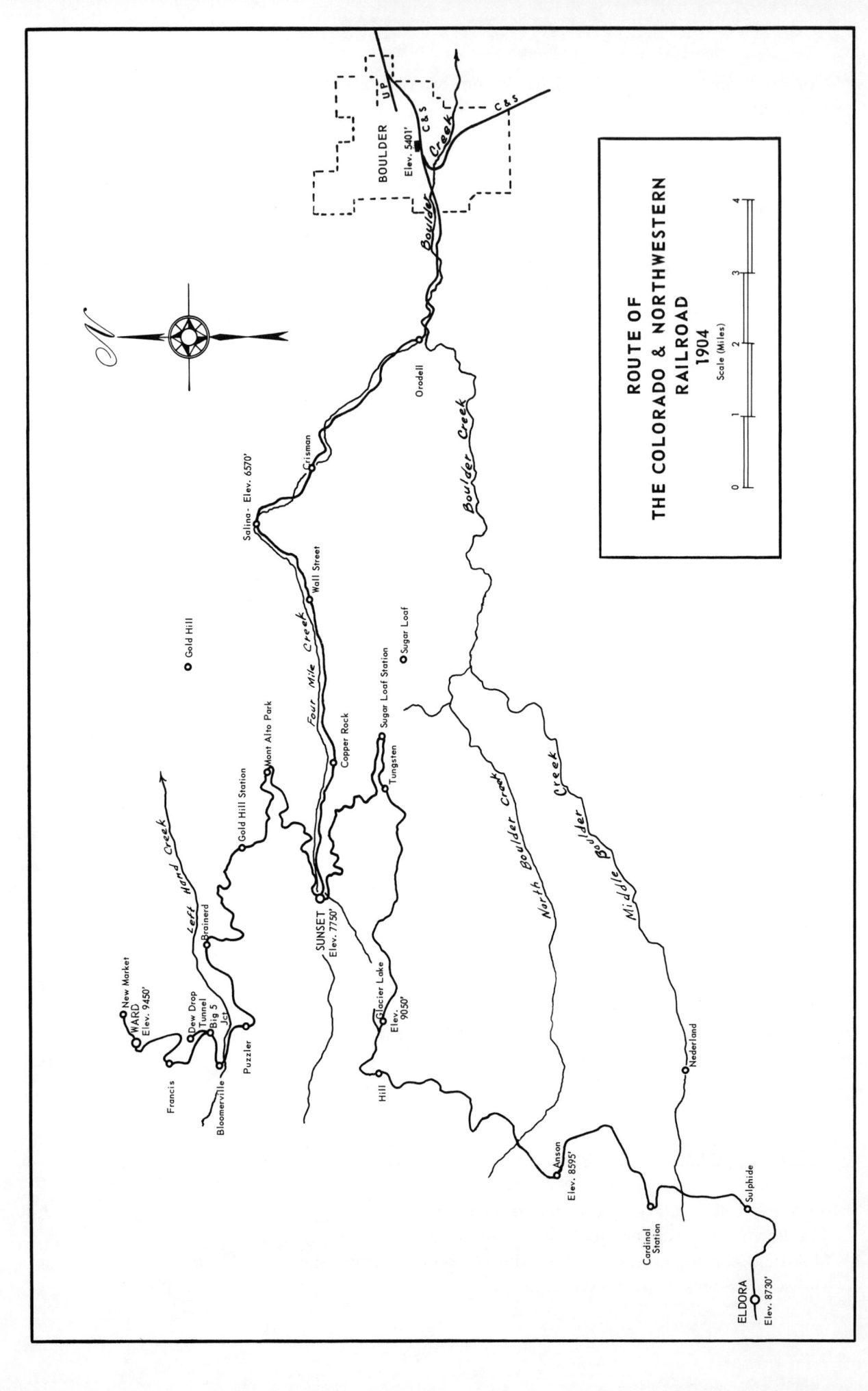

1903 (Cont'd)

	Miles
Electric Line between Cripple Creek and High Line crossing No. 1 (later Fairview, then Badger) (sg)	1.9

The steam line was electrified from Victor Junction (later Pisgah Junction)[26] to accommodate the electric cars. This eliminated the heavier grades on the High Line up Poverty Gulch and Gold Hill. The change was made by sections; first, from Cripple Creek to High Line Crossing No. 2, near Moon Anchor station, and later between Crossing No. 2 and Crossing No. 1. The change was completed over the first section in March and the second section after the middle of September.

Total	4.4

1904

CONSTRUCTION

CHICAGO BURLINGTON & QUINCY

Vaughn Mine Spur—from the original line of the Lyons Branch 0.46 mile south of Irvington, southeast to the Vaughn Mine (sg) — 0.5

The New Baker Mine which opened in 1905 also was served by this spur.

COLORADO & NORTHWESTERN

Sunset to Eldora (ng) — 20.1

The line followed a winding route between the two stations; first southeasterly on a grade constructed in 1893 by the GSL&P for a proposed extension of its narrow gauge line, then west to its maximum altitude of 9,050 feet at Glacier Lake, 1,300 feet higher than Sunset. From there the direction was west for a short distance, then north and around a loop to a southwesterly course along mountain sides to Eldora on Middle Boulder Creek. An excursion ran to the end of the track a short distance from the Eldora station on December 29. The track was completed about December 31 and the first official time card issued on that date showed a scheduled daily train between Boulder and Eldora.

COLORADO & SOUTHEASTERN

From a connection with the D&RG at Barnes, west to Barnes Junction (sg) — 2.8

In addition to this trackage the company acquired 1.07 miles of C&S track between Barnes Junction and Hastings and 2.45 miles between Hastings and Delagua from the Victor Fuel Company, giving it a continuous line of 6.27 miles between Barnes to Delagua.

A view of Sunset taken after 1909. The track following the stream eastward down the canyon is the *Colorado & Northwestern* line from Boulder. The Ward Branch is at left and the Eldora Branch is seen climbing the wall of the canyon at right.—(L. C. McClure Photo—Denver Public Library, Western History Dep't)

A *Denver, Northwestern & Pacific* train on the depot spur at Arrow.—(L. C. McClure Photo—Denver Public Library—Western History Dep't)

1904 (Cont'd)

COLORADO & SOUTHERN

Miles

From the main line 2.4 miles south of Forbes, southwesterly to Thor Mine (sg) — 0.7

Night Hawk Branch extended (ng) — 0.2

Lowery Quarry Spur—from Wilds on Arkins Branch, north to Lowery Quarry (sg) — 2.8

Matchless Mine Spur—from the main line 1.2 miles north of Louisville west and southwest to the Matchless Mine (sg) — 2.4

The spur was completed in February.

COLORADO SPRINGS & CRIPPLE CREEK DISTRICT

Gold Sovereign Spur—Los Angeles Station on the electric High Line to Gold Sovereign and Dexter Mines (sg) — 0.5

DENVER & NORTHWESTERN (Electric)

From Clear Creek Junction, 1.5 rail miles west of Lakeside on the Leyden line, southwesterly to Golden (3 ft. 6 in.) — 8.5

The rails and poles were in place as far as Ford Street in Golden the second week of March and hourly service to and from that point began April 10. A week later cars were using a loop through the business section to a permanent terminal at Third Street and Washington Avenue.

DENVER & RIO GRANDE

Loma Branch—extended from Maitland to Strong (sg) — 7.6

This extension, built under the charter of the Rio Grande Railroad Company, was completed to Strong on December 31 and placed in service in January of the following year.

New line from a point south of Nathrop to Buena Vista (sg) — 9.3

This was a realignment to reduce curvature and grade.

DENVER NORTHWESTERN & PACIFIC

Coal Creek to Arrowhead (later Arrow) (sg) — 53.8

From Coal Creek the line skirted the eastern escarpment of the foothills, then swung westward along the steep slopes of South Boulder Canon. From the head of the canyon the track continued along South Boulder Creek to Mammoth (later Tolland), situated in a small valley at the foot of the main mountain range. A short distance farther it began its ascent of the main range via a series of switchbacks and curves and on grades up to 4 percent.

1904 (Cont'd)

In this scene on the south slope of Bull Hill in the Cripple Creek District we see the Electric High Line of the CS&CCD The unelectrified track at left is the spur to the Blue Bird Mine, The train in the distance is on the Golden Circle track superimposed along the west slope of Battle Mountain. At the extreme middle right a Midland Terminal train is approaching Eclipse Gulch.—(L. C. McClure Photo—Denver Public Library, Western History Dep't)

TIME TABLE

WESTWARD No. 1 Daily. A. M.	ELEVATION		STATIONS		Miles from Denver	EASTWARD No. 2 Daily P. M.
8.00	5170	Leave	**DENVER**	Arrive	0.	5.30
8.20	5215	"	Utah Junction	"	3.60	5.07
8.26	5268	"	Ralston	"	7.26	5.00
8.36	5687	"	Leyden Junction	"	13.28	4.51
8.46	6162	"	Arena	"	18.18	4.40
9.02	6783	"	Plainview	"	24.81	4 23
9.26	7457	"	Crescent	"	31.92	4.00
9.47	7958	"	Gato	"	37.25	3.41
10.01	8367	"	Rollinsville	"	42.15	3.31
10.20	8889	"	**TOLLAND**	"	47.36	3.15
10.35	9380	"	Ladora	"	52.47	3.03
10.49	9905	"	Antelope	"	56.31	2.49
11.07	10860	"	Jenny Lake	"	61.35	2.31
11.32	11660	"	Rollins Pass	"	65.75	2.05
11.47	10980	"	Loop Siding	"	69.63	1.51
12.05	10158	"	Fawn Creek	"	73.93	1.35
12.20	9585	Arrive	**ARROW HEAD**	Leave	76.77	1.20
P. M.			(PRESENT TERMINUS)			P. M.

Trains leave D. N-W. & P. Ry. Depot, Delgany St., bet. 15th and 16th Sts.

1904 (Cont'd)

Miles

It crossed the Continental Divide at Rollins Pass (Corona), altitude 11,660 feet, the highest point in the United States reached by a standard gauge railroad operated with adhesion power. Continuing its meandering course it descended the western slope of the range to Arrowhead, some 2,000 feet below the pass. The main track was completed to that point on September 18 and six days later a spur track for the station was finished. Regular passenger service, which had been in operation to Mammoth since June 23, was extended to Arrowhead on October 4. That was the terminus for scheduled trains for nearly a year.

DURANGO RAILWAY & REALTY COMPANY

Extended to La Plata County Fair Grounds (sg) 0.5

FLORENCE & CRIPPLE CREEK

Beacon Hill Branch—extended from a point near the El Paso Mine to the Henry Adney Mine (ng) 1.6
    There were five switchbacks on this extension which also served the CK&N and Old Gold Mines.

GREAT WESTERN

Johnstown to Milliken (sg) 2.6

RIO GRANDE & PAGOSA SPRINGS[27]

Chambers to Flaugh (ng) 7.0
    Flaugh was the northern terminus of the railroad, a few miles short of its original objective.

SILVERTON NORTHERN

Extended from Eureka to Animas Forks (ng) 4.0
    A specific completion date was not resolved from available records but it appears to have been in late August or sometime in September. By August 20 the rails were two miles from Animas Forks and on October 5 it was reported that traffic over the line was well established.[28]

TRINIDAD ELECTRIC RAILWAY (Electric) (Southern Colorado Power & Railway Co., 1908—Colorado Railway Light and

1904 (Cont'd)

The power of this *Uintah RR* Shay engine appears to be taxed to near capacity as it pulls a 5-car mixed train around a sharp curve.—(Denver Public Library, Western History Department)

1904 (Cont'd)

	Miles
Power Co., 1909, Trinidad Electric Transmission Railway & Gas Co., 1911)	
From the intersection of East Main and Maple Streets in Trinidad, west and south to Starkville (sg)	7.5[29]
Branch—Piedmont to Sopris (sg)	1.1

The main line to Starkville and the branch to Sopris were completed about the middle of April. After a number of trial runs two special cars ran round-trip between Trinidad, Starkville and Sopris on April 29. A time table for the line was published May 5. The company also operated street railway lines in Trinidad.

UINTAH

From a connection with the D&RG at Mack, 9 miles west of Grand Junction, north and northwesterly to the Utah State line (ng) — 50.8

The line terminated at Dragon, Utah (later extended to Watson, Utah). It had the steepest gradient of any steam railroad operated with adhesion power in Colorado, 7.5 percent in places, and curves up to 66 degrees. Its primary purpose was to transport gilsonite from the deposits in eastern Utah. The track reached Dragon, Utah, four miles west of the Colorado state line, around October 1.

Total	184.3

ABANDONMENTS

COLORADO & SOUTHERN

Minnequa Junction to Bessemer Junction (sg)	0.8

DENVER & RIO GRANDE

Aberdeen Quarry Branch (ng)	4.5
Old line between Buena Vista and a point south of Nathrop (sg)	9.6
Santa Clara Junction to Old Rouse (sg)	1.4
Total	16.3

Laying track on the DNW&P in Middle Park near Fraser.—(State Historical Society of Colorado)

1905

CONSTRUCTION | Miles

ARGENTINE CENTRAL (Georgetown & Grays Peak, 1913; Argentine & Grays Peak, 1913)

From a connection with the C&S at Silver Plume to Sidney Tunnel (ng) — *8.0*

Using two switchbacks the track ascended the north slope of Pendleton Mountain on grades reported to be as much as 6 percent and greater.

CHICAGO BURLINGTON & QUINCY

Vulcan Mine Spur—from the Lyons Branch about 1.5 miles south of Lafayette, westerly to the Vulcan Mine (sg) — *1.1*

Standard Mine Spur—from a connection 510 feet from the end of the Vaughn Mine Spur, southerly to end of track 800 feet south of the Standard Mine (sg) — *0.5*

COLORADO & SOUTHERN

Wellington north to end of track (sg) — *1.2*
Waverly Branch—Wellington west to Waverly (sg) — *4.7*
  Both of the above sections of track were constructed by the Fort Collins Development Railway Company.

Standard gauge to dual gauge—from Denver via Louisville to Allison
  This conversion was made to accommodate C&NW narrow gauge trains between Boulder and Denver. A third rail had previously been laid between Boulder and Allison.

COLORADO EASTERN

From 23rd Street in Denver northerly to Franklin Junction (sg) — *2.1*
  This standard gauge track, independent of the narrow gauge line, was entirely within Denver County.

DENVER & RIO GRANDE
Farmington Branch—from Carbon Junction, 2.4 track miles east of Durango, south to New Mexico state line (sg) — *18.2*

This was the Colorado portion of an isolated standard gauge line which paralleled the Animas River to Farmington, New Mexico. The line was completed to Farmington in September.

The DNW&P station at Hot Sulphur Springs soon after the rails reached there in 1905. The view is toward the east.—(L. C. McClure Photo—State Hist. Society of Colo.)

The Green Mountain Branch of the *Silverton Northern* at Old Hundred Mill with a D&RG box car resting on the spur. The main track at right continues to the Green Mountain Mine further up the gulch.—(State Historical Society of Colorado)

1905 (Cont'd)

Miles

Narrow gauge to dual gauge—Durango to Carbon Junction.
    This unusual conversion was to allow standard gauge rolling stock on the Farmington Branch to operate into Durango.

DENVER NORTHWESTERN & PACIFIC

Arrow to Hot Sulphur Springs (sg)   *34.0*
    The line continued its descent of the western slope of the Continental Divide to the head of Middle Park. From there it followed the Fraser River in a northwesterly course through the site of present-day Granby to the Grand (later Colorado) River where it swung toward the west and continued a short distance to Hot Sulphur Springs, at the head of Byers Canon. The railhead reached the village on August 20 and on that day a special train with railroad officials and guests aboard arrived at the end of the track. On September 15 a two-section excursion arrived from Denver but it was December 3 before a regular schedule became effective.

GREAT WESTERN

Windsor to Eaton (sg)   *12.6*
    On October 20 a special train for GW officials pulled into Eaton on the completed track.

Johnstown to Liberty (sg)   *12.0*
    This section of track was completed near the end of the year and accepted from the construction company on March 8, 1906.

GILPIN TRAMWAY

Banta Hill Extension—near Frontenac Mine to end of track on Banta Hill (2 ft.)   *2.8*

NORTHWESTERN TERMINAL

Utah Junction to 15th and Delgany Streets in Denver (sg)   *3.2*
    This trackage was completed by DNW&P in December and has since been operated by parent companies as a separate corporation. Its purpose was to provide access into Denver for DNW&P trains.

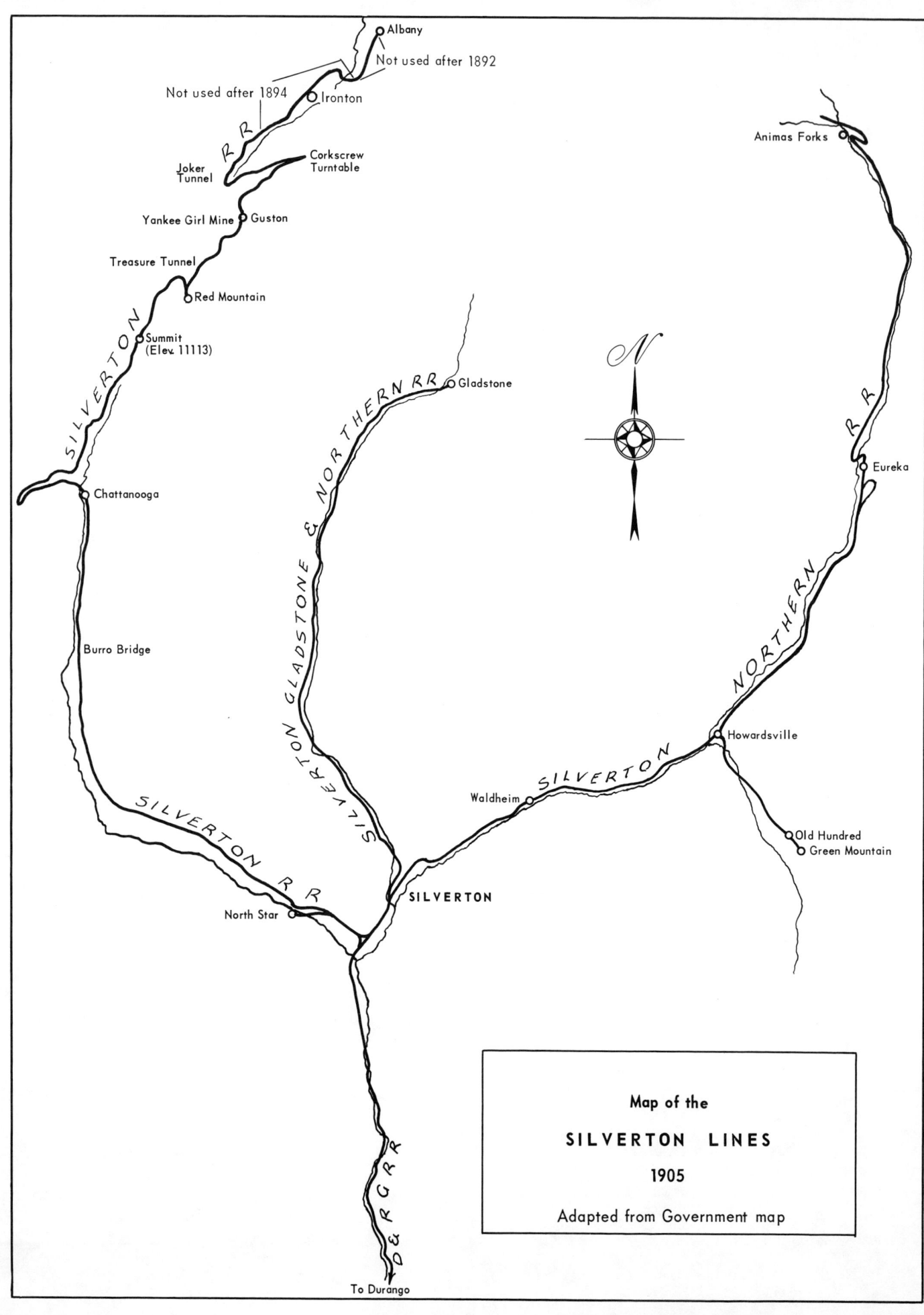

1905 (Cont'd)

SILVERTON NORTHERN

	Miles
Green Mountain Branch—from the main line at Howardsville southeast up Cunningham Gulch to Green Mountain Mine (ng)	1.6

The tracklayers reached the mine on September 25 and within a few days trains were delivering machinery and building material for the construction of a mill on the mine property.

Total	102.0

ABANDONMENTS

COLORADO & SOUTHERN

	Miles
Stout Branch reduced to Lord's (sg)	2.9

COLORADO SPRINGS & CRIPPLE CREEK DISTRICT

	Miles
High Line Electric—Fairview to Midway (sg)	1.2

This was the last section of the original electric line between Cripple Creek and Midway. Early in the year the cars were re-routed over the CS&CCD main line to Hoosier Pass, thence over the Altman Branch to Midway.

DENVER & RIO GRANDE

	Miles
Oak Creek Branch—Oak Creek Junction at Florence to Oak Creek Mines (sg)	2.6
Total	6.7

The half-mile Argentine Central spur to Vidler Tunnel is shown in this McClure photograph from above Waldorf. The large building in the foreground is the Waldorf Mill which was circled by the main line. The prominent grade winding along the hills above Vidler Tunnel is a wagon road to Argentine Pass.—(Denver Public Library, Western History Department)

The *Argentine Central* terminated at the summit of Mt. McClellan where tourists could view the spectacular scenery in all directions.—(L. C. McClure Photo—State Hist. Society of Colo.)

1906

| CONSTRUCTION | Miles |

ARGENTINE CENTRAL

Sidney Tunnel to Waldorf (ng) — 1.0
  On the last day of January the tracklayers reached Waldorf where a gold spike ceremony was held.
Spur—Waldorf to Vidler Tunnel (ng) — 0.5
Waldorf to end of track at McClellan (ng) — 6.9
  Four switchbacks were used to reach the 13,000-foot altitude at end of track. Completion of the track was celebrated on August 1 with a second gold spike ceremony.

ARKANSAS VALLEY[30] (Atchison, Topeka & Santa Fe, 1907)

From the main line of the AT&SF at Rocky Ford, northeasterly and easterly to Buchtel (sg) — 16.1
From the main line of the AT&SF at Lamar, north to Lay's Junction (later Kornman, now Wilson Junction) (sg) — 4.9
Lay's Junction west to Keesee (sg) — 9.3
  Freight service between Lamar and points on the line began about the third week in September.
May Valley Spur—Lay's Junction north to May Valley (sg) — 3.7
Big Bend Spur—Wiley north to Big Bend (sg) — 4.2
  The rails were in place on all the above lines by December 22.

HOLLY & SWINK (Atchison, Topeka & Santa Fe, 1907)

From the main line of the AT&SF at Holly, northwest and west to Bristol (sg) — 13.2
  The laying of track was completed to Bristol the latter part of August. Two daily freights were placed in service the second week of October.
From the main line of the AT&SF at Swink, north to a connection with the AV at Shelton Junction (sg) — 5.2
  The H&S track was completed to the connection in September.

CHICAGO BURLINGTON & QUINCY

Parkdale Mine Spur—from the Lyons Branch 0.36 mile north of Irvington, southerly to the Parkdale Mine (formerly Blue Ribbon Mine) (sg) — 1.3
Pluto Mine Spur—from Lyons Branch about 0.44 mile south of the Lafayette station to Pluto Mine (sg) — 0.3

Argentine Central locomotive No. 4, one of seven Shay engines owned by the railroad. —(L. C. McClure Photo—Denver Public Library, Western History Dep't)

A McClure photo of Kremmling taken from the north soon after the DNW&P tracks reached that point. —(Denver Public Library, Western History Department)

1906 (Cont'd)

COLORADO & SOUTHERN

Miles

Ingleside Branch—from Bellevue Junction, 5.1 miles west of Fort Collins on the Stout Branch, north to Ingleside Quarry (sg) — 9.9

Black Hollow Branch—from Black Hollow Junction, 3 miles east of Fort Collins, east to Black Hollow (sg) — 8.7

From end of track north of Wellington to Dixon — 2.1

> The above three segments were built under the charter of the Colorado Railroad Company, a C&S satellite which had absorbed the Fort Collins Development Railway. Other scattered sections of track were later built under its charter and leased and operated by C&S. It was merged with the parent company in 1930.

Sunnyside Mine Spur—from the C&S main line near Webb, east to Sunnyside Mine No. 2 (sg) — 0.4

> This was an extension of a short stub off the main line which served Sunnyside Mine No. 1, opened in 1900.

COLORADO & WYOMING

Piedmont Branch—Sopris to Piedmont (sg) — 0.8

> Access to this disconnected branch was over 1.5 miles of C&S trackage between Long's Junction to Sopris.

From Cuatro Junction (established 1 mile west of Tercio) to end of track — 0.7

CRYSTAL RIVER & SAN JUAN

From the end of the Crystal River railroad at Placita, south and southeasterly to Marble (sg) — 7.3

> The track was completed to Marble on November 23. The company had previously leased the CR track between Placita and Redstone and later leased the entire CR line.

DENVER & RIO GRANDE

Longsdale to Cokedale (sg) — 0.9

> This piece of track was reached via AT&SF tracks from Trinidad to Jansen, thence over C&W tracks to Longsdale.

Narrow gauge to standard gauge:
  Grand Junction to Montrose
  North Fork Branch—Delta to Somerset

1906(Cont'd)

After the conversion of D&RG tracks to standard gauge between Grand Junction and Montrose, dual-gauge tracks continued in use at the latter place for the accommodation of equipment on the Gunnison and Ouray lines. (At right) A D&RG freight with No. 628 at the head in the Montrose Yards. (Below): A 6-car D&RG passenger train arriving in the yard. The coal in the cars on the right is probably from Crested Butte.—
(F. A. Rice Collection—Western History Collection, Univ. of Colo. Libraries)

164

1906 (Cont'd)

DENVER NORTHWESTERN & PACIFIC

Miles

From the railhead at Hot Sulphur Springs to a point 2.15 miles west of Kremmling (sg) — 18.6

    Immediately west of Hot Sulphur Springs the track ran through Byers Canon for its entire length of about two miles, then along the hills bordering the Grand River to a point near the head of Gore Canon. Train service was extended to Kremmling on June 15.

GREAT WESTERN

Liberty to Longmont (sg) — 6.1

    Sugar beet shipments over this section of track began on November 10. Evidently early operations were by the construction company as the line was not turned over to GW until April 8, 1907.

RIO GRANDE SOUTHERN

May Day Branch—from the main line at May Day, 3.6 track miles south of Hesperus, to May Day mine (ng) — 1.9

    The branch was completed and opened for traffic in June.[31]

                                            Total — 124.0

ABANDONMENTS

CHICAGO BURLINGTON & QUINCY

From the New Mitchell Mine spur to Gladstone Mine (sg) — 0.2

COLORADO MIDLAND

A section of the original main line from Snowden toward Leadville (sg) — 5.7

    This was a little used section of the original line which looped through Leadville. Most of the traffic for the mining district had been routed via Arkansas Junction.

SILVERTON RAILROAD

From Paymaster Mine ore track to Joker Tunnel (ng) — 0.8

                                            Total — 6.7

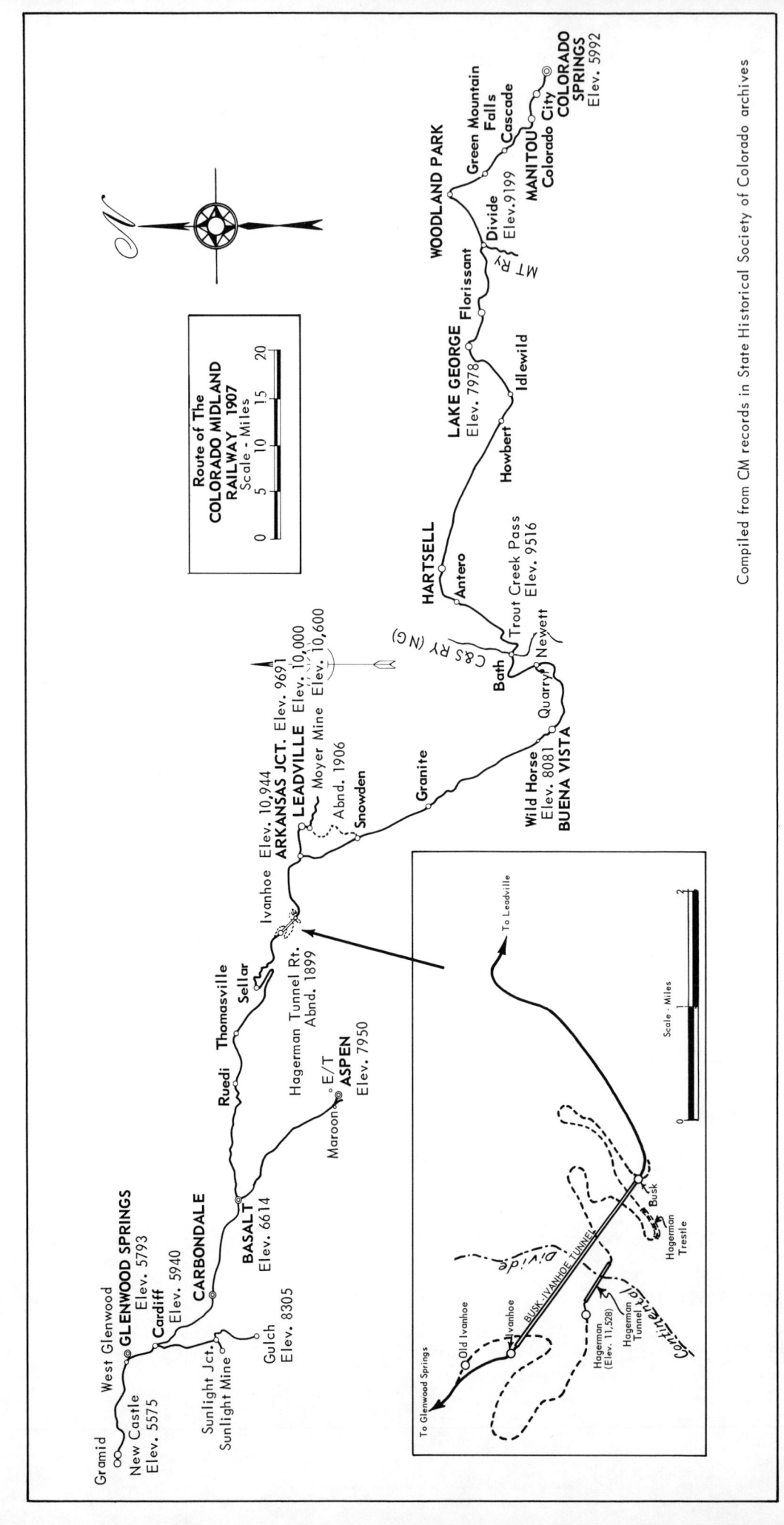

1907

| CONSTRUCTION | Miles |

ATCHISON TOPEKA & SANTA FE

Keesee to a point west of Hasty (sg)	*18.2*
Las Animas to Waveland (sg)	*2.9*
Waveland to Buchtel (sg)	*14.8*

In August 1906 AT&SF acquired the AV and H&S properties and in March 1907 assumed control of the two lines and took over construction.

Grand Valley Branch—from Newdale on the main line between Swink and Rocky Ford, south and west to Hawley (sg) — *5.9*

CHICAGO BURLINGTON & QUINCY

From the main line of the Lyons Branch 1.4 miles south of Eversman, westerly to Sunnyside Mine No. 2 (sg) — *0.7*

COLORADO & SOUTHEASTERN

Chandler Junction on the AT&SF to D&RG Junction (sg) — *0.7*

This short track, which connected AT&SF and D&RG coal branches near Florence, was 110 miles from the C&SE Barnes-Delagua trackage. It was leased and operated jointly by the D&RG and AT&SF.

COLORADO & SOUTHERN

Electric Mine spur—From the Lafayette Branch, 1.4 miles east of Louisville, north to Electric Mine (sg) — *0.6*

The spur also served the Northern Colorado Power Company plant.

From the Rugby Spur 0.45 mile from its initial point, southwesterly to Rapson Mine (sg) — *1.5*

DENVER & RIO GRANDE

From Tropic Junction, on the main line west of La Veta, northwest to Tropic Mine (sg) — *2.0*

From Bulkley Junction, 3.2 miles east of Crested Butte, to Bulkley Mine (ng) — *0.6*

Loma Branch extended from Strong to Big Four (Kebler No. 2 mine) (sg) — *1.8*

This extension was completed at the end of the year and placed in service January 20, 1908. Construction was under the charter of the Rio Grande Railroad Company.

1907 (Cont'd)

(Upper) The rails of the DNW&P passing through a series of tunnels in Gore Canon. (Lower) A construction crew unloads rock near the west end of the canon. The grade toward Yarmony appears in the distance along Piney Ridge.—(Both photos—L. C. McClure—Denver Public Library, Western History Dep't)

1907 (Cont'd)

	Miles

DENVER & SOUTH PLATTE (Electric)

Englewood to Littleton (3 ft-6 in) — 4.2
  Track and poles were in place and cars were operating to the north end of Littleton by September 23. The track was completed to the foot of Main Street about November 8 and regular service to and from that point began on November 10.

DENVER NORTHWESTERN & PACIFIC

From the railhead west of Kremmling, west to Yarmony (sg) — 17.5
  For over one-third of the distance the road was built alongside the Grand River through Gore Canon, the walls of which rose to heights approaching two thousand feet in places. The track was completed to Yarmony about October 10 and train service was extended to that station November 1.

ELDORADO SPRINGS RAILWAY (Denver & Interurban, 1908)

Marshall to Eldorado Springs (sg) — 3.0
  This short railroad which connected with the C&S at Marshall was built to serve a resort at Eldorado Springs. It was completed in May and excursion trains from Boulder operated over the line on Memorial Day. The following year it was electrified and transferred by deed to the Denver & Interurban. (See 1908.)

GILPIN RAILROAD[32]

From the Saratoga Branch to the Anchor Mine (2 ft.) — 1.5
From the main line at Chase Gulch to the Tucker Mine (2 ft.) — 0.7

GREAT WESTERN

Officer Junction to Windsor (sg) — 7.0
  This segment from the main line six miles east of Loveland joined the disconnected track built to Eaton in 1905, forming what later became the Eaton Branch. It was completed late in the year and turned over to GW January 18, 1908.

ROCKY MOUNTAIN

From a connection with the DNW&P about one-half mile west of Granby to lumber mills on the south fork of Grand River (now Colorado River) above Monarch (sg) — 13.6

1907(Cont'd)

This railway car operated between Marshall and Eldorado Springs, before the line was electrified.—(From a magazine, "Souvenir of Denver," published 1907—State Hist. Society of Colo.)

1907 (Cont'd)

	Miles
Following the stream, first northeasterly, then southeasterly, the track was completed and placed in operation in June.	

UNION PACIFIC

From the Brighton-Boulder Branch at the present site of St. Vrains,[33] north and east to Grant Mine (sg)	6.3
From Diamond (later Baum Mine Junction), 3.7 miles north of the initial point of the above line, west to Baum mine (sg)	1.1

WALSENBURG & WESTERN (Colorado & Southern, 1930)

Walsenburg to McNally Mine (sg)	1.4
About half of the line was constructed by the Huerfano Fuel Company. It was merged with the Colorado Railroad in 1911 and operated by C&S within the framework of that subsidiary.	
Total	106.0

1908

CONSTRUCTION

ATCHISON TOPEKA & SANTA FE

From the end of track west of Hasty to Waveland (sg)	6.4
This section was completed about January 17 and a special train ran from Las Animas to Lamar on January 20.	
Bristol west to Lay's Junction (sg)	17.0
The last rail and switches were placed on this final section of the AV branch on May 1. The first train over the entire route between Rocky Ford and Holly was a May 2 special for Arkansas Valley bankers. On May 28 another special train was operated for the accommodation of newsmen. Regular service began July 1.	

CHICAGO BURLINGTON & QUINCY

Capital Mine Spur—from the original track of the Lyons Branch 0.8 mile south of Irvington, south to Capital Mine (sg)	0.4

1908(Cont'd)

The first D&I cars were shuttled through Boulder over C&S tracks. Operations had barely begun when this 1908 photo was snapped.—(Denver Public Library, Western History Department)

The cold weather did not stop the construction crew from laying the last stretch of DNW&P track into Steamboat Springs on December 13, 1908. The view below is from the north side of the river looking southwest.—(State Historical Society of Colorado)

1908 (Cont'd)

COLORADO & SOUTHERN

Miles

From Trout Creek, on old South Park line, to Macune (ng) *1.6*
> This was a reconstruction necessitated by a washout in Box Canon. The rails were laid on the original grade of the track vacated by the 1884 DSP&P route change.

From Semper, 6.0 miles north of Utah Junction on the Denver-Cheyenne route, northerly to Louisville Junction (dg) *7.4*
> This new track was built for the use of steam trains. The old line alongside was leased to the Denver & Interurban for electric operations.

Louisville Junction via the Monarch Mine to Webb (sg) *0.9*
> Steam trains were routed over this section of track which was constructed under the Colorado Railroad charter. The original main line between Marshall Junction and Webb was electrified for the use of Denver & Interurban cars.

DENVER & INTERURBAN (Electric)

From the Globeville Station, at 52nd and Washington Streets at the north boundary of Denver, to a point about 2,500 feet north of Utah Junction, thence alongside the C&S tracks to Semper (sg) *8.1*
> The track was completed in June.

Track in Boulder from the C&S main line at Twelfth Street (now Broadway), north to Pearl Street, thence east on Pearl to the Louisville route of the C&S (sg) *1.8*
> Owned by the C&S, the Denver & Interurban operated between Denver and Boulder, running over its own tracks to Semper and over the old track of the C&S from Semper to D&I Junction, a new junction for electric operations a short distance south of Louisville Junction. From that point to Boulder the cars used C&S tracks which had been electrified via both Marshall and Louisville. After reaching Boulder D&I cars diverged from the C&S lines and passed through town on its own tracks via Twelfth and Pearl Streets.[34] Operations between Globeville and downtown Denver were over a standard gauge[35] line of the Denver City Tramway Company. On June 23 a special car operated round trip over the line and regular service was inaugurated July 27. The company also operated a branch between Marshall and Eldorado Springs, as noted under 1907.

DENVER & RIO GRANDE

From Louviers on the main line south of Denver, westerly to Dupont Powder Plant (sg) *1.2*

1908 (Cont'd)

	Miles

DENVER & SOUTH PLATTE (Electric)

From Littleton west across the South Platte River to Bowles Park (3 ft. 6 in.) — *0.8*

DENVER NORTHWESTERN & PACIFIC

Yarmony to Steamboat Springs (sg) — *68.1*
  After following the Grand River for nearly 50 miles the track left that stream 6 miles west of Yarmony to begin its climb northward across the Gore Mountain Range to the Yampa Valley. Some of the most difficult construction on the entire road was required over sections of this route. On December 13 the track-laying machine reached Steamboat Springs on the Yampa River and regularly scheduled service to that point began January 19, 1909. Steamboat Springs was the western terminus of the railroad until 1913.

SOUTHERN COLORADO POWER & RAILWAY COMPANY (Electric) (formerly Trinidad Electric Railway)

Cokedale Branch—from the Starkville line at the C&W quarry west of Jansen, westerly to Cokedale (sg) — *4.0*
  The line was opened for public traffic on March 21. Cars operated to and from the Trinidad terminal using the Starkville line east of the C&W quarry.

UNION PACIFIC

From a point on the Denver-Cheyenne line about 4 miles north of Carr to the Colorado-Wyoming boundary (sg) — *3.8*
  This was the Colorado portion of a new route which would allow trains to enter Cheyenne from the west. It was opened for traffic to Cheyenne on December 6.

Puritan Branch—from Parkdale Junction, on Denver & Boulder Valley Branch, north to Puritan (sg) — *3.1*
  This branch, built by Parkdale Fuel Company and operated by UP, was opened for traffic June 1. Title passed to UP about 1915.

Johnson to McKissick (sg) — *0.9*
  There is evidence that the track was at least partially laid the previous year and classified as a siding.

Total — *125.5*

1908 (Cont'd)

ABANDONMENTS | Miles

COLORADO & SOUTHERN

Long Canon Branch—from a point near Long's Junction to the New Mexico state line (sg) — 10.7
  This was the Colorado portion of a cut-back from Pels, New Mexico.
Trout Creek to Schwanders (ng) — 1.1
  This section of track through Box Creek Canon on the old South Park line had been washed out.

COLORADO SPRINGS & CRIPPLE CREEK DISTRICT

Economic Mill Spur (sg) — 0.5

RIO GRANDE SOUTHERN

Ute Coal Branch—Ute Junction to Ute Mine (ng) — 1.9

UNION PACIFIC

Original main line between a point north of Carr and the Colorado-Wyoming boundary (sg) — 4.7
  This was part of the line built by the DP in 1869 and merged into the UP system in 1880. The Wyoming portion was also abandoned.

Total — 18.9

A construction train on the *Denver, Laramie & Northwestern* in 1909.—(Denver Public Library, Western History Department)

Everyone got into the act to pose for this photo of an autocar on the *Beaver, Penrose & Northern* at Penrose.—(Denver Public Library, Westen History Department)

1909

| CONSTRUCTION | Miles |

BEAVER PENROSE & NORTHERN

From Beaver, on the D&RG main line about 22 miles west of Pueblo, north and west to Penrose (sg)   *6.5*
    The laying of steel was completed in time for an unscheduled passenger train to run over the road on May 23. The formal opening on June 3 was the occasion for a special train for railroad officials and newsmen.

COLORADO & SOUTHERN

Silica Branch—from the main line of the old South Park line at Waterton, east and south to Silica (ng)   *3.9*
    Construction of this branch was under the charter of Colorado Railroad Company. It was opened for operation in August.
Ideal Mine Spur—From the main line 5 miles south of Walsenburg to Ideal Mine (sg)   *2.3*

DENVER & RIO GRANDE

Du Pont Junction, north of Trinidad, to Du Pont Powder Works (sg)   *1.2*

DENVER LARAMIE & NORTHWESTERN (Denver Laramie & Northern, 1917)

Utah Junction northeasterly to a point near Fort St. Vrain (sg)   *36.3*
    This was the first segment of a railroad which would terminate at Greeley, far short of its stated goal. It paralleled the Platte River on the west side opposite the UP main line. Access into Denver was over the Northwestern Terminal track between Utah Junction and the Moffat Station.

GRAND JUNCTION & GRAND RIVER VALLEY (Electric) (Grand River Valley, 1914)

Trackage within Grand Junction (sg)   *1.6*
    A total of 3.2 miles was built during the year but half the trackage was for the exclusive use of street railway service.

1909 (Cont'd)

(Right) Station and yard facilities of the *San Luis Southern* at San Acacio, October 14, 1910.—(Original photo, O. T. Davis. J. C. Thode print—State Historical Society of Colorado)

(Below) The first passenger train to operate over the *San Luis Southern* was this 3-car special which made a round-trip run between Blanca and San Acacio on April 14, 1910.—(Denver Public Library, Western History Department)

1909 (Cont'd)

UNION PACIFIC

	Miles
Dent Branch—From Sand Creek Junction, 5 miles north of the Denver Union Terminal, to St. Vrains (sg)	17.4

The line was opened for business on November 1.

Total	69.2

ABANDONMENTS

COLORADO & SOUTHERN

	Miles
Stout Branch reduced to a point near Malaby's Spur (sg)	4.0
Long Canon Branch reduced (sg)	0.4

CRYSTAL RIVER

Coal Basin Branch (ng)	11.8
Total	16.2

1910

CONSTRUCTION

DENVER & INTERMOUNTAIN

	Miles
Ruby Spur—from the D&IM main line on East Street in Golden, southwesterly along city streets to Ruby Quarry (sg)	0.8

A specific completion date was not found but the rails were reported to have been laid as far as Washington Avenue by December 1 and clay was being shipped from the quarry by January 26, 1911.[36]

DENVER GOLDEN & MORRISON (Denver & Intermountain, 1920)

From a connection with the D&IM at Wyman east of Golden, south to clay pits at Apex (sg)	1.8

DENVER LARAMIE & NORTHWESTERN

From the railhead near Fort St. Vrain, north to Milliken (sg)	3.9
Milliken northeasterly to Greeley (sg)	12.6

The laying of steel was completed to the southern limit of Greeley on May 5. Construction of the final 1.36 miles within the city

1910 (Cont'd)

The abandoned grade of the old *South Park line* winds down the mountain slopes from Alpine Tunnel at upper center, around Sherrod Loop in the foreground and on toward Quartz and Gunnison. This section west of the Continental Divide was abandoned by C&S in 1910 but the tracks remained in place for another 13 years.—(Dow Helmers Photo—Denver Public Library, Western History Dep't)

1910 (Cont'd)

was under the charter of the Greeley Terminal Railway Company, a wholly owned subsidiary. On May 29 trains were placed in service using a short section of street railway to a temporary depot at Eighth Street and Seventh Avenue. On June 5 the track was completed to Ninth Street, one block beyond the site of the permanent depot.

Miles

GRAND JUNCTION & GRAND RIVER VALLEY (Electric)

Grand Junction northwesterly to Fruita (sg)   *16.2*
  The track of this electric interurban road zigzagged through the orchard and farm area between the two towns. The last rail was laid at Fruita the first week of July and regularly scheduled cars were placed in service July 14.

KANSAS-COLORADO (Colorado-Kansas, 1911; Colorado Railroad, Inc., 1938)

From Victoria Street in Pueblo westward to AT&SF tracks (sg)[37]   *1.5*

TREASURY MOUNTAIN

From a junction with the CR&SJ at Marble, to Strauss Quarry (sg)   *4.0*
  This short railroad was built to haul marble from a quarry on a mountainside south of the town of Marble. The steep grade required the construction of two switchbacks and the use of a geared locomotive. Construction of the line was completed on August 18.

SAN LUIS SOUTHERN (San Luis Valley Southern, 1928; Southern San Luis Valley, 1955)

From a connection with the D&RG at Blanca, south to Jaroso (sg)   *31.7*
  This railroad was opened for traffic as far as San Acacio, 15.8 miles from Blanca, on April 14 and to Jaroso by September 1.

UNION PACIFIC

Dent Branch—from Grant Junction at Firestone to the UP mainline at La Salle Junction (sg)   *23.1*
  This final segment of the Dent Branch was opened for traffic on November 1. The 1.4 miles from Grant Junction to Grant Mine became Grant Mine Spur (later Russell Mine Spur).

1910 (Cont'd)

	Miles
Greeley Branch—from Greeley Junction, on the main line 2.3 miles north of Greeley, east and northeast to Briggsdale (sg)	26.2
The branch was opened for traffic on May 22.	
Pleasant Valley Branch—Cloverly, on the Greeley Branch 3.7 miles east of Greeley Junction, north to Hungerford (sg)	13.2
This line was also opened for traffic on May 22.	
Pleasant Valley Branch extended to New Hungerford (later Purcell) (sg)	1.0
Train operations over this extension began August 9.	
Total	136.0

ABANDONMENTS

COLORADO & SOUTHERN

From Cohen Spur, 4 miles south of Garos, to Macune (ng)	24.6
A flood on Trout Creek caused extensive damage to a section of the line and the volume of business would not warrant restoration. The tracks were not removed until 1922.	
Hancock to Quartz (ng)	13.6
A cave-in at Alpine Tunnel isolated this and other trackage west of the Continental Divide. The tracks were removed in 1923.	

UNION PACIFIC

Erie to Lehigh Mine (sg)	1.3
This is the year in which the mine closed. The track removal date was not ascertained.	
Total	39.5

1911

CONSTRUCTION

COLORADO & SOUTHERN

From near the Southwestern Mine tipple, northwesterly to the Jewel Mine (later Jewel-Creston) (sg)	0.8
Berwind Branch extended to Toller Mine (sg)	0.9
This trackage was built by the Cedar Hill Coal and Coke Company and purchased by C&S.	
Morrison Branch extended (ng)	0.2
The extension was completed in June.	
From a point 1.3 miles south of the end of the Dixon extension north of Wellington, northerly to the Wyoming state line (sg)	19.7

1911 (Cont'd)

Miles

This was the Colorado portion of an extension to Cheyenne, Wyoming, constructed under the name of the Colorado Railroad Company. The last rail was laid on October 7 and the line was formally opened for traffic on October 14 with an excursion train from Denver to Cheyenne. Regular passenger service began October 15 and freight trains were placed in service over the line on November 6. The remaining section of the old track to Dixon was named Dixon Spur.

Southern Junction to Walsenburg Junction (sg)   *46.5*

C&S and D&RG constructed adjacent lines between Southern Junction and Walsenburg to be operated as a paired double track (see D&RG below). The rails of both roads reached Walsenburg within a seven-day period in early October but the need for additional ballasting delayed the opening for revenue trains until November 1. The C&S track was constructed under the Colorado Railroad charter. This section, together with the new section north of Wellington, completed a continuous north-south C&S line across the state.

DENVER & RIO GRANDE

Southern Junction to Walsenburg (sg)   *46.5*

This more direct route adjacent to the C&S was about 5.5 miles shorter than the original line. From a crossing of the old line 16 miles north, it ran directly into Walsenburg, by-passing Cuchara Junction. Sections of the original line continued in use until 1936.

Connection wtih C&S at Parlin (ng)   *0.4*

Alpine Tunnel was closed in 1910, isolating C&S trackage west of the Continental Divide on the old South Park line to Gunnison and Baldwin. D&RG took over operation of the section between Parlin and Quartz, and built a short connecting track between the two railroads. It also leased the Baldwin Branch at that time and in return the D&RG Blue River Branch was turned over to C&S for operation. D&RG acquired complete ownership of the Baldwin Branch in 1937.

Dual gauge to standard gauge:
  Pueblo to Florence
  Chandler Junction to Cleora (2 miles east of Salida)
  Pueblo to Minnequa

COLORADO-KANSAS (formerly Kansas-Colorado)

From Pueblo northwest to Turkey Creek (sg)   *14.8*

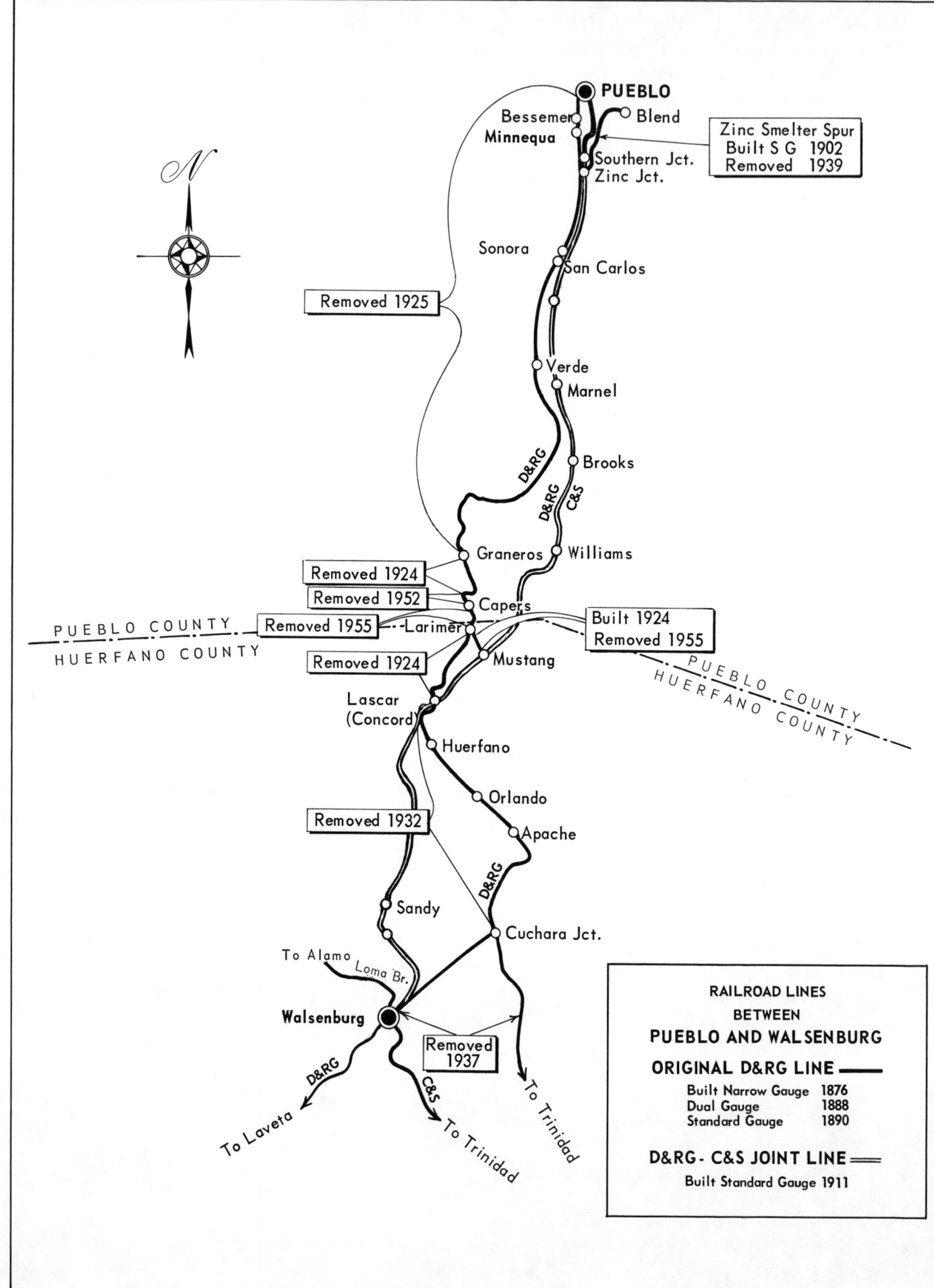

1911 (Cont'd)

	Miles

DENVER & INTERURBAN

Westminster Line—from the D&I main line at Westminster Station, north along Bradburn Boulevard to Westminster University (now Belleview College) (sg) — 1.8

LARAMIE HAHNS PEAK & PACIFIC (Colorado, Wyoming & Eastern, 1914; Northern Colorado & Eastern, 1924; Laramie, North Park & Western, 1924; Union Pacific, 1951)

Colorado-Wyoming boundary to Coalmont (sg) — 43.9

   This railroad originated at Laramie, Wyoming in 1901 but did not reach the Colorado state line until ten years later. The tracklayers reached Walden, 27 track miles south of the state line, on October 10 and the last rail was spiked down at Coalmont on November 16. After a succession of reorganizations UP acquired title to the road in 1936. It continued to operate under its fourth corporate name, Laramie, North Park & Western, until 1951 when it became the Coalmont Branch of the UP.

UNION PACIFIC

From Dent, on the Dent Branch 7 miles west of La Salle Junction, northwest to Fort Collins (sg) — 25.1

   The main track was completed July 1 and regular freight and passenger service began July 15.

Total — 200.6

ABANDONMENTS

COLORADO & SOUTHERN

Parlin to Gunnison (ng) — 12.0

   The track was not dismantled until 1923.

RIO GRANDE & PAGOSA SPRINGS

Blanco to Flaugh (ng) — 8.0

Total — 20.0

1911(Cont'd)

This photo of the C&S-D&I station at Westminster was taken before construction of the branch to Westminster College. The tracks of the branch turned into the street at right.—(L. C. McClure Photo—Denver Public Library, Western History Dep't)

A D&I car is headed toward Boulder at the foot of the mountains in the distance. Note the 3-rail C&S track to the right of the electric line.—(L. C. McClure Photo, Denver Public Library, Western History Dep't)

1911 (Cont'd)

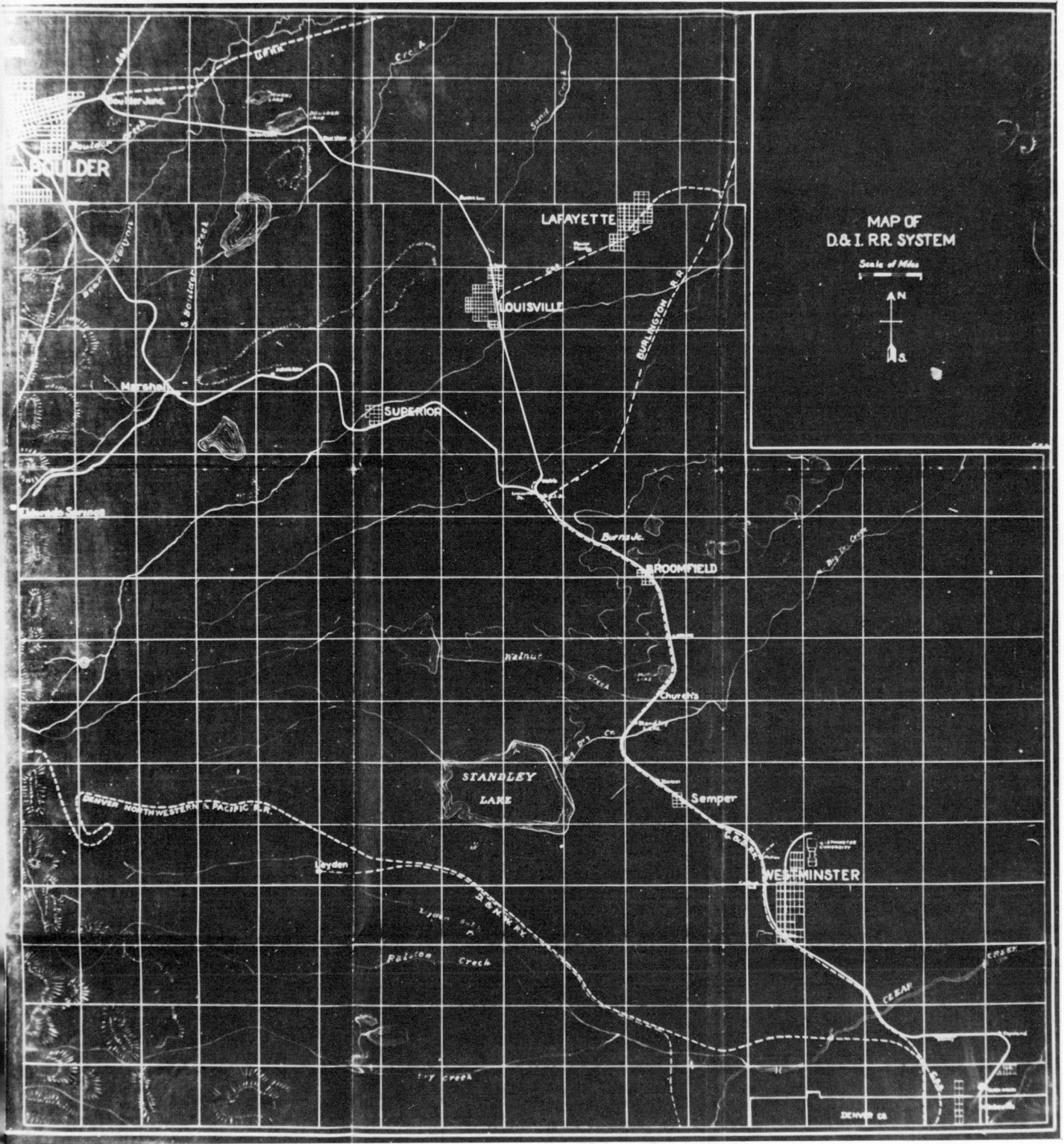

Map of *Denver & Interurban Railroad System.*—(Courtesy J. B. Schoolland)

1912

Colorado-Kansas Locomotive No. 1 standing on the line near Stone City.—(Denver Public Library—Western History Department)

(Below) A C&S engine and caboose standing in one of the larger cuts on the C&S-D&RG parallel line between Southern Junction and Walsenburg on March 28, 1912.—(J.E. Thode Collection)

1912

CONSTRUCTION	Miles
COLORADO-KANSAS	
Turkey Creek to Stone City (sg)	8.0
Completion of the railroad was celebrated on June 12 with a special train and festivities at Stone City.	
DENVER & RIO GRANDE	
Reliance Branch—Reliance Junction, west of La Veta, to Ojo (sg)	5.4
The tracks were laid on a section of the abandoned grade of the Veta Pass narrow gauge route to a coal mine at Ojo.	
Total	13.4

ABANDONMENTS	Miles
ATCHISON TOPEKA & SANTA FE	
Spur to Santa Fe Quarry[38]	1.1
CHICAGO BURLINGTON & QUINCY	
Spur from Lyons Branch south of Eversman to Sunnyside Mine No. 2 (sg)	0.7
COLORADO & SOUTHERN	
Keystone Extension reduced (ng)	0.2
Total	2.0

1912 (Cont'd)

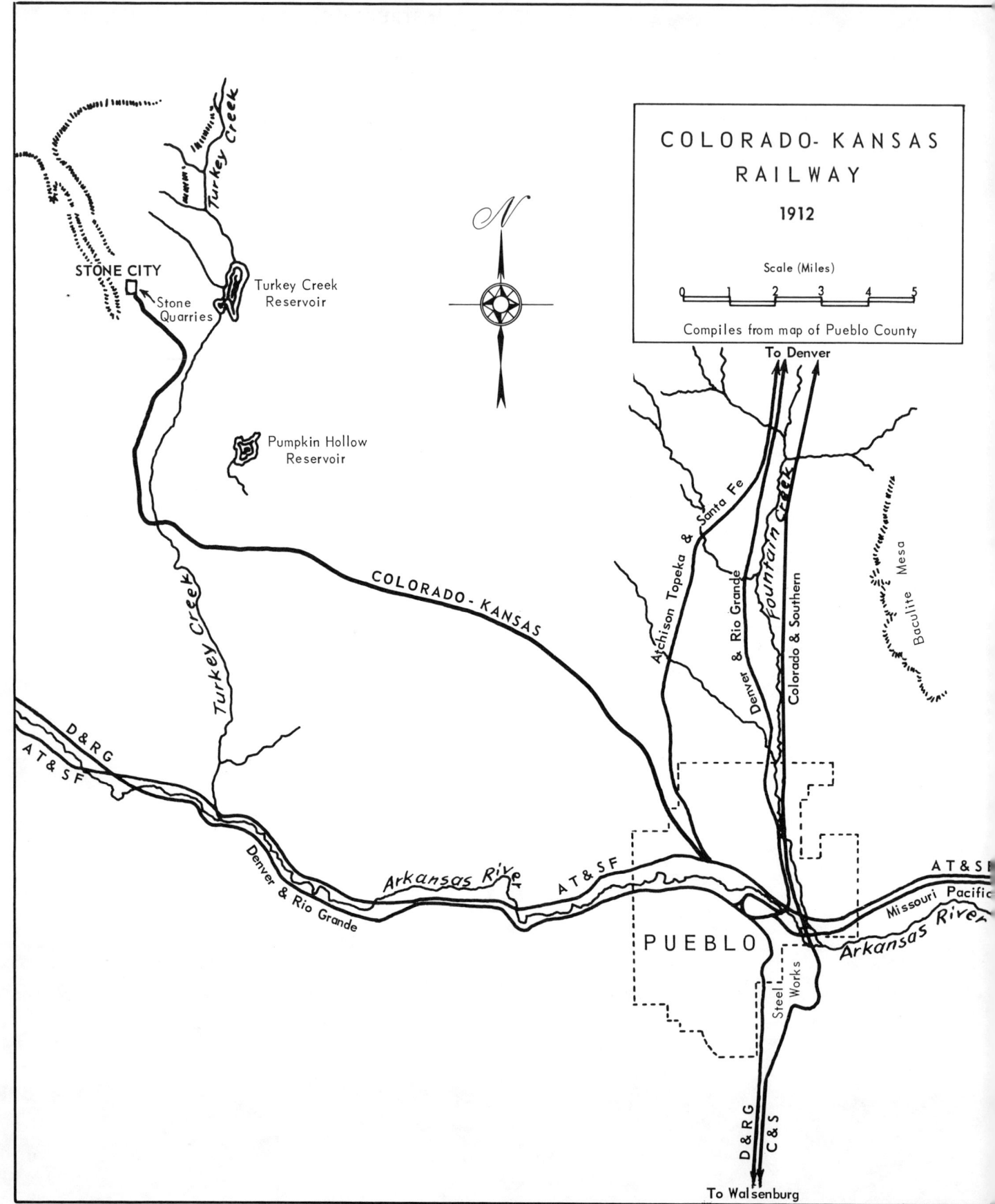

1913

| CONSTRUCTION | Miles |

DENVER & RIO GRANDE

Narrow gauge to dual gauge—Leadville to Graham Park Junction
Narrow gauge to standard gauge—Graham Park Junction to Wolftone Junction.

DENVER & SALT LAKE (formerly Denver, Northwestern & Pacific)

Steamboat Springs to Craig (sg) — *41.2*
  The route of this final extension of the Moffat Road was westerly through the valley of the Yampa River. The tracklaying outfit reached the depot site at Craig on November 19 and on December 1 three-day-a-week mixed train service was established between Craig and Steamboat Springs. On May 31, 1914 Craig became the western terminus for a regularly scheduled passenger train originating at Denver.

NORTHWESTERN TERMINAL

From a connection with the Denver, Laramie & Northwestern 0.62 mile north of Utah Junction, easterly to a connection with the UP near East 48th Avenue and York Street in Denver (sg) — *3.4*
Spur from Stockyard Junction on above line to Denver Stockyards (sg) — *1.3*
  This trackage of the Northwestern Terminal was known as the East Denver Belt Line. It was completed early in the year by DNW&P (D&SL shortly thereafter) and operated by the parent company.

SAN LUIS CENTRAL

From a connection with D&RG at Sugar Junction, 2.5 miles east of Monte Vista, north to Center (sg) — *12.2*
  The laying of steel was completed on August 26 and the first regular train arrived at Center September 1. D&RG trackage was used between Sugar Junction and Monte Vista.

Total — *58.1*

1913 (Cont'd)

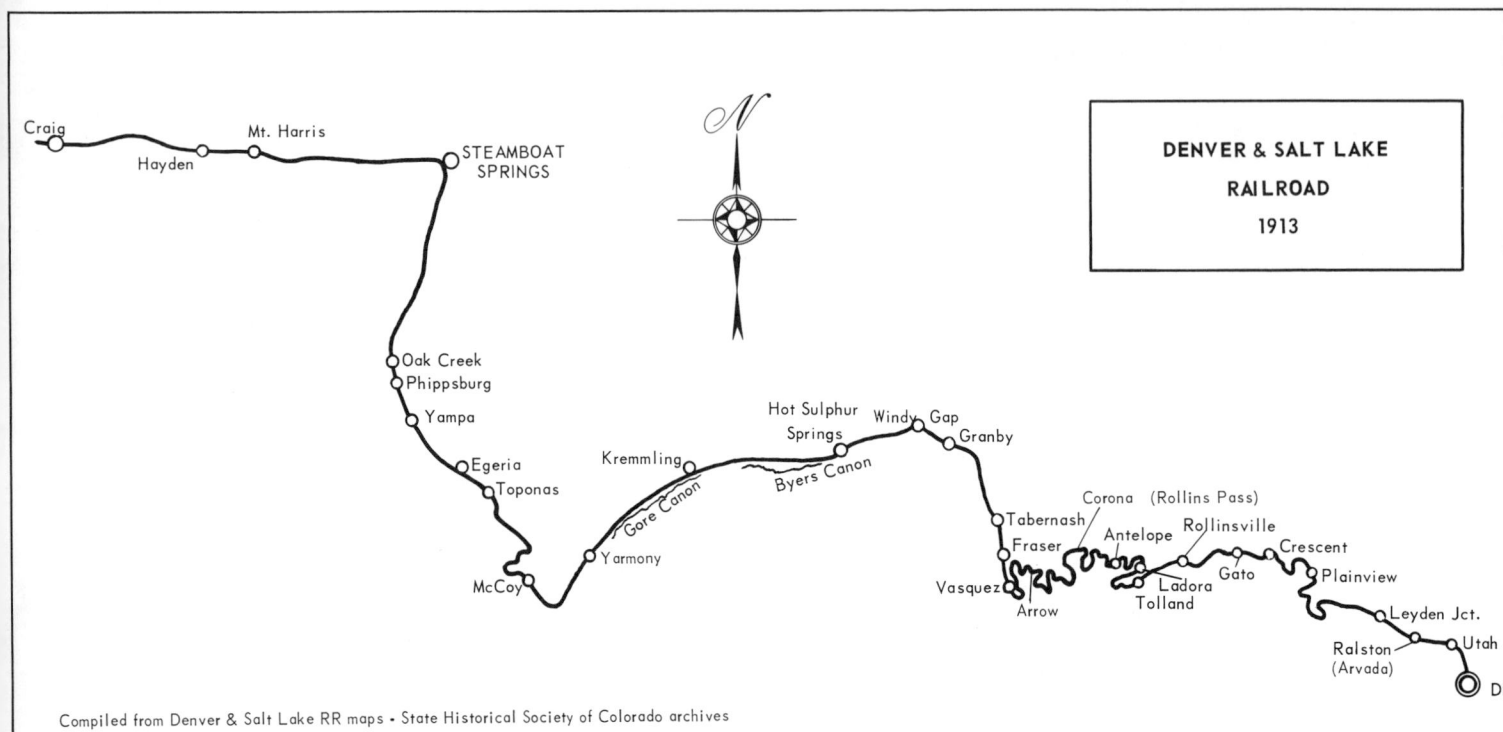

San Luis Central No. 1 at Center in September 1950. This 2-8-0 Baldwin was the only steam locomotive owned by the railroad.—(Author's collection)

1913 (Cont'd)

ABANDONMENTS

	Miles
COLORADO & WYOMING	
Cuatro Junction to Cuatro (sg)	*1.3*
RIO GRANDE & PAGOSA SPRINGS	
Edith to Blanco (ng)	*16.0*
Total	*17.3*

1914

CONSTRUCTION

DENVER & RIO GRANDE

Dual gauge to standard gauge:
    Florence to Chandler Junction
    Chandler Junction to Fremont Mine
    Coal Creek Branch

ABANDONMENTS

	Miles
COLORADO & SOUTHERN	
Lowery Quarry Spur (sg)	*2.8*
A section of 0.4 mile remained until 1917 for use as a siding.	
GILPIN RAILROAD	
Trackage in Central City mining district (2 ft)[39]	*2.3*
RIO GRANDE & PAGOSA SPRINGS	
Edith to the state line (ng)	*0.2*
This was the Colorado portion of the section between Edith and Lumberton, New Mexico, all of which was abandoned in 1914.	
TREASURY MOUNTAIN	
Marble to Strauss Quarry (sg)[40]	*4.0*
Total	*9.3*

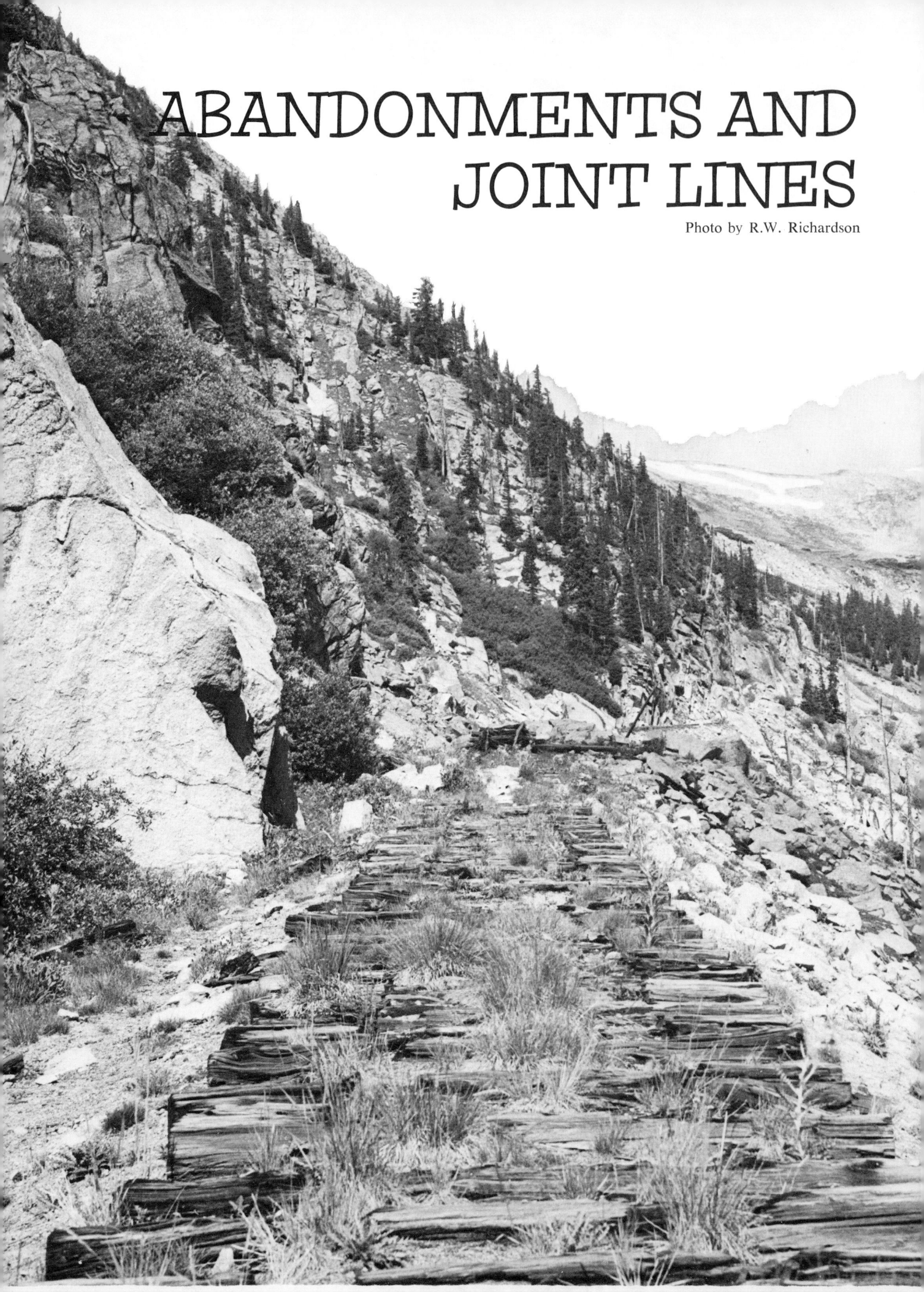

ABANDONMENTS AND JOINT LINES

Photo by R.W. Richardson

PART IV

Beginning with 1915 abandonments dominated the physical aspects of Colorado's railroad history, with total mileage declining nearly two thousand miles by the end of 1966. Many of the railroads built during the heyday of construction were either completely eliminated from the State's system or substantially reduced in mileage. Major abandonments were confined mostly to the mountains and areas adjacent to the eastern foothills, with a relatively small occurrence on the eastern plains.

As lines were abandoned a number of once-thriving communities found themselves without railroads. Among these were the mining towns west of Golden, the Cripple Creek District, the South Park area, the Blue River Valley and the Ten Mile Mining District, the Gunnison Valley and nearby mining areas, the Crystal River Valley, Westcliffe, Pagosa Springs and Telluride. The largest single abandonment occurred in 1919 when the Colorado Midland was officially granted permission to remove its tracks between Divide and New Castle. That, combined with the demise of two shorter railroads in the same year, gave 1919 the dubious distinction of being the biggest railroad abandonment year in Colorado history.

Duplicate trackage between points was frequently eliminated by shifting operations from one railroad to another parallel line. Prominent among these was the transfer of C&S traffic between Denver and Pueblo to the AT&SF. This eventually led to removal of all but a short appendage at each end of the C&S line between the two cities, thus severing the only continuous north-south railroad across the state. In 1918 the AT&SF and the D&RG began operating their lines between Denver and Pueblo as a paired double track with trackage rights to the C&S over both lines. After a section of the Santa Fe line west of Pueblo was damaged by a 1921 flood it shifted operations to the parallel Rio Grande as far as Portland. Later it abandoned its track west of Portland and used Rio Grande tracks entirely between Pueblo and Canon City. The Rio Grande line between Walsenburg and Trinidad was abandoned after a section of track was washed out by a 1936 flood. Thereafter all DR&GW trains operated over C&S tracks between the two towns.

Major new construction occurred in only a few scattered years after the 1913 mileage peak. In 1927 the Santa Fe opened a branch line in southeastern Colorado extending westward from Kansas through Springfield to Pritchett. Ten years later the same company completed a connecting link from the south via Springfield to the AT&SF main line a short distance east of Las Animas. That was the last major section of new railroad constructed in the state. Back in 1928 the world-famous Moffat Tunnel was completed through the Continental Divide west of Denver, eliminating the long climb for D&SL trains over Rollins Pass and cutting 23 miles from the distance by rail to the western slope of the Rockies. The 38-mile Dotsero Cutoff between the DS&L and D&RGW main lines was completed in 1934, reducing the rail distance between Denver and Salt Lake City by 173 miles.

1915

The McGregor Coal Mine south of Milner, with several D&SL cars on the loading and holding tracks.—(L. C. McClure Photo—Denver Public Library, Western History Dep't)

The Wilbur Loop on the F&CC railroad 7 miles south of Victor was a popular subject for photographers. In this L. C. McClure photograph taken a few years before the line was abandoned we see a three-coach passenger train on the upper level headed downgrade. A portion of the middle level can be seen in the center of the picture and at right the track makes a reverse curve and continues south toward Wilbur in the upper part of Phantom Canon.—(Denver Public Library, Western History Department)

1915

CONSTRUCTION

	Miles

COLORADO & SOUTHERN

Berwind Branch extended from Toller Mine to Bear Canon Mine No. 3 (sg) — 1.0
   The extension was placed in service in August.

DENVER & SALT LAKE

From the main line 0.85 mile west of Milner, southerly to McGregor (McNeal) Mine (sg) — 1.1

From the main line 0.55 mile east of Milner, southerly to Curtis Mine (sg) — 2.0
   Construction of the above spurs was financed by the respective coal companies.

UNION PACIFIC

From Shamrock Junction on the Puritan Mine Branch to Shamrock Mine (sg) — 1.0

Total — 5.1

ABANDONMENTS

COLORADO EASTERN

Denver to Scranton (ng) — 16.6
From 23rd Street to Franklin Junction in Denver (sg) — 2.1

CANON CITY & CRIPPLE CREEK

Canon City to Oro Junta (ng) — 7.2

FLORENCE & CRIPPLE CREEK

Florence to Victor (ng) — 34.6
Branch—Vesta Junction to ore reduction mills (ng) — 1.9
   Operations between Florence and Victor ceased in 1912 following a damaging flood in Phantom Canon but formal abandonment was delayed for three years. The section between Victor and Cripple Creek and the Golden Circle line between Victor and Midway (Vista Grande) continued to operate as a narrow gauge until 1917 under the corporate name of Cripple Creek & Colorado Springs Railroad.

1915 (Cont'd)

	Miles
NOLAND LAND & TRANSFER COMPANY (formerly Stone Mountain Railroad & Quarry Company)	
Noland (Tower) to Beach Hill (sg)	3.5[1]
The rails were removed the following year and sold to the Routt-Pinnacle Coal Company.	
Total	65.9

1916

CONSTRUCTION

COLORADO & SOUTHERN

Dual gauge to standard gauge—Denver to Boulder
    This marked the end of DB&W service into Denver.

ROUTT-PINNACLE COAL COMPANY (American Power & Coal Company, 1924)

From the main line of the D&SL 2.36 miles east of Mt. Harris, south to Routt-Pinnacle Mine (sg)	1.8

WOLF CREEK

From the main line of the D&SL at Mt. Harris, northerly to the property of the International Fuel Company (sg)	1.0
This short railroad was operated and maintained by the D&SL (later D&RGW).	
Total	2.8

ABANDONMENTS

ATCHISON TOPEKA & SANTA FE

Spur to Curtis and Danville coal mines (sg)	2.2

CHICAGO ROCK ISLAND & PACIFIC

Spur from main line to Rapson No. 2 Mine (sg)[2]	1.1

1916 (Cont'd)

COLORADO & SOUTHERN

	Miles
Night Hawk Branch—South Platte to Night Hawk (ng)	4.3

The track was immediately removed except a short section at South Platte which was put into side track.

DENVER & INTERURBAN

	Miles
Line to Westminster University (sg)	1.8
Total	9.4

1917

CONSTRUCTION

COLORADO & SOUTHERN

	Miles
Berwind Branch extended to end of track at Bear Canon Mine (sg)	0.7

CRIPPLE CREEK & COLORADO SPRINGS

Narrow gauge to standard gauge:
    Bull Hill Junction to Midway (Vista Grande)
    Bull Hill Branch—from a point near the Last Dollar Mine to a point near the Vindicator Mine.

Dual gauge to standard gauge
    Near Vindicator Mine to Bull Hill (Cripple Creek Sampler site)
    The connection at Bull Hill Junction was eliminated and the two lines were joined with a short standard gauge track north of the Last Dollar Mine.
    From the switch for the Mary McKinney Mine spur on the Cripple Creek-Victor Line to the junction of the Beacon Hill Branch, thence on the Beacon Hill Branch to the El Paso Mine.
    A narrow gauge spur to the Mary McKinney Mine was converted to standard gauge and connected with the MT main line at the mine.

Following these conversions the line was operated with MT equipment. The two railroads were under common ownership at the time but were separate legal entities. MT purchased outright all remaining CC&CS trackage in 1921.

1917 (Cont'd)

DENVER & RIO GRANDE

Miles

Reilly Canon Branch—from Cokedale northwesterly up Reilly Canon to end of track at Bon Carbo (sg) — 7.2

> This extension, placed in operation in November, was built for the American Smelting & Refining Company but conveyed to D&RG after completion. A connecting track of 0.85 mile through the Cokedale yards, was acquired from the refining company in 1929.

Dual gauge to standard gauge—Leadville to Graham Park Junction.

Narrow gauge to standard gauge—Graham Park Junction to Ibex.

ELK CREEK COAL COMPANY (Amalgamated Development Corporation, 1920; Blue Seal Coal Company, 1921)

From a connection with the D&SL near Milner, southerly to Elk Creek Mine (sg) — 2.5

> This short railroad was built to haul coal from the mine to the D&SL tracks.

UNION PACIFIC

Eureka Mine Spur—from the Puritan Branch north to Eureka (Munroe) Mine (sg) — 0.6

Total — 11.0

ABANDONMENTS

ATCHISON TOPEKA & SANTA FE

Arkansas Valley Branch—Rocky Ford to Fenton[3] (sg) — 3.4

> No through traffic had passed over this section of track since 1910 when a bridge across the Arkansas was washed out. A short section of track at Rocky Ford was retained to service a sugar factory and for car storage.

CHICAGO BURLINGTON & QUINCY

Parkdale Mine spur (sg) — 1.3

COLORADO & SOUTHERN

Falcon to Wann Brick Yard, 3.5 miles north of Gulf Junction at Pueblo (sg)[4] — 47.4

1917 (Cont'd)

	Miles

This was a section of the old main line originally constructed by D&NO in 1882. All C&S through traffic had operated over AT&SF tracks between Denver & Pueblo since 1899.[5] Removal of the tracks to the northern edge of Pueblo began in 1917 and was completed in 1919, thus again leaving C&S with disconnected segments of main line trackage. The remaining section within Pueblo was connected with the AT&SF east of Fountain Creek in 1921 after the C&S bridge across the creek was washed out. It has continued in use as an industrial spur.

	Miles
Manitou Junction to the AT&SF track in Colorado Springs (sg)	8.1
Arkins Branch reduced (sg)	0.6

CRIPPLE CREEK & COLORADO SPRINGS

Victor to Cripple Creek except a short section near the Mary McKinney Mine which was converted to standard gauge (sg)	5.6
Victor to Bull Hill Junction (ng)	3.3
Beacon Hill Branch—from El Paso Mine to Henry Adney Mine (ng)	1.6

DENVER & RIO GRANDE

Sonora to a point near Graneros (sg)[6] — 18.1

This was an interior section of the original main line between Pueblo and Walsenburg. The remaining sections became branches; the Sonora Branch which connected with the new main line at Sonora Junction, near Minnequa, and the Graneros Branch with a main line connection at Lascar, 13.3 track miles north of Cuchara Junction.

Castle Rock Quarry Spur reduced from Hathaway to O'Brien's Quarry (sg) — 1.4

DENVER LARAMIE & NORTHERN (formerly Denver Laramie & Northwestern)

From 0.62 miles north of Utah Junction to Boulder Valley Junction (where the line crossed the Brighton-Boulder branch of the UP) (sg) — 17.0

The 28.2 mile section between Boulder Valley Junction and Elm was sold to the Great Western Railway and the 0.62 mile section north from Utah Junction was later conveyed to D&SL. The balance of the track was removed soon after abandonment.

Denver & Rio Grande Railroad
IN COLORADO AND NEW MEXICO
1916

Courtesy Colorado Railroad Museum

1917 (Cont'd)

	Miles
Elm to Greeley (sg)	8.4
The track was removed soon after abandonment except the 1.36 miles of Greeley Terminal Railway trackage which evidently remained in place until 1937.[7]	

GILPIN RAILROAD

All remaining trackage between Black Hawk and Banta Hill, including branches (2 ft.) — 16.3

ROCKY MOUNTAIN

Near Granby to end of track at Monarch (sg) — 13.6
All trackage of this railroad was taken up the following year.

Total — 146.1

1918

CONSTRUCTION

UNION PACIFIC

State Mine Junction, on Boulder Branch, to State Mine (sg) — 2.2

ABANDONMENTS

CHICAGO BURLINGTON & QUINCY

Tower Junction to Noland (Tower) (sg) — 3.7

COLORADO & SOUTHERN

Lafayette Branch reduced (sg) — 0.8
Stout Branch—from Bellevue Junction to end of track (sg) — 3.0
A stub of 0.18 mile was retained as side track. The balance was dismantled soon after abandonment.

DENVER & INTERURBAN

From the junction with the C&S tracks at Twelfth Street (now Broadway) in Boulder, north to Pearl Street, thence east on Pearl to the C&S cross-over near 28th Street (sg) — 1.2
D&I cars thereafter used C&S tracks which had been electrified between Twelfth Street and the Pearl Street cross-over.

1918 (Cont'd)

	Miles
GEORGETOWN & GRAYS PEAK (Also known as Argentine & Grays Peak. Formerly Argentine Central.)	
Entire line—Silver Plume to McClellan, including Vidler spur (ng) The track was removed in 1921.	16.4
Total	25.1

1919

CONSTRUCTION

CHICAGO BURLINGTON & QUINCY

From the Lyons Branch about 1.8 miles south of Erie, easterly to Columbine Mine (sg) — 2.1

ABANDONMENTS

BEAVER PENROSE & NORTHERN

Entire line—Beaver to Penrose (sg) — 6.5

COLORADO & SOUTHERN

Morrison Branch reduced (ng) — 0.4
Garfield Quarry Branch (2.75 mi.) and Soda Lake Spur (0.25 mi.) (ng) — 3.0

COLORADO MIDLAND[8]

Divide to New Castle (sg)	195.0
Jerome Park Branch (sg)	16.5
Aspen Branch (sg)	18.4
Mine branches at Aspen (sg)	0.9
Leadville to Arkansas Junction (sg)	3.8
Mine branches in Leadville district	5.8

Trackage between Colorado Springs and Divide and the terminal facilities at Colorado City were sold to the Midland Terminal Railway. D&RG purchased 1.7 miles of main track running west from the passenger station at Aspen, along with adjoining sidings and spurs. The remaining track was dismantled in 1921.

1919 (Cont'd)

DENVER BOULDER & WESTERN

	Miles
Boulder to Eldora (ng)	33.4
Sunset to Ward and extension to New Market (ng)	14.0
Spur to Dew Drop (Adit) Tunnel (ng)	0.7

In July 1920, after most of the line had been dismantled, the Colorado Supreme Court reversed the decision of the PUC and ordered operations to be resumed. The order was never carried out.

GREAT WESTERN

Between Wattenberg and Boulder Valley Junction (sg)	1.2

The rails were removed the following year and installed on the main line between Officer Junction and Johnstown.

Total 299.6

A *Denver, Boulder & Western* passenger train with a one-coach consist at the end of the line at Eldora shortly before abandonment.— (State Historical Society of Colorado)

The Great Western Ry. Co.

LONGMONT AND EATON DISTRICT

TIME TABLE No. 9 — April 1st, 1920

NORTH BOUND				SOUTH BOUND	
Motor Passenger *First Class*	Motor Passenger *First Class*	Distance from Longmont	STATIONS	Distance from Eaton	Motor Passenger *First Class*	Motor Passenger *First Class*
No. 1				**No. 2**	
	Daily Ex. Sun. Lv. 4 20 pm		C. B. & Q. JUNCTION LONGMONT	42.1	Daily Ex. Sun Ar. 9 20 am	
			3.2			
	f	3.2	FOSTER	38.9	f	
			1.6			
	f 4 32	4.8	KIRKLAND	37.3	f 9 05	
			1.3			
	f	6.1	LIBERTY	36.0	f	
			2.0			
	s 4 45	8.1	MEAD	34.0	s 8 55	
			4.1			
	f 4 55	12.2	WALKER	29.9	f 8 42	
			2.2			
	f	14.4	BUNYAN	27.7	f	
			1.0			
	f	15.4	EVANSTON	26.7	f	
			2.4			
	s 5 10	17.8	JOHNSTOWN	24.3	s 8 30	
			2.2			
	f	20.0	HARDMAN	22.1	f	
			1.0			
	f	21.0	RAGAN	21.1	f	
			2.1			
	Ar. 5 25 pm Lv. 6 00 pm	23.1	OFFICER JUNCTION	19.0	Lv. 8 15 Ar. 7 32	
			0.1			
		23.2	U. P. CROSSING	18.9		
			0.0			
	f	23.2	KELIM	18.9	f	
			1.3			
	f	24.5	GOVE	17.6	f	
			1.3			
	f	25.8	LOREY	16.3	f	
			4.3			
	s 6 15	30.1	WINDSOR	12.0	s 7 15	
			0.0			
		30.1	C. & S. CROSSING	12.0		
			1.8			
	f	31.9	BRUCE	10.2	f	
			2.1			
	s 6 25	34.0	SEVERANCE	8.1	s 7 05	
			3.5			
	f	37.5	HURICH	4.6	f	
			1.0			
	f	38.5	TUBER	3.6	f	
			1.0			
	f	39.5	GATES	2.6	f	
			2.3			
		41.8	U. P. CROSSING			
			0.3			
	Ar. 6 45 pm	42.1	EATON		Lv. 6 45 am	
	(2 25)				(2 35)	

LOVELAND AND OFFICER DISTRICT

No. 5 Daily Ex. Sun.	No. 3 Daily Ex. Sun.		STATIONS		No. 4 Daily Ex. Sun.	No. 6 Daily Ex. Sun.
Lv. 5 25 pm	Lv. 7 32 am	23.1	OFFICER JUNCTION	19.0	Ar. 8 15 am	Ar. 6 00 pm
			2.3			
f	f	25.4	BIRD	21.3	f	f
			3.7			
Ar. 5 40 pm	Ar. 7 50 am	29.1	LOVELAND	25.0	Lv. 7 50 am	Lv. 5 40 pm
(.15)	(.18)				(.25)	(.20)

Time Table No. 9—April 1, 1920

Distance from Johnstown	JOHNSTOWN and WATTENBERG DISTRICT		Distance from Johnstown	JOHNSTOWN and WELTY DISTRICT
	JOHNSTOWN			JOHNSTOWN
2.6	MILLIKEN		1.2	CLARK
6.0	U. P. CROSSING	Intermittent Freight Service on Johnstown-Wattenberg, Johnstown-Welty and Milliken-Elm Districts	2.3	PULLIAM
6.7	FORT ST. VRAIN		4.1	BUDA
10.5	HODGSON		5.1	KAHLER
13.0	MOORE		6.2	WELTY
15.6	WULFEKUHLER		Distance from Milliken	MILLIKEN and ELM DISTRICT
16.8	VOLLMAR			
20.5	TRACEYVILLE			MILLIKEN
23.0	ADY		0.1	U. P. CROSSING
			1.7	ADNA
24.1	WATTENBERG		4.3	ELM

SPECIAL RULES AND INSTRUCTIONS

North bound trains are superior to south bound trains of the same class.

Passenger trains must not exceed 35 miles an hour and freight trains 20 miles an hour.

Freight service performed daily except Sunday.

s—Indicates regular stop.

f—Indicates stop on signal.

REGISTER STATIONS—Longmont, Johnstown, Officer Junction, Eaton and Loveland.

WATER STATIONS—Longmont and Loveland.

FUEL STATIONS—Longmont and Loveland.

WYES—Longmont, Johnstown, Officer Junction, Windsor, Eaton, Loveland and Wattenberg.

TRACK SCALES—Longmont, Milliken, Loveland and Windsor.

AGENCIES AND TELEPHONES—Longmont, Mead, Johnstown, Windsor, Severance, Eaton, Loveland, Milliken and Wattenberg.

RULES GOVERNING CROSSINGS

All trains will come to full stop at least two hundred feet from Union Pacific crossing at Kelim, and Colorado & Southern crossing at Windsor, and ascertain that track is clear before crossing.

Union Pacific crossing at Eaton is mechanically controlled. All trains arriving at and leaving Eaton will be governed by signals displayed by towerman.

Trains approaching Eaton must be under perfect control. One long blast of whistle will inform towerman that train wishes to go down straight track or north leg of wye, and two short and one long blast of whistle will indicate that train wishes to go down track leading to factory.

Trains leaving Eaton will signal towerman with four short blasts of whistle, but in no case will trains pass over derail until proper signal is displayed by towerman.

Union Pacific crossing on Elm District at Milliken is protected by gate and derails set normally against Great Western Railway trains. This gate must be left in its normal position and must not be closed until trains have cleared derails, and when closed must be locked.

Union Pacific crossing on Wattenberg District at Wild Cat is mechanically controlled, and its use will be governed by signals from towerman.

WARNING TO EMPLOYES OF DANGER

The Company does not block switches, frogs or guard rails.

There are buildings, coal platforms, stock yards, beet dumps, water crane frames, telephone and electric light poles, scales, switch stands, overhead and guy wires, elevated tracks, sheds, which are located on main line and on sidings, and all employes are required to familiarize themselves with same and to protect themselves from injury on account thereof.

Derails are installed in side tracks where requirements demand and must be kept in derailing position when not in use, whether siding is occupied or not.

All trains will approach road crossing at Tuber under perfect control; both track and road crossing at this point are in a cut, which makes crossing hazardous.

1920

	CONSTRUCTION	Miles

MIDLAND TERMINAL

Taylor Switchback—Taylor to La Bella Junction (sg) | | *1.0*
    This trackage was used as a passenger train route through Victor. From Taylor it switched back on the old Golden Circle (CC&CS) grade for 0.5 mile, thence on a new grade to a connection with the extension of the Victor Branch at La Bella Junction, near the switch at Strong Junction.

GREAT WESTERN

Duke Spur—Maloy to Duke (sg) | | *1.7*
    The spur was completed and ready for service in September.

Total | | *2.7*

ABANDONMENT

DURANGO RAILWAY & REALTY COMPANY (Electric)

Entire line—Durango to Animas City (sg) | | *2.5*

1921

CONSTRUCTION

UNION PACIFIC

Clayton Junction on the Boulder Valley Branch to Clayton Mine (sg) | | *0.5*
    Construction of this spur was financed by the Clayton Coal Company.

Sterling Mine Junction on the Dent Branch to Sterling Mine (sg) | | *0.8*
    This spur in the Erie coal mining district was built by the Grand Junction Mining and Fuel Company (later reorganized as the McNeil Coal Corporation).

Firestone Junction on the Dent Branch to Firestone Mine (sg) | | *0.5*

U. S. Hospital Branch—from Sable on the main line east of Denver, south to Bunell (Fitzsimons Army Hospital) (sg) | | *1.3*
    This spur was built by the U.S. government and operated by UP under contract.

Total | | *3.1*

1921 (Cont'd)

ABANDONMENTS

	Miles

BLUE SEAL COAL COMPANY (formerly Elk Creek Coal Company)

Milner to end of line at Elk Creek Mine (sg) — 2.5

DENVER & INTERURBAN

Globeville to C&S tracks near Utah Junction (sg) — 2.8
  The Denver terminus for D&I cars was shifted to Union Station which was reached via C&S tracks from a point about 2,500 feet north of Utah Junction.

Total — 5.3

1922

CONSTRUCTION

None during the year.

ABANDONMENTS

COLORADO & SOUTHERN

D&I Junction to Webb (sg) — 0.7
  D&I operations via Louisville were shifted from this section of track to the newer section between the two points via Monarch Mine. The abandoned track was dismantled in 1927 along with other trackage used by D&I.
Spur to Sunnyside Mine No. 2 (sg) — 0.4

DENVER & RIO GRANDE WESTERN (formerly Denver & Rio Grande which was renamed with a change in ownership in 1921)
Grand Junction to Sugar Factory (sg) — 1.2

SILVERTON RAILROAD

Silverton to Joker Tunnel (ng) — 14.0
  The rails were not removed until 1926.[9]

Total — 16.3

1923

CONSTRUCTION
Miles

DENVER & RIO GRANDE WESTERN

Loma Branch—extended from Kebler No. 2 Mine (formerly Big Four) to end of track at Alamo (sg) — 4.2

    Construction was fnanced by Alamo Coal Company but title to the track was transferred to D&RGW soon after its completion.

Dual gauge to narrow gauge—Durango to Carbon Junction

Standard gauge to narrow gauge—Carbon Junction to state line.

    With these "reverse" conversions all railroads serving southwestern Colorado were again exclusively narrow gauge.

ABANDONMENTS

COLORADO SPRINGS & CRIPPLE CREEK DISTRICT[10]

	Miles
Short Line District—Colorado Springs to Vindicator Junction (sg)	41.0
Colorado City Branch (sg)	1.9
Connection with AT&SF at Colorado Springs (sg)	1.2
High Line District—Cripple Creek to Victor except 0.8 mile between the Last Dollar and Gold Sovereign Mines (sg)	11.5
Low Line District—Victor to Pisgah Junction (sg)	4.3
Hoosier Pass Cutoff—Cameron to Hoosier Pass (sg)	1.7
Raven Hill Spur (sg)	0.5
Blue Bird Spur (sg)	0.3
Eagle Sampler Branch (sg)	1.1

DENVER & RIO GRANDE WESTERN

Blue River Branch—from the initial point in the Leadville yards to Dillon (ng) — 36.3

    The tracks were removed the following year. There had been little traffic over the line for about 15 years.

Calumet Branch—Hecla Junction to Calumet (ng) — 7.1

    Except for a short section from Hecla Junction east, this branch had not been used since 1897. Washouts and removal of rails by others left only about 5.5 miles of reclaimable track.[11]

DENVER & SALT LAKE

Spur to Curtis Mine (sg) — 2.0

1923 (Cont'd)

TRINIDAD ELECTRIC TRANSMISSION RAILWAY & GAS COMPANY

	Miles
Trinidad to Starkville (sg)	7.5
Sopris Branch (sg)	1.1
Cokedale Branch (sg)	4.0
Total	121.5

1924

CONSTRUCTION

DENVER & RIO GRANDE WESTERN

From Mustang, on the main line between Pueblo and Walsenburg, to Larimer on the Graneros Branch (sg) — 1.5

This connecting track, together with 1.4 miles of track on the Graneros Branch became the Capers Branch.

DOLORES PARADOX & GRAND JUNCTION (Colorado & Southwestern, 1945)

From the Rio Grande Southern at Dolores, west and north to McPhee (ng) — 5.0

Owned by the New Mexico Lumber Company (later Montezuma Lumber Company), this railroad was built to transport lumber, supplies and passengers between Dolores and McPhee. The tracks reached McPhee in late May or early June. In addition to this common carrier line, the company operated up to 60 miles of logging branches extending from its mill at McPhee into the cutting areas of Montezuma National Forest. The logging trains were replaced by trucks in 1933.

UNION PACIFIC

Fort Collins to Buckeye (sg) — 17.2

Ths extenson into a farming and ranching community northwest of Fort Collins was opened for traffic September 1.

Total — 23.7

1924 (Cont'd)

ABANDONMENTS | Miles

COLORADO & SOUTHERN

Long's Junction to end of track (sg)	0.6
The track was dismantled the following year.	
Buena Vista to Hancock[12] (ng)	30.8
Spur to Fox Mine near Marshall (sg)	1.0

DENVER & RIO GRANDE WESTERN

Castle Rock Quarry Spur—Castle Rock to end of track at Hathaway Quarry (sg)	2.9
Coal Creek Branch—Florence to Coal Creek Mine No. 2 (sg)	3.2
Sonora Branch—Sonora Junction to end of track at Sonora (sg)	4.7
The track was removed the following year.	
Graneros Branch:	
Lascar to Larimer (sg)[13]	4.3
From a point near Capers to Graneros (sg)[13]	2.8
Total	50.3

1925

CONSTRUCTION

CHICAGO BURLINGTON & QUINCY

Tampa Beet Spur—from Tampa on the main line between Roggen and Keenesburg, south to Sheehan, thence west to Sloan (sg)	9.0

DENVER & RIO GRANDE WESTERN

Dual gauge to standard gauge:
    Salida to Malta
    Malta to Eilers

ABANDONMENTS

AMERICAN POWER & COAL COMPANY

Track between D&SL connection and Routt-Pinnacle Mine (sg)	1.8

BOOK CLIFF

Grand Junction to Carpenter (ng)	11.5

1925 (Cont'd)

This L. C. McClure photo of the head house of the Gray Creek Coal Mine on the C&S branch was taken several years before its closing.— (Denver Public Library, Western History Department)

1925 (Cont'd)

COLORADO & SOUTHERN

	Miles
Dixon Spur reduced (sg)	0.7
Gray Creek Branch reduced (sg)	7.3
Total	21.3

1926

CONSTRUCTION

ATCHISON TOPEKA & SANTA FE

Colorado-Kansas boundary via Springfield to Pritchett (sg) — 47.2

This was the Colorado portion of a branch originating at Satanta, Kansas. Construction was under the charter of a subsidiary, the Dodge City & Cimarron Valley Railway Company. The rails were laid as far as Springfield by November 5 and the last spike was driven at Pritchett on November 24. The branch was opened for revenue traffic February 1, 1927.

UNION PACIFIC

From Ripple on the Fort Collins-Buckeye extension, east to Orcutt (sg) — 2.4

This spur, built to serve an old field north of Fort Collins, was placed in operation November 14.

Total — 49.6

ABANDONMENTS

CALUMET FUEL COMPANY

Franklin Junction to Perrins (ng) — 4.7
This railroad had been operated by RGS since 1906.

COLORADO & SOUTHERN

Arkins Branch—Wilds to Arkins (sg) — 2.3
Remaining section of Dixon Spur (sg) — 0.6

DENVER & INTERURBAN (Electric)

Near Utah Junction to Semper (sg) — 5.3

1926 (Cont'd)

	Miles
Branch to Eldorado Springs (sg)	3.0
Remaining trackage in Boulder between the C&S tracks at the Pearl Street crossing and the Junction with the Louisville Branch (sg)	0.6

All D&I trackage was taken up in 1927.

DENVER & RIO GRANDE WESTERN

Crestone Branch—Moffat to Cottonwood[14] (ng) — 17.0

There had been no regular service over this branch for several years. Evidently there was little, if any, track in place on the 5.52 miles beyond Crestone at the time abandonment was granted. The 11.44 miles of track between Moffat and Crestone was removed in 1929.

Aspen Branch—part of main line track and various mine spurs at Aspen (sg) — 3.0

DENVER & SOUTH PLATTE (Electric)

Englewood to Littleton (3'6") — 4.2

RIO GRANDE SOUTHERN

May Day Branch (ng) — 1.9

Total — 42.6

The Imperial Coal Mine in Weld County, served by the Boulder Branch of the UP.— (Author's collection)

1927

CONSTRUCTION

	Miles

DENVER & RIO GRANDE WESTERN

New Pacific Mine Spur—New Pacific Junction near Pictou on Loma Branch to New Pacific Mine (sg) — 2.7

UNION PACIFIC

Imperial Mine Spur—State Mine Junction to Imperial Mine (sg) — 0.6
    In addition to the main spur nearly a mile of siding and spur tracks were built at the mine.

Total — 3.3

ABANDONMENTS

ATCHISON TOPEKA & SANTA FE

Pueblo to Portland (sg) — 26.1
    AT&SF trains had been operating over D&RGW tracks between the two points under temporary detour arrangements since 1921 when sections of its own track were severely damaged by an Arkansas River flood. The original order was for permanent abandonment but was later modified to apply only as long as the AT&SF used that part of the D&RGW railroad.[15]

CHICAGO BURLINGTON & QUINCY

New Mitchell Mine Spur (sg) — 0.6

COLORADO & SOUTHERN

Gray Creek Branch—Beshoar Junction to end of track (sg) — 0.6
From Semper to a point 1.1 track miles south of Louisville Junction (sg) — 6.3
    This section of the original C&S main line was used by D&I under lease from 1908 until it discontinued operations near the end of 1926.
From the Torrid (Rugby) Mine on the Rugby Spur to end of track at Primrose Mine (sg) — 0.4

Total — 34.0

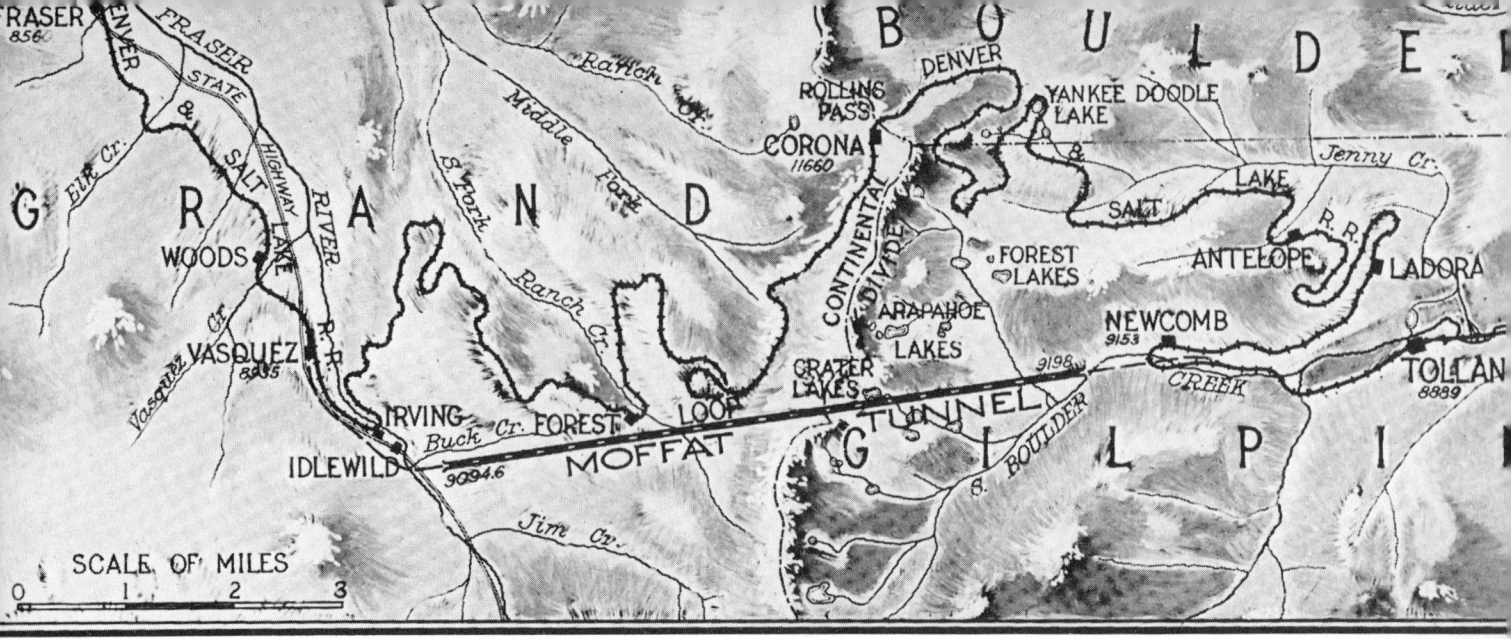

Map—Moffat Tunnel area

The east portal of Moffat Tunnel during the late construction period.

The west portal as it appeared soon after the tunnel was completed. The surrounding scenery has changed considerably over the years. The aspen trees have disappeared, the evergreens have grown to greater heights and U.S. Highway 40 crosses over the tunnel just above the portal.—(Both photos—State Hist. Society of Colo.)

The opening of Moffat Tunnel brought an end to the operating burdens caused by winter and spring snow on the Rollins Pass route.
(Above) A DS&L rotary snow plow and train stalled by a slide at an unidentified location below the summit in 1927, the final year of operations over the pass. (Left) Another 1927 photo showing a D&SL train with a rotary snow plow approaching Corona from the west.—
(Both photos—Blaine Markle Collection, State Hist. Society of Colo.)

1928

CONSTRUCTION | Miles

MOFFAT TUNNEL COMMISSION

From a point near Newcomb west through Moffat Tunnel to a point near Vasquez (Moffat Tunnel 6.2 mi., approaches 2.7 mi.) (sg) — 8.9

The track of the tunnel and approaches were leased to the D&SL. The new route via the tunnel was 22.8 miles shorter than over Rollins Pass and 2,421 feet lower in maximum altitude, being 9,239 ft. at the apex of the tunnel. The tunnel was officially opened on February 26 with an elaborate ceremony climaxed with the passage of the first passenger train through the bore.[16]

ABANDONMENTS

COLORADO & SOUTHERN

Black Hawk-Central City line reduced (ng) — 0.5
  There had been no traffic over this line since 1925.
From the main line north of Louisville to Matchless (Paramount) Mine (sg) — 1.9
From Forbes Mine Spur to Majestic Mine (sg) — 1.5
Forbes to Forbes Mine (sg) — 1.7

Total — 5.6

1929

CONSTRUCTION

COLORADO & SOUTHERN

Ingleside branch extended from a point 2.2 miles south of Ingleside Quarry, north to Rex (sg) — 4.7

Construction was under the Colorado Railroad charter. The branch later became Ingleside Spur, and in the 1960's was renamed Rex Spur.

ABANDONMENTS

DENVER & RIO GRANDE WESTERN

Floresta Branch—Crested Butte to Floresta (ng) — 10.7
Engleville Branch—Engleville Junction to Engleville (sg) — 6.4
  The track was dismantled the following year.

Total — 17.1

1929 (Cont'd)

After the abandonment of the rails to Floresta, Crested Butte continued to be an important shipping point for coal from the nearby Colorado Fuel & Iron Corporation mine. The poultry flock on the main line appears to be oblivious to any prospective traffic.—(Ronfor Photo—State Historical Society of Colorado)

1930

CONSTRUCTION | Miles

DENVER & RIO GRANDE WESTERN

North Fork Branch extended from Somerset to Oliver Mine (sg) | 1.6
Narrow gauge to dual gauge—Alamosa to Hooper.

ABANDONMENTS

COLORADO & WYOMING

Piedmont Branch—Sopris to Piedmont Mine (sg) | 0.8

MIDLAND TERMINAL

Taylor Switchback—Taylor to Portland (Independence)[17] Mill (sg) | 1.2

Total | 2.0

1931

CONSTRUCTION

None during the year.

ABANDONMENTS

ATCHISON TOPEKA & SANTA FE

Arkansas Valley Branch—Shelton Junction to Fenton (sg) | 2.4
    This was the remaining section of the line between Rocky Ford and Shelton Junction built by the Arkansas Valley Railway Company in 1906.

COLORADO & SOUTHERN

Balance of Black-Hawk Central City Line (ng) | 3.6
Spur at Ingleside—from the junction with the new main line to Ingleside Quarry | 2.2
    The extension from south of the quarry in 1929 left part of the original track extending from the new line, forming a spur. Since the limestone deposits at its terminus were exhausted the spur was no longer needed.

1931 (Cont'd)

COLORADO & WYOMING *Miles*

Primero Branch reduced (sg)   0.4

Total   8.6

1932

CONSTRUCTION

None during the year.

ABANDONMENTS

COLORADO & SOUTHERN

Marshall Branch—from Water Street (now Canyon Boulevard) in Boulder to the Crown Mine Spur between Superior and Marshall (sg)   7.6

COLORADO & WYOMING

Hezron Branch—Hezron Junction to Hezron (sg)   1.7

COLORADO SPRINGS & INTERURBAN

Colorado Springs to Manitou (sg)   5.9
    The entire Colorado Springs street car system was replaced by buses May 1, 1932.[18]

DENVER & RIO GRANDE WESTERN

Calcite Branch—Howard to end of track at Calcite (sg)   5.8
    The track was not removed until 1936. Some traffic might possibly have passed over the line after the official abandonment date.

Lascar to Cuchara Junction (sg)   13.3
    This was another section of the original Pueblo-Walsenburg main line.

Total   34.3

1933

Lake City, from the south, shortly before the D&RGW branch was abandoned. The railroad facilities are at extreme right.—(Denver Public Library, Western History Department)

1933 (Cont'd)

	Miles
CONSTRUCTION	

None during the year.

ABANDONMENTS

COLORADO & SOUTHERN

Morrison Branch—Sheridan Junction to Morrison (ng) — 9.8
A 6.3-mile segment from Morrison east was dismantled the following year and the remaining 3.5 miles in 1938.

COLORADO & WYOMING

Primero Branch—Primero Junction to end of track (sg) — 2.6

DENVER & RIO GRANDE WESTERN

Lake City Branch—Lake Junction to Lake City (ng) — 35.8
The branch was sold in 1934. The purchaser organized the San Cristobal Railway but operations over the line by that company were very limited. It was dismantled in 1936.

Total — 48.2

1934

Three views of the Dotsero Cutoff soon after completion. (Above) Looking down on Colorado River above Burns, June 12, 1934. (Below) Looking eastward from above the upper tunnel, June 12, 1934. (Opposite page) Looking south at station 1234, May 9, 1934. —(D&RGW Collection—State Hist. Society of Colo.)

1934 (Cont'd)

Looking east from the east portal of Sweetwater Tunnel, June 12, 1934.— (D&RGW Collection—State Hist. Society of Colo.)

1934 (Cont'd)

CONSTRUCTION | Miles

DENVER & SALT LAKE WESTERN (Denver & Rio Grande Western, 1947)

Dotsero Cutoff—From the D&RGW main line at Dotsero to the D&SL at Orestod (sg) | 38.1
    This connection between the two railroads shortened the rail distance between Denver and Salt Lake City by 173 miles. The D&SLW was a subsidiary of the D&SL but was constructed and operated exclusively by D&RGW. The rails were connected with the D&SL at Orestod on May 7[19] and on June 15 a through freight train from Denver passed over the line enroute to Salt Lake City. The following day several passenger trains carried participants to a celebration at Bond, 0.7 mile west of Orestod. Regular passenger service over the cutoff was inaugurated May 17. D&RGW trains used D&SL tracks between Denver and the cutoff under previous arrangements.[20]

ABANDONMENT

COLORADO & SOUTHERN

Parlin to Quartz (ng)[21] | 18.5
    D&RGW, which had operated this section of the old South Park line since 1911, joined C&S in the abandonment petition. The abandoned trackage included the D&RGW connection at Parlin.

1935

CONSTRUCTION

None during the year.

ABANDONMENTS

DENVER & RIO GRANDE WESTERN

Pagosa Springs Branch—Pagosa Junction to Pagosa Springs (ng) | 30.8
    This was the former Rio Grande, Pagosa and Northern, acquired by D&RG in 1908.
Tropic Branch—Oakdale Junction (formerly Tropic Junction) to Tropic Mine (sg) | 2.0
    There had been no service over this branch since 1932.

1935 (Cont'd)

Grand River Valley cars at Grand Junction, probably in the early 1920's. Note the designation "Colorado Fruit Belt Route" on the letterboard of car 76. —(State Historical Society of Colorado)

1935 (Cont'd)

DENVER & SALT LAKE

Miles

From a point near Newcomb, via Corona, to a point near Vasquez (sg) — 31.7
> This was the original main line over Rollins Pass. It had not been used since early 1928, when operations were routed through Moffat Tunnel, except for a few days in 1929 when there was a minor cave-in in the tunnel. Dismantling was completed in 1937.

GRAND RIVER VALLEY (Electric) (Formerly Grand Junction & Grand River Valley)

Entire line—Grand Junction to Fruita (sg) — 17.8
> Passenger service was discontinued in 1928 but freight service continued until abandonment.

Total — 82.3

1936

CONSTRUCTION

CHICAGO BURLINGTON & QUINCY

Vulcan Mine Branch extended south and west to New Centennial Mine (sg) — 0.8

ABANDONMENTS

CHICAGO BURLINGTON & QUINCY

Capitol Mine Spur (sg) — 0.4

COLORADO & SOUTHERN

From the south switch at Connors to Falcon (sg) — 65.5
> The track was removed within the year except a one-mile section which remained until the last month of 1938. The part remaining between South Denver and Connors was later named Connors Spur.

From a point near Superior to Crown Mine (sg) — 1.6
> The remaining section between Coalton and Superior became the Industrial Branch and later the Industrial Spur.

1936 (Cont'd)

SILVERTON NORTHERN

Miles

Eureka to Animas Forks (ng) — 0.4

There had been no trains over this section of track since the early 1920's.[22]

Green Mountain Branch—Howardsville to Green Mountain Mine (ng) — 1.6

Total — 73.1

1937

CONSTRUCTION

ATCHISON TOPEKA & SANTA FE

From the main line of the AT&SF at Las Animas Junction, south and southeasterly to North Junction on the Satanta, Kansas-Pritchett, Colorado branch, 1.3 miles west of Springfield (sg)[23] — 61.1

From the Colorado-Oklahoma boundary north to South Junction on the Satanta-Pritchett branch 0.5 mile east of Springfield (sg) — 29.8

These two segments were the Colorado portion of a line connecting Amarillo, Texas with the main line of the Santa Fe 2.5 miles east of Las Animas. Construction was under the Dodge City and Cimarron Valley charter. Tracks of the Satanta, Kansas-Pritchett, Colorado line were used between North Junction and South Junction, a distance of 1.8 miles. The tracks were in place and ballasted by January 28 and on February 1 special excursions from Denver and La Junta to Amarillo passed over the road. A daily mixed train was put in service February 2.[24]

Total — 90.9

ABANDONMENTS

COLORADO & SOUTHEASTERN

Barnes to Barnes Junction (sg)[25] — 2.7

The connection at Barnes Junction had been eliminated by abandonment of the D&RGW Walsenburg-Trinidad line. (See Denver and Rio Grane Western below.)

COLORADO & SOUTHERN

Arkins Branch reduced (sg) — 4.0

South Park Line:
Waterton to Climax (ng) — 116.8

1937 (Cont'd)

	Miles
L.M.B. Junction to Blind Tom Mine (Mineral Belt Line) (dg)	2.4
Leadville terminal trackage from a point south of the Leadville station to end of track (ng)	0.8
Dickey to Keystone (ng)	6.8
Kokomo to Wilfley's Mill (ng)	1.1
Como to Cohen Spur (ng)	20.4
Garos to Alma (ng)	15.4
Hilltop Junction to Leavick (ng)	11.3

All the abandoned track was removed the following year except a section between Waterton and South Platte which remained until 1942. The 14.8-mile section between Leadville and Climax, isolated from all other C&S trackage by the abandonment, is operated today as a standard gauge spur with exchange facilities with the D&RGW at Leadville.

Chicosa Junction to Forbes Junction (sg)	1.2

This short connection between the C&S and D&RGW tracks north of Trinidad had been operated by D&RGW for a number of years.

DENVER & RIO GRANDE WESTERN

Westcliffe Branch—Texas Creek to Westcliffe (sg)	25.5
Blende Spur—Zinc Junction to Blende (sg)	3.4
Cuchara Junction to Trinidad (sg)	40.1
Cuchara Junction toward Walsenburg (sg)	3.3
Rouse Junction to a point near Mayne (sg)	4.2
DuPont Junction to Powder Works (sg)	1.2

After a flood destroyed a section of D&RGW tracks between Cuchara Junction and Rouse Junction in August 1936, traffic was diverted over the C&S between Walsenburg and Trinidad under a temporary detour arrangement. Later that year D&RGW was granted trackage rights over the C&S between the two points. Short connecting tracks were built at Walsenburg (247 feet by C&S) and at Trinidad (165 feet by D&RGW).

New Pacific Mine Spur—New Pacific Junction to New Pacific Mine (sg)	2.7

SILVERTON NORTHERN

Silverton to Gladstone[26] (ng)	7.3

This was the former SG&N, acquired by SN in 1915. The line had not been used since 1924.

Total	267.0

The Eagle coal mine in Weld county is served by a short spur from the Boulder Branch of the UP.—(Author's collection)

(Right) *Great Western* Locomotive No. 90, a 2-10-0, rests at Loveland, October 10, 1939. (Below) No. 90 at the head end of a string of sugar beet cars on the Eaton Branch, October 1960. Note the different lettering style and the modified pilot. It was one of the last standard gauge steam locomotives to be used in road service in Colorado.—(Both photos—Author's collection)

1938

CONSTRUCTION

	Miles

COLORADO & SOUTHERN

Narrow gauge to dual gauge—from the end of dual gauge track south of Denver to Sheridan Junction.

ABANDONMENTS

COLORADO & SOUTHERN

Sopris Branch (formerly Long Canon Branch)—
Trinidad to Sopris (sg) — *3.9*
    The remaining C&S trackage between Sopris and Long's Junction was reached via AT&SF tracks from Trinidad to Jansen, thence over the C&W to Long's Junction. C&S had been operating over parts of AT&SF since 1934.[27]
Hastings Branch—Ludlow to Barnes (sg) — *1.3*
Industrial Spur reduced to a point near Superior (sg) — *0.5*

DENVER & RIO GRANDE WESTERN

Reliance Branch—Reliance Junction to Ojo (sg) — *5.4*

Total — *11.1*

1939

CONSTRUCTION

COLORADO & SOUTHERN

Narrow gauge to dual gauge—Sheridan Junction to Chatfield.

UNION PACIFIC

Eagle Mine Spur—from National, 1.9 miles west of St. Vrains on the Boulder Branch, southerly to Eagle Mine (sg) — *0.7*
    In addition to the main spur, extensive switching and storage tracks were constructed at the mine.

ABANDONMENTS

CHICAGO BURLINGTON & QUINCY

Standard Mine Spur (sg) — *0.9*

1939(Cont'd)

	Miles
COLORADO & SOUTHERN	
Berwind Branch—from Bear Canon Mine No. 6 to end of track. (sg)	0.7
A short section remained for use as side track until 1945.	
Clear Creek Line—Idaho Springs to Silver Plume (ng)	16.9
DENVER & RIO GRANDE WESTERN	
Manitou Branch—reduced from Manitou to 28th Street in Colorado Springs (sg)	2.6
GREAT WESTERN	
Duke Spur—Maloy to Duke (sg)	1.7
UINTAH	
Mack to Colorado state line (ng)	50.8
The entire line from Mack to Watson, Utah was abandoned, including two short branches in Utah.	
UNION PACIFIC	
Puritan Mine Spur—from Shamrock Junction on the Puritan Branch to Puritan Mine (sg)	0.7
Total	74.3

1940

CONSTRUCTION

ATCHISON TOPEKA & SANTA FE

Main line track relocation between a point 1.6 miles west of Prowers to about 0.4 mile east of Las Animas Junction (sg)   *21.3*
    This was a new alignment above the level of a reservoir to be formed by the construction of a dam across the Arkansas River at Caddoa. The distance was lengthened by only 0.3 mile. Train operations over the new route began December 30.

1940 (Cont'd)

DENVER & RIO GRANDE WESTERN

Miles

Dual gauge to standard gauge—Eilers to Leadville

UNION PACIFIC

From Boulder Branch 0.5 mile west of St. Vrains to Washington Mine (sg)   *1.5*
    Construction of this track was financed by the Clayton Coal Company, owner of the mine. Extensive switching and storage tracks were also constructed at the mine.

                                                         Total   *22.8*

ABANDONMENTS

ATCHISON TOPEKA & SANTA FE

Old main line between Prowers and Las Animas Junction (sg)   *21.0*

COLORADO & SOUTHERN

Aguilar Branch—from a point near the Aguilar station to end of branch (sg)   *2.4*
Balance of Sopris Branch—Long's Junction to Sopris (sg)   *1.5*
Sopris Mine Spur (sg)   *0.7*
    This spur had previously been reclassified as side track.

COLORADO & WYOMING

Thompson Mine Spur (sg)   *1.3*

DENVER & RIO GRANDE WESTERN

Ryan Cut-off—Leadville to Leadville Junction (sg)   *2.9*
California Gulch Branch (Iron Silver Mine Branch) reduced (sg)   *0.3*

UNION PACIFIC

Eureka Mine Spur—from Puritan Branch to Munroe and Eureka Mines (sg)   *0.6*

                                                    Total   *30.7*

1941

Crystal River & San Juan train with No. 1 at the head on the final run from Marble to Carbondale.—(State Historical Society of Colorado)

1941

CONSTRUCTION

	Miles

CHICAGO ROCK ISLAND & PACIFIC

Elsmere south to Peterson Field (sg) — 3.5
About the first mile of this track followed the alignment of the old line to McFerran Mine.

DENVER & INTERMOUNTAIN

Remington Arms Plant Spur (later Denver Federal Center Spur)—from a point near Morningside station, south to the plant (sg) — 1.7
The spur was constructed at U.S. government expense by an association of railroads which had trackage rights over the D&IM. All operations over the spur were conducted by D&IM[28] until later taken over by the U.S. government.

Total — 5.2

ABANDONMENTS

COLORADO & SOUTHERN

Clear Creek Line—from a point 0.53 mile west of the Golden depot to end of track at Idaho Springs (ng) — 21.8
Black Hawk Branch—Forks Creek to Black Hawk (ng) — 7.8
Silica Branch—Waterton to Silica (ng) — 3.9
Dual gauge to standard gauge:
    Golden to Church's Brick Yard
    Golden to Denver

CRYSTAL RIVER

Carbondale to Placita (sg) — 20.7

CRYSTAL RIVER & SAN JUAN

Placita to Marble (sg) — 7.3

DENVER & RIO GRANDE WESTERN

Santa Fe Branch—Antonito to state line (ng) — 5.6
This was the Colorado portion of an abandonment which also included that part of the branch in New Mexico.

1941 (Cont'd)

	Miles
Rouse Branch—from Mayne Junction to Pryor (near Monson) (sg)	2.4
The connection with the C&S was moved from Mayne Junction to Monson. A short connecting track was built at that point, 477 feet by C&S and 947 feet by D&RGW.	
California Gulch Branch reduced (sg)[29]	0.8
Graham Park Branch:	
Graham Park Junction to Wolftone Mine (sg)	1.6
Wolftone Junction to North Moyer (sg)	2.0
Total	73.9

1942

CONSTRUCTION

COLORADO & SOUTHERN

Dual gauge to standard gauge—Denver to Chatfield

UNION PACIFIC

	Miles
Spur from Roydale, 5 miles east of Denver (Pullman), to the boundary of the Rocky Mountain Arsenal reservation (sg)	2.2
An extensive system of government-owned tracks was constructed within the reservation.	

ABANDONMENTS

COLORADO & SOUTHERN

	Miles
Chatfield to South Platte (dg)	15.5
Clear Creek Line—From Washington Avenue in Golden to end of track (sg)	0.5

DENVER & RIO GRANDE WESTERN

	Miles
Loma Branch—Alamo No. 2 Mine to Alamo (sg)	0.9
Durango to San Juan Smelter (ng)	1.0
Orient Branch—Villa Grove to Orient (ng)	8.2
Fremont Branch—Fremont Junction to Fremont Mine (sg)	1.9

1942 (Cont'd)

	Miles
SILVERTON NORTHERN	
Silverton to Eureka (ng)	8.4
The line had been dormant for about ten years except for an occasional train.	
UNION PACIFIC	
Spur track—Firestone Junction to Firestone Mine (sg)	0.5
Total	36.9

1943

CONSTRUCTION

COLORADO & SOUTHERN

Narrow gauge to standard gauge—Leadville to Climax

ABANDONMENTS

	Miles
COLORADO & SOUTHERN	
From the main line to end of track at Jewell-Creston Mine (sg)	1.6
DENVER & RIO GRANDE WESTERN	
Overland Junction to Overland Park (sg)	0.6
Castleton to end of D&RGW track on Kubler Branch (ng)	1.6
ROCKY MOUNTAIN FUEL COMPANY	
From the end of the D&RGW track north of Castelton to Kubler Mine (sg)	1.8
The mine had been closed since about 1937.	
UNION PACIFIC	
Pleasant Valley Branch—Galeton to Purcell (sg)	8.8
State Coal Mine Spur—State Mine Junction to State Mine (sg)	2.2
Clayton Junction to Clayton Mine (sg)	0.5
Total	17.1

1943 (Cont'd)

C&S Engine No. 76 heads the last narrow gauge train on the Leadville-Climax line on August 25, 1943. After this run standard gauge equipment went into operation and the two inside rails were removed.—(CB&Q RR Photo—State Hist. Society of Colo.)

1944

CONSTRUCTION · Miles

None during the year.

ABANDONMENTS · Miles

COLORADO & SOUTHEASTERN

Chandler Junction to D&RG Junction (sg) · 0.7

DENVER & RIO GRANDE WESTERN
Chandler Creek Branch—Chandler Junction to Chandler Mine (sg) · 4.6
Ibex Branch—Leadville to Ibex (sg) · 7.2
Fryer Hill Branch—Chrysolite Junction to mines on Fryer Hill (sg) · 1.3

Total · *13.8*

1945

CONSTRUCTION

None during the year.

1946

CONSTRUCTION

None during the year.

ABANDONMENTS

CHICAGO BURLINGTON & QUINCY

From main line of Lyons Branch south of Erie to Columbine Mine (sg) · 2.1
    The track was not dismantled until sometime after 1950.

DENVER & RIO GRANDE WESTERN

Baldwin Branch—from a point near Castleton to end of track near Baldwin (ng) · 2.1

1946 (Cont'd)

UNION PACIFIC — Miles

Ripple to Orcutt (sg) — 2.4

Total — 6.6

1947

Under a reorganization effective April 11, 1947, the Denver & Salt Lake, the Denver & Salt Lake Western (Dotsero Cut-off) and the Rio Grande Junction railroads were merged with the Denver & Rio Grande Western. At the same time the Northwestern Terminal was leased to D&RGW.

CONSTRUCTION

None during the year.

ABANDONMENTS

ATCHISON TOPEKA & SANTA FE

Two sections of main line trackage between Portland and Canon City (sg) — 10.4
    Trackage rights were granted over D&RGW tracks from Adobe, near Portland, to Canon City.
Rockvale Branch:
    Clelland south to D&RGW tracks (including both legs of a wye (sg) — 0.8
    Rockvale to Kenwood (sg) — 4.0

COLORADO & SOUTHERN

Industrial Spur—Coalton to Superior (sg) — 3.6
    After the closing of the Industrial Mine at Superior this remaining trackage of the former line to Boulder via Marshall was no longer needed.

DENVER & RIO GRANDE WESTERN

Crested Butte Branch—Crested Butte to Anthracite (ng) — 4.1
Bulkley Junction to Bulkley Mine (ng) — 0.6
Spur to McGregor (McNeal) Mine (sg) — 1.8

1947 (Cont'd)

GREAT WESTERN — *Miles*

Wattenberg Branch—from a point 0.5 mile south of Milliken to the end of the branch (sg) — *21.7*

UNION PACIFIC

Grant (Russell) Mine Spur—Grant Junction to end of track (sg) — *1.4*

Total — *48.4*

1948

CONSTRUCTION

None during the year.

ABANDONMENTS

CHICAGO BURLINGTON & QUINCY

Centennial (Vulcan) Mine Spur—from Lyons Branch to new Centennial Mine (sg) — *1.9*
   The track was not immediately removed.

COLORADO & SOUTHERN

From the main line south of Forbes to end of track at Thor Mine (sg) — *0.7*

COLORADO & SOUTHWESTERN

Dolores to McPhee (ng) — *5.0*

DENVER & RIO GRANDE WESTERN

From a point near Sapinero, between Gunnison and Montrose, westerly to a point near Cedar Creek (ng) — *26.6*
   The track was removed during July of the following year.

1948 (Cont'd)

All locomotives owned by the MT at the time of abandonment were scrapped in 1948 and 1949. (Above) Engine 59 was the last to be scrapped at the Colorado City shops.—(R. W. Richardson Photo—Colorado Railroad Museum Collection. (Right) No. 59 in the Colorado City yards in 1939.—(Author's Collection)

1948 (Cont'd)

Removing rails on the *Midland Terminal* near Woodland Park in 1949. The engine at the head of the dismantler's train was the only diesel ever to operate on the line.—(R. W. Richardson photo—Colorado Railroad Museum Collection)

1948 (Cont'd)

MIDLAND TERMINAL

	Miles
Colorado Springs to Cripple Creek (sg)	55.9
Victor Branch—Victor Junction to end of track at Portland Mill (sg)	1.0
Beacon Hill Branch—Mary McKinney Mine to El Paso Mine (sg)	1.0
Former Golden Circle trackage (sg)	4.9
Golden Cycle Spur at Colorado Springs	1.0
Portland-Ajax Branch (sg)	1.6

All tracks were removed in 1949.

Total 99.6

1949

CONSTRUCTION

UNION PACIFIC

Lincoln Mine Spur—from Dent Branch near St. Vrains, east to Lincoln Mine (sg)   0.9

DENVER & RIO GRANDE WESTERN

From the main line of the Craig Branch 1.9 miles west of Miner, to the strip mine of the Osage Coal Company (sg)   1.2

Total 2.1

ABANDONMENTS

COLORADO & SOUTHERN

Golden Branch—from Clear Creek Junction,[30] at Mile Post 2.60, westerly to a point near Zuni (sg)   1.6

C&S acquired trackage rights over the D&RGW between Prospect and Zuni.

DENVER & RIO GRANDE WESTERN

Rouse Branch—Monson to Rouse (sg)   2.5

1949 (Cont'd)

DENVER TRAMWAY COMPANY   *Miles*

Barnum Junction to Barnum (3 ft.-6 in.)   3.0
    This was the former DL&G branch built as standard gauge in 1892 and later operated as a part of the Denver street railway system. The gauge was changed in 1921 to conform with other street car tracks.

                                                                      Total   7.1

1950

CONSTRUCTION

CHICAGO ROCK ISLAND & PACIFIC

Sandown Cutoff—From Sandown Junction on the UP main line east of Denver, northwesterly to a connection with the Northwestern Terminal at Belt (sg)[31]   4.3
    The line was placed in service February 1, 1951.

ABANDONMENTS

COLORADO & SOUTHERN

Chatfield Branch—Sheridan Junction to Chatfield (sg)   6.5
Rugby Spur—from the initial point of the Rapson Mine spur to the end of track at Torrid (Rugby) Mine (sg)   1.3

DENVER & RIO GRANDE WESTERN

Reilly Canon Branch—Longsdale to Bon Carbo (sg)   8.9
Ouray Branch—from a point near the Ouray depot to end of track (ng)   0.2
San Luis Valley Line—Mears Junction to Hooper (ng)   53.2

DENVER & INTERMOUNTAIN

Lakeside to Arvada Junction (Electric) (3 ft.-6 in.)   2.3
Arvada Junction to Leyden Mines (dg)   8.6
Clear Creek Junction (in Arvada) to Golden (Electric) (3 ft.-6 in.)   8.5
    These were the former D&NW lines, owned at the time by Denver Tramway Company and operated by D&IM.

                                                                      Total   89.5

1950 (Cont'd)

(Above) The last train to operate north of Moffat over D&RGW's San Luis Valley Branch was this non-revenue special photographed as it approached the north end of the 51-mile tangent near Villa Grove on February 15, 1951. (Opposite page) A dismantling train and crew removing rails from the branch in the spring of 1951. Snow capped peaks of the Sangre de Cristo Range rise abruptly from the level valley floor in the background.—(Both photos—R. W. Richardson)

1950 (Cont'd)

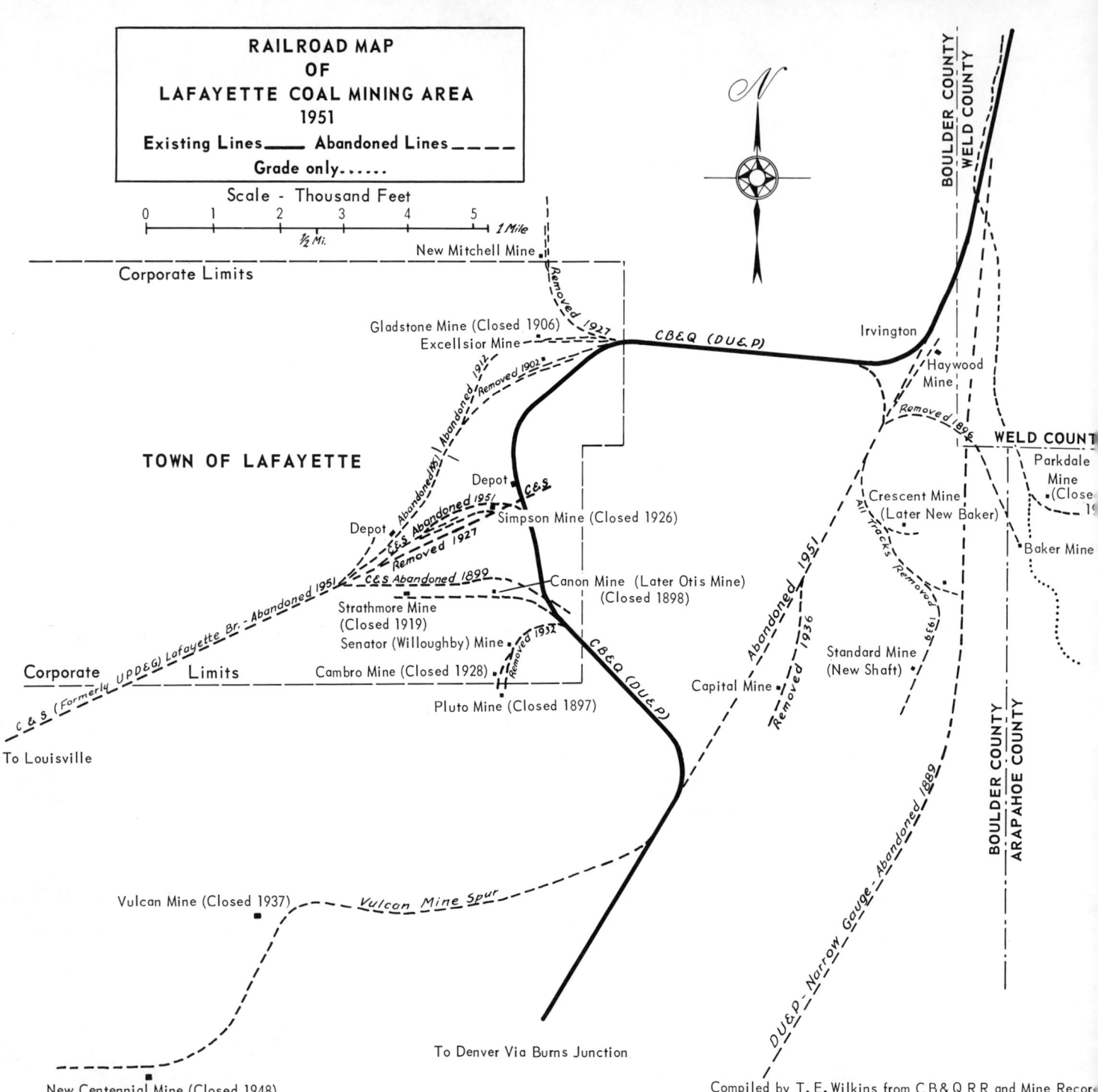

1951

CONSTRUCTION

Miles

DENVER & RIO GRANDE WESTERN

Dual gauge to standard gauge—from a point near Alamosa to Hooper.

ABANDONMENTS

CHICAGO BURLINGTON & QUINCY

Original trackage of the Lyons Branch between the two connections with the loop through Lafayette (sg)	*1.5*
South leg of wye at Irvington (sg)	*0.3*

COLORADO & SOUTHERN

Lafayette Branch—Louisville to Lafayette (sg) — *2.2*

WOLF CREEK[32]

From the D&SL at Mt. Harris to end of track (sg) — *1.0*
    Only about 4,000 feet of track was in use at the time of abandonment.

Total — *5.0*

1952

CONSTRUCTION

COLORADO & WYOMING

From Weston northwesterly to Allen Mine (sg) — *9.5*

DENVER & RIO GRANDE WESTERN

Rocky Spur—From Rocky on the Moffat Tunnel Route 18 miles west of Denver, northeasterly to an Atomic Energy Commission plant (Dow Chemical Company) on Rocky Flats (sg) — *4.0*

Total — *13.5*

1952 (Cont'd)

Miles

COLORADO & WYOMING

ABANDONMENTS

From Weston to end of line at Tercio (sg) — 11.6
    Mining operations had been shifted from the coal mines at Tercio to the Allen Mine.

COLORADO & SOUTHEASTERN

Barnes Junction to Delagua (sg) — 3.6

COLORADO & SOUTHERN

Balance of Aguilar Branch—Acme Junction to end of track at Aguilar (sg) — 1.9

DENVER & RIO GRANDE WESTERN

From a point near Cedar Creek to Ouray Junction at Montrose (ng) — 10.0
Ouray Branch—Ridgway to end of track at Ouray (ng) — 10.1
    Dismantling of both these narrow gauge segments was completed the following year.
Capers Branch reduced (sg) — 0.3

RIO GRANDE SOUTHERN

Ridgway to Durango (ng) — 162.6
Telluride Branch—Vance Junction to Pandora (ng) — 9.8

Total — 209.9

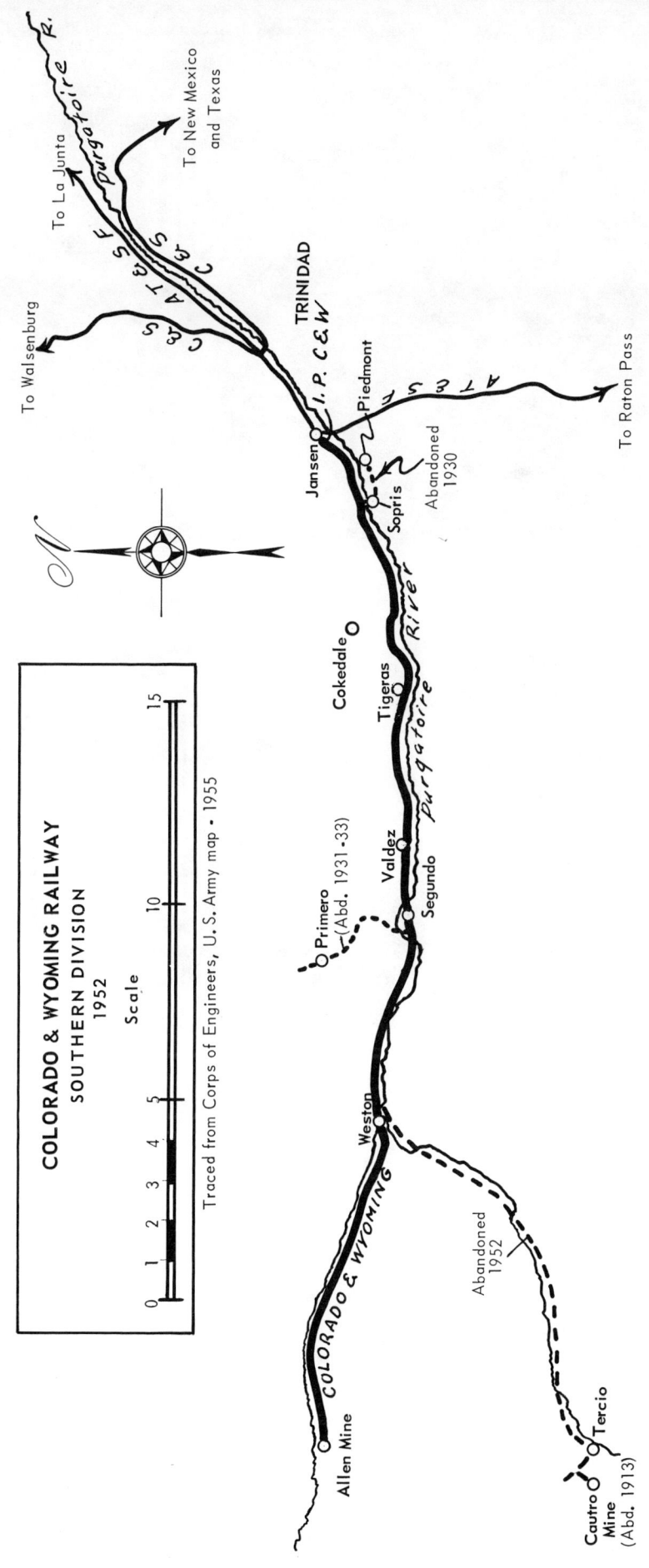

1952 (Cont'd)

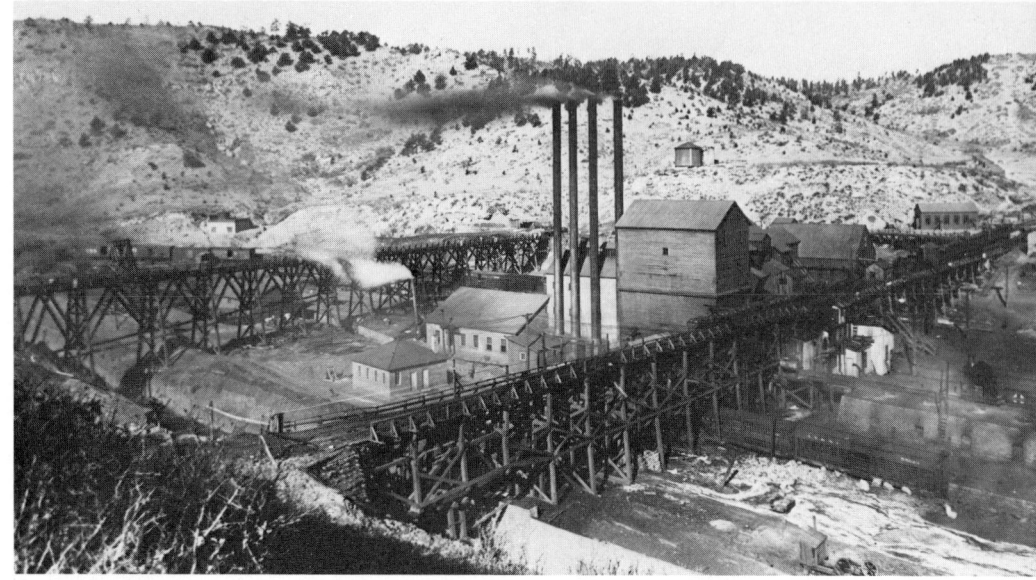

The Victor American Fuel Company mine at Delagua. Although served by the *Colorado and Southeastern*, Santa Fe cars are dominant in the yards on the right.—(L. C. McClure Photo—Denver Public Library, Western History Dep't)

This impressive *Colorado & Wyoming* station building at Segundo is in use today as a residence for an official of the road.—(Author's collection)

Rio Grande Southern railroad facilities at Rico on June 25, 1952, two and one-half months after ICC granted permission to abandon the line.—(Photo by Ted Gay—Lloyd J. Hendricks Collection)

The final operation to Ouray occurred on a snowy March 21, 1953 when D&RGW engine No. 318 was dispatched to pick up the remaining cars in the yard.—(R. W. Richardson photo)

As the rails were removed from the RGS they were hauled by dismantling trains to points accessible by motor trucks. This November 1952 photo shows rails and equipment assembled at Dallas Divide.— (R. W. Richardson photo—Colorado Railroad Museum Collection)

(Above) Preparatory to changing the gauge of the D&RGW Montrose-Ridgway Branch, standard gauge ties were added at intervals and bridges were strengthened to accommodate heavier equipment. The crew in this early 1953 photo is at a small bridge about ten miles south of Montrose.—(R. W. Richardson photo)

(Right) The conversion from narrow gauge was accomplished by moving the rails over to standard gauge width. —(D&RGW Collection, State Hist. Society of Colo.)

1953

CONSTRUCTION

Miles

DENVER & RIO GRANDE

Narrow gauge to standard gauge—Montrose to Ridgway

ABANDONMENTS

DENVER & INTERMOUNTAIN

Golden east to Simms Street (near Morningside) (sg)	5.6
The entire line between Denver and Golden was included in the abandonment but the section between Denver and Simms Street was purchased by the Associated Railroads[33] primarily to serve the Denver Federal Center.	
Ruby Quarry Spur (sg)	0.8
Morrison Spur (the former Denver, Golden & Morrison trackage) (sg)	2.7

DENVER & RIO GRANDE WESTERN

Loma Branch—from Kebler No. 2 mine to Alamo No. 2 Mine (sg)	1.2
Total	10.3

1954

CONSTRUCTION

None during the year.

ABANDONMENTS

COLORADO & SOUTHERN

Wellington to Waverly (sg)	4.7
Ludlow to Barnes Junction (sg)	1.2
This trackage had previously been reclassified as side track.	

DENVER & RIO GRANDE WESTERN

Capers Branch—Mustang to Capers (sg)	2.6
The track was removed the following year.	

1954 (Cont'd)

The final run on the D&RGW west of Gunnison left Sapinero on October 5, 1954. (Opposite page above) Making up the train at Sapinero with engine 268. (Opposite page below) The train with a consist of 21 empty box cars and an outfit car passing Elk Creek tank.
(Above) A stop was made at Iola where five stock cars were added to the consist.
—(R. W. Richardson photos)

1954 (Cont'd)

(Opposite page) Dismantling train on the D&RGW Baldwin Branch south of Castleton. Engine 268 at the head end was the last operating C-16 Baldwin 2-8-0. It was built in 1882, the same year the branch was constructed by the DSP&P. (Opposite page, above) Ex RGS No. 7 "Galloping Goose" headed the dismantling train on the D&RGW Crested Butte Branch. The mountain in the background is Crested Butte, for which the nearby town was named. (Above) The last train over Marshall Pass on the west approach to the summit with a consist of empty cars which had been assembled at Gunnison. Note the helper engine ahead of the caboose. The date is May 1955.
—(R. W. Richardson Photos)

(Right) A D&RGW dismantling crew at Shawano on the west side of Marshall Pass in the summer of 1955.—(R. W. Richardson Photo)

(Below) A southbound *San Luis Valley Southern* freight at Rattlesnake Canyon trestle south of Blanca in April 1951, six years before this section of track was abandoned. The peak in the distance is Mt. Blanca, fourth highest in Colorado. —(R. W. Richardson photo)

1954 (Cont'd)

	Miles
Gunnison Lines:[34]	
Poncha Junction to end of track at Saperino (ng)	93.5
Crested Butte Branch—Gunnison to Crested Butte (ng)	28.2
Baldwin Branch—Gunnison to end of track (ng)	15.8

The abandoned trackage of the Gunnison lines was removed in 1955.

Total	146.0

1955

CONSTRUCTION

None during the year.

ABANDONMENT

COLORADO & SOUTHERN

Berwind Branch—Ludlow to terminus at Bear Canon Mine No. 6 (sg)	4.9

1956

CONSTRUCTION

DENVER & RIO GRANDE WESTERN

Narrow gauge to standard gauge—Monarch Branch—Salida to Monarch.

1957

CONSTRUCTION

None during the year.

ABANDONMENTS

COLORADO RAILROAD, INC. (Formerly Colorado-Kansas)

Pueblo to Stone City (sg)	21.3
Trackage at Pueblo (sg)	1.5

1957 (Cont'd)

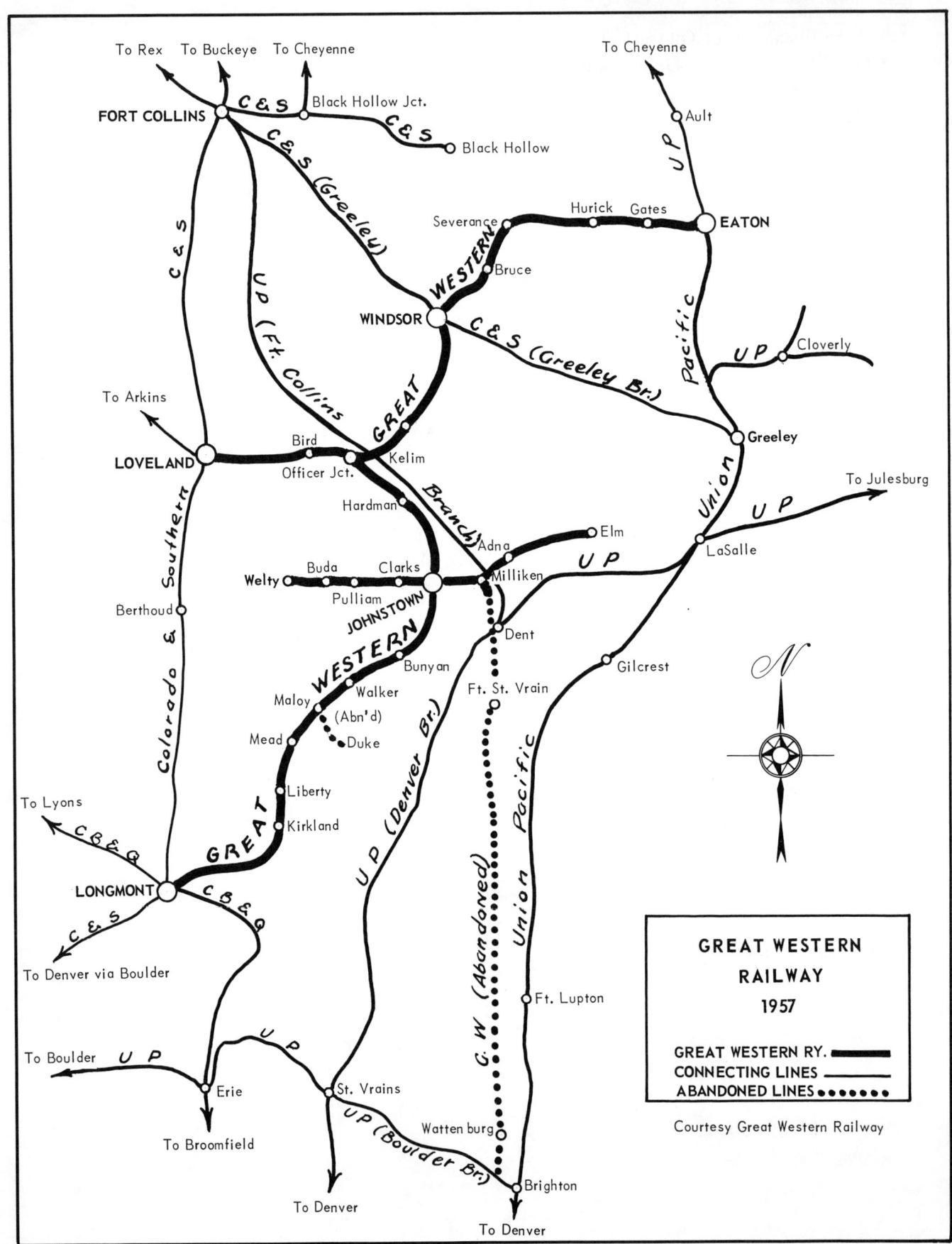

1957 (Cont'd)

GREAT WESTERN

	Miles
Stub of the former Wattenberg Branch at Milliken reduced (sg)	0.3

SOUTHERN SAN LUIS VALLEY

From a point 1.5 miles south of McClintock to end of line at Jarosa (sg)	30.2
Total	53.3

1958

CONSTRUCTION

None during the year.

ABANDONMENTS

COLORADO & SOUTHERN

Golden Branch—Zuni to C&S Junction (sg) — 0.7
   C&S acquired trackage rights over the D&RGW main line between the two points.

DENVER & RIO GRANDE WESTERN

Valley Line (Hooper Spur)—Garland Junction at Alamosa to end of track at Hooper (sg) — 20.2
   The track was dismantled in 1959 except a short stub north of the junction.

Loma Branch—Calumet No. 2 Mine to Kebler No. 2 (sg) — 7.0
   The track was removed the following year.

UNION PACIFIC

Baum Mine Junction to Baum Mine (sg) — 1.1

Total — 29.0

1959

CONSTRUCTION

None during the year.

ABANDONMENT | Miles

SOUTHERN SAN LUIS VALLEY

From a point 0.5 mile south of McClintock to end of track (sg) | 1.0
    The remaining portion of the railroad was retained for seasonal switching service.

1960

CONSTRUCTION

None during the year.

ABANDONMENT

COLORADO & SOUTHERN

From a connection with the Boulder Branch of the UP near 28th Street in Boulder to the end of the track near Broadway (sg) | 1.2
    This was the C&S portion of a spur track from the main line at Ara (Mile Post 21.97) which had been used for access to the Boulder depot since abandonment of the track between Boulder and the Crown Mine spur in 1932. It was part of the standard gauge line built by UP in 1881 toward Boulder Canon and was acquired by C&S in the 1899 transfer of UPD&G properties. In reaching the Boulder station C&S had utilized under trackage rights a 0.35 mile segment of the UP between a connection at Ara and the switch near 28th Street. This trackage was not included in the abandonment. C&S retained its 0.2 mile connection with the UP at Ara for use as a transfer track.

1961

CONSTRUCTION

DENVER & RIO GRANDE WESTERN

From a connection with the Rocky Spur about 1 mile west of the A.E.C. plant, north to the Idealite Company plant (sg) | 2.2

1961 (Cont'd)

ABANDONMENT

	Miles
CHICAGO ROCK ISLAND & PACIFIC	
Spur from Elsmere to Peterson Field (sg)	3.5

1962

CONSTRUCTION

DENVER & RIO GRANDE WESTERN

Energy Spur—from Hitchens on the main line of the Craig Branch 9 miles west of Steamboat Springs, southwesterly to mines at Energy (sg) — 12.6
  Construction of this spur was completed September 2.

New line between Gato and Allison on the Alamosa-Durango narrow gauge line (ng) — 11.3
  This was a track relocation above the high water line of a reservoir to be created by the construction of a dam on the San Juan River.

Total — 23.9

ABANDONMENTS

COLORADO & SOUTHERN

Rugby to Rapson Mine (sg) — 1.9

DENVER & RIO GRANDE WESTERN

Original line between Gato and Allison (ng) — 7.6
  This trackage was within the area to be covered by the reservoir on the San Juan River.

Loma Branch—from Calumet No. 2 Mine to end of track (sg) — 0.4

Fort Logan Branch—from 0.7 mile west of Military Junction to Fort Logan (sg) — 1.1
  The track was removed the following year.

Spur to Osage Coal Company strip mine (sg) — 1.2

Total — 12.2

This frame depot at Boulder was located on Water Street (now Canyon Blvd.) between 9th and 10th streets. Completed by the UP in May 1883, it served the *Denver & Boulder Valley,* the *Colorado Central* and the *Greeley, Salt Lake & Pacific* narrow gauge line. It replaced the original D&BV station which stood near 23rd and Pearl streets.—(J. B. Sturtevant photo—Denver Public Library, Martin R. Parsons Collection, from Boulder Historical Society)

UP completed this stone passenger station at 14th and Water streets in Boulder in September 1890. Frequently referred to by the citizenry as "Union Station," it was used by all passenger trains entering and leaving Boulder until 1958.—(J. B. Sturtevant photo—University of Colorado Museum Collection.)

Ownership of the Boulder passenger station passed to the C&S in 1899. The following year a pavilion type waiting room was added to the west end.—(State Historical Society of Colorado)

(Above) The present Boulder passenger and freight station was constructed by C&S in 1958 near Ara, a point on the main line near the eastern edge of the city. In the same year trackage to the facilities on Water street was reclassified as side track for freight traffic only and was finally retired in 1960.—(Author's collection)

(Left) The UP station at St. Vrains at the crossing of the Boulder Valley Branch (across picture in foreground) and the Dent Branch. The date of the photograph is 1967, shortly before the station was closed and dismantled.—(Author's collection)

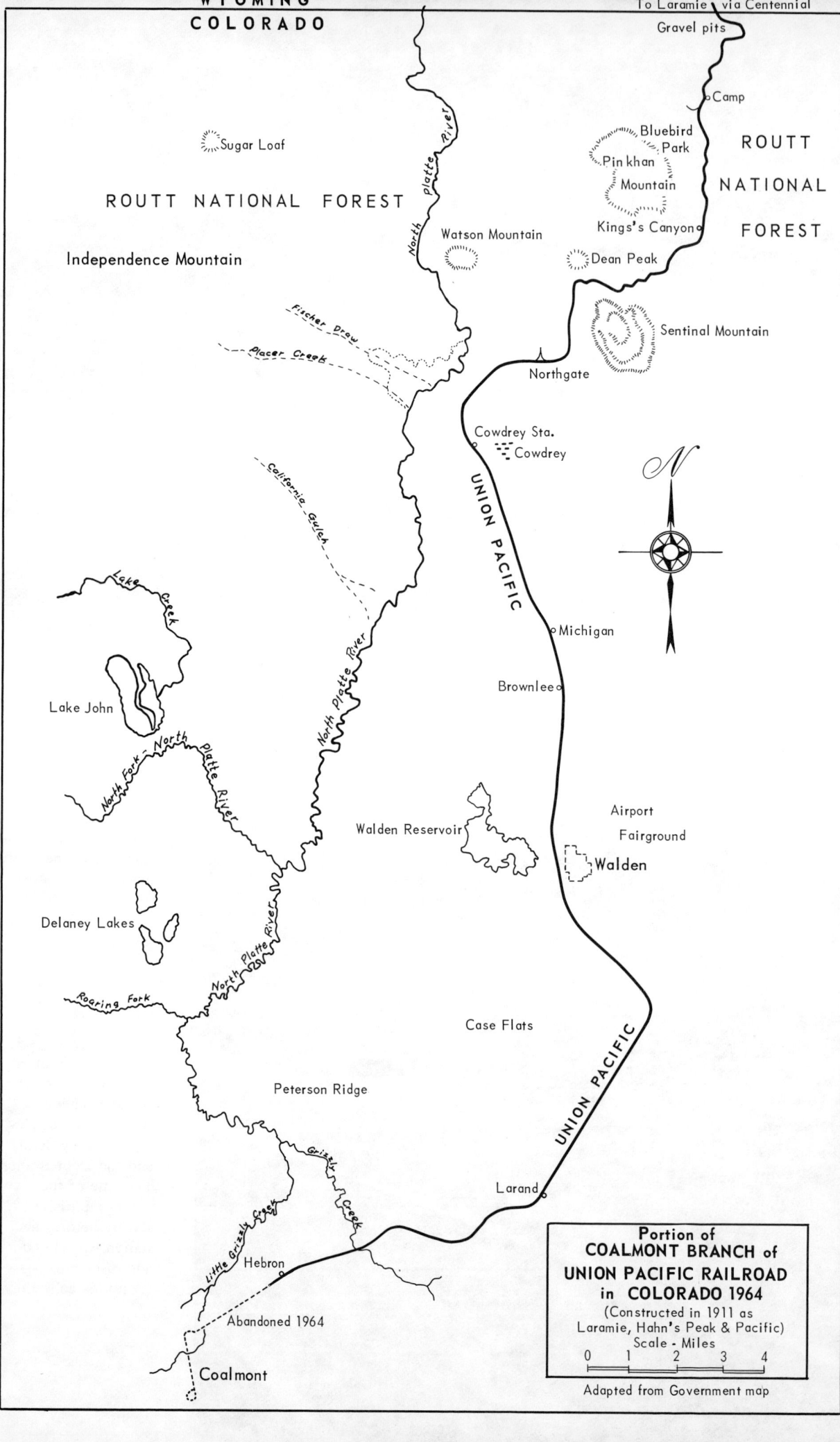

1963

CONSTRUCTION

	Miles

DENVER & RIO GRANDE WESTERN

Hayden Power Plant Spur from Hayden, 16.5 miles east of Craig, south of Power Plant (sg) — 2.8

    Construction of the spur was financed by the power company but operated by D&RGW.

ABANDONMENT

DENVER & RIO GRANDE WESTERN

California Gulch Branch—Oro Junction to end of track (sg) — 2.2

1964

CONSTRUCTION

None during the year.

ABANDONMENTS

DENVER & RIO GRANDE

Fort Logan Branch—From the main line at Military Junction to end of track (sg) — 0.7

    The track was removed in 1967 except the south leg of a wye which connects with the main line a short distance south of Military Junction.

UNION PACIFIC

Boulder Branch—from the Platte River at Brighton to a point near Yoxall (sg) — 4.6

    This broke the continuity of the branch. The short stub east of the Platte River is used to serve small industries in Brighton. Trains serving the western section are switched from the Dent Branch at St. Vrains.

Coalmont Branch—reduced from 0.4 mile west of Hebron to end of track at Coalmont (sg) — 3.8

Total — 9.1

AT&SF locomotive 312 on east bound "Grand Canyon" Trinidad, Colo. Oct. 25, 1967.— (Photo by L.J. Hendricks)

1965

CONSTRUCTION

None during the year.

ABANDONMENTS

Miles

UNION PACIFIC

Greeley Branch—reduced from end of track at Briggsdale to Mathews (sg)	14.3
Fort Collins Branch—reduced from end of track at Buckeye to a point 0.8 mile west of Boettcher (sg)	10.9
Sterling Mine Spur (sg)	0.8
Total	26.0

1966

CONSTRUCTION

None during the year.

ABANDONMENTS

ATCHISON TOPEKA & SANTA FE

Grand Valley Branch—Newdale to Hawley (sg) — 5.9
 The track was removed the following year except for a short stub extending south from Newdale.

DENVER & RIO GRANDE WESTERN

Loma Junction to end of track (sg) — 8.7
 The track of this last segment of the Loma Branch was removed the following year.

Total — 14.6

NOTES

Part I

1. (sg) denotes standard gauge track, 4 ft.-8½ in. between the rails.

2. The KP was linked with eastern rail lines at Kansas City, Missouri by means of the first permanent railroad bridge to span the Missouri River. That bridge was built in 1869, whereas the UP was not connected with railroads on the east side of the river with a permanent bridge until 1872.

3. (ng) denotes narrow gauge track. By definition narrow gauge is any track smaller than the standard gauge width of 4 ft.-8½ in. between the rails. In this report only the 3-ft. gauge is designated as narrow gauge. Other gauges smaller than standard are indicated by specific measurement, such as (2 ft.) or (3 ft.-6 in)

4. A dual gauge track (dg) is one with more than two rails, usually three, for the accommodation of equipment of different gauges.

5. The route was projected via Boulder and Longmont to Greeley, thence down the Platte River Valley to Julesburg. At the time Julesburg was about 5 miles west of its present site at a location now known as Weir.

6. *Rocky Mountain News*, Oct. 11, 1872, p. 2 and *Colorado Transcript,* Oct. 16, 1872, p. 3.

7. At the time Granada was on the south side of the Arkansas River near the mouth of Granada Creek, 3.5 miles east of its present location. It was reestablished at its present site in 1876.—*Las Animas Leader,* Nov. 15, 1873, p. 1 and *Colorado Magazine,* Vol. 18, No. 2, 1941.

8. West Las Animas was established on the south side of the Arkansas River about the time the railroad reached that point. It became Las Animas in 1886, The original town of Las Animas was about six miles east—*Colorado Magazine,* Vol. 18, No. 6, 1941.

9. All except 67 miles of the grade had been completed by the end of 1873. —*Colorado Central Railroad, Report of the Board of Directors,* 1873, Division Engineer's Report, pp 21-22.

10. At the time Rocky Ford was a small settlement on the Arkansas River three miles northeast of its present location. After the railroad was built through the area the post office was moved and he town was reestablished at its present site.—*Colorado Magazine,* Vol. 19, No. 5, Sept. 1942, p. 181.

11. Garland City was a temporary construction town 6.5 miles east of Fort Garland, near the eastern edge of the San Luis Valley. It was abandoned soon after the arrival of the railroad.

12. For an account of events leading up to the struggle for the route over Raton Pass and the dramatic seizure by AT&SF see *Santa Fe: The Railroad that Built an Empire,* James Marshall, 1945; *Steel Rails to Santa Fe,* L. L. Waters, 1950; or *Rebel of the Rockies,* Robert G. Athearn, 1962.

13. See *Colorado Transcript* or *Golden Weekly Globe,* issues of Feb. 27, 1878, for the procedure followed in the transfer of trackage.

14. The controversy between AT&SF and D&RG over the route through Royal Gorge, often referred to as "Royal Gorge War", is described in a number of works. Short accounts are given in *Santa Fe: The Railroad that Built an Empire,* James Marshall, 1945; *Rebel of the Rockies,* Robert G. Athearn, 1962; and *Kansas West,* George L. Anderson, 1963.

15. *Railroad Gazette,* Jan. 16, 1880 which shows the track reaching a point 116 miles from Denver at the end of the year. That would place it nearly four miles east of the summit of Trout Creek Pass.

16. Mileage is from *Colorado State Archives and Records Service,* Records of the State Board of Equalization for 1892 and succeeding years. However, *History of Clear Creek County,* O. L. Baskin, p. 375 and "History of Jefferson County", E. L. Berthoud, nd, p. 18, each show four miles of track laid and operated. Contemporary news items and an examination of the old grade indicate that 1.7 miles was probably the extent of the rails.— See *Colorado Transcript,* June 18, 1879, p. 3; July 16, 1879, p. 3; July 23, 1879, p. 3 and Dec. 31, 1879, p. 3.

Part II

1. *Colorado Transcript,* Nov. 3, 1880, p. 2.
2. The grade was constructed earlier by the AT&SF but was transferred to the D&RG under terms of the Royal Gorge decision. The details of the transfer had not been completed at the time the DSP&P track reached this point.
3. DSP&P used DR&G tracks between Buena Vista and Leadville under a joint operating agreement between the two companies.
4. No specific record was found showing the year in which the Golden & Ralston was abandoned but evidence indicates that 1880 was the most probable year. *Golden Weekly Globe,* Aug. 2, 1879 mentions a plan to widen the track to standard gauge as far as the Belcher Stone Quarries, indicating it existed on that date. According to Elmer O. Davis in his article "The Circle Railroad" in *Engineers Bulletin,* June 1958, rail from the line was used on the Denver Circle Railroad. (See 1881, this report.) A report of the Golden Board of Trade which appeared in *Colorado Transcript,* Dec. 31, 1879, mentioned the Golden & Ralston as one of the railroads serving Golden but it was not included in a similar report which appeared in the Jan. 5, 1881 edition of the newspaper.
5. *Colorado Transcript,* Oct. 5, 1881, p. 2; *Denver Daily Times*, Oct. 31, 1881, p. 1; Nov. 2, 1881, p. 3; Nov. 5, 1881, p. 3 and *Rocky Mountain News,* Nov. 5, 1881, p. 2 and Nov. 6, 1881, p. 8.
6. For informative accounts of the location and construction of Alpine Tunnel see *The Denver, South Park & Pacific*, M. C. Poor, 1949 and *Historic Alpine Tunnel,* Dow Helmers, 1963. The latter is devoted entirely to the tunnel.
7. Most sources agree that the line reached the summit of Boreas Pass in 1881. However, according to M. C. Poor in *The Denver, South Park & Pacific* the laying of the rails to the summit was delayed until May of the following year.
8. The Denver & Rio Grande Western *Railway* Company was a Utah corporation formed in 1882 and is not to be confused with the Denver & Rio Grande *Railroad* Company, incorporated in 1920 to take over the Denver & Rio Grande Railroad. Part of the construction west of the Colorado state line was by D&RG construction crews for the account of the Utah corporation.
9. *Report of the Board of Directors of the Denver and Rio Grande Railway Company for the year 1882* (D&RG A. R., 1882). According to the *Corporate History of the Denver Rio Grande Railroad Company,* 1919, (D&RG C. H.) the completion date was July 11. A special edition of *La Plata Miner* (Silverton), issued July 4, announced that the road had reached Silverton as of that date.
10. Mileage figures for the Denver Circle were scaled from the 1957 USGS map of Denver and Vicinity after superimposing described routes thereon.
11. See *Fairplay Flume,* Sept. 7, 1882, p. 3, col. 3

12. *Railway Age,* 1884, p. 281. An earlier issue, Feb. 22, 1883, p. 103, reported 6.0 miles completed in 1882. *Boulder News & Courier,* Nov. 24, 1882, p. 3 reported that track had been laid almost to Orodelphan (3.5 miles), near the mouth of Four Mile Canon. The Jan. 5, 1883 issue of the same newspaper, p. 1, reported about 10.0 miles completed as of that date.
13. Ralston station was north of North Table Mountain, 4.4 rail miles from Golden. Former stations with that name were on the original CC line which ran on the east side of North Table Mountain. The first such station was 3.0 miles north and the second was 4.7 miles north of Golden Junction.
14. Acording to historical records of the C&S Ry. Co. this track was abandoned in 1885. The removal date is from correspondence dated July 16 and August 13, 1888 from UP Division Engineer William Ashton to Superintendent J. K. Choate.
15. The first building was erected on the present campus in 1900. *Rocky Mountain News,* April 23, 1934, p. 17, Sec. B. See also *Denver University Historical Papers,* Library of the State Historical Society of Colorado.
16. Letter from William Ashton to V. G. Bogue, UP Chief Enigneer, dated Oct. 29, 1887.
17. Mileage for this initial section of the Gilpin Tramway is partly estimated.
18. The mileage is partly estimated. The track was later extended to the Concrete Mine and became the Concrete Branch Switchback.
19. The course of the Arkansas River through Pueblo at that time was several blocks north of its present channel. The newer, more contained channel along the bluffs south of Union Station was constructed following a destructive flood in June 1921.
20. See Silverton Democrat, Nov. 5, 1887, p 3.
21. Poor's Manual of Railroads (Poor's Manual), 1889, p. 480.
22. According to production records in the State Mine Inspection Division, Colorado Department of Natural Resources, Denver, the Thompson Mine operated only in 1888 with a total output of 113 tons.
23. The trackage rights over the D&RG were formally relinquished in 1928. However, on account of non-usage the D&RG trackage was eliminated from Rock Island's record of operated mileage on Jan. 1, 1919.—*Chicago, Rock Island & Pacific Annual Report for 1919.*
24. "Denver & Rio Grande-Development of Physical Property in Chronological Narrative."—Arthur Ridgway, Jan. 1, 1921 (Unpublished)
25. At different times during its existence this line was also referred to as Maxwell Branch, Catskill Branch, Vasquez Branch, Pels Branch and finally the section between Trinidad and Long's Junction became the Sopris Branch.
26. Mileages for the Silverton Railroad are from an 1892 survey by R. L. Kelly, locating engineer, and from Colorado State Board of Equalization reports.
27. This company and its successors operated a street railway system in Colorado Springs. In addition to the Manitou line, other of its lines extended beyond the boundaries of the city although they were not strictly interurban in character. These included a line to Stratton Park, southwest of the city, via Cheyenne Boulevard with a branch to Broadmoor; a spur from the Broadmoor line south and east to Myron Stratton Home; a line to Roswell, north of Colorado Springs; another which ran east and northeast of the city to Austin Bluffs via Nob Hill and a line to Prospect Lake and Evergreen Cemetery, east of the city limits. The line to Austin Bluffs was cut back to Nob Hill in 1894 and further reduced in 1917. That part of

the Roswell line outside the Colorado Springs city limits was abandoned in 1925. In early 1930 the line to Stratton Park was reduced and service to the park was transferred to the extended Broadmoor line.—*Colorado Springs Gazette*, various issues, 1887 to 1932; *The Book of Colorado Springs*, M. D. and E. R. Ormes, 1933 and *Electric Railway Journal*, Vol. 34, Oct. 1909, p. 509.

28. See 1882, this report, Denver & Rio Grande—Utah Extension, and Note 8, Part II, above.
29. Telegram dated Feb. 16, 1891, William A. Ashton to E. C. Smeed, UP Chief Engineer, Omaha.
30. *Rocky Mountain News,* Dec. 20, 1891, p. 4 (Durango date line, Dec. 19) According to *Corporate History of The Rio Grande Southern Railroad Company,* 1919 (RGS Corporate History), the south section was completed to Muldoon on Dec. 6, 1891 and the section between Rico and Muldoon on Jan. 6, 1892. *First Annual Report to the Stockholders of the Rio Grande Southern Railroad Company* for the year ending June 30, 1892 stated that the entire line was completed and turned over by the construction company on Feb. 1, 1892 and that operation by the railroad company commenced on the same date. That would indicate that prior operations were by the construction company.

Part III

1. Reports of both the Interstate Commerce Commission and the Colorado Tax Commision give 1914 as the peak year of railroad mileage in Colorado. However, mileage for a Denver & Salt Lake R. R. Co. extension which was completed and placed in operation in late 1913 was not included in reports of either agency until the following year.
2. A part of the track was first converted to dual gauge but the inside rail remained in place for only a short time.
3. RGS Corporate History.
4. *Colorado State Archives and Records Service,* Records of the State Board of Equalization; Crystal River Ry. Co. annual reports for the years 1893 and 1898. Notations on the reports for 1893 through 1897 state that the track was never used.
5. *The Morning Journal* (Cripple Creek), Dec. 16, 1894, p. 1.
6. Available records of the Denver, Leadville & Gunnison and its successors do not reveal the year in which this section of track was actually abandoned. According to the *Biennial Report of the Inspector of Coal Mines* (Colorado) for 1895-1896, the old Baldwin Mine, which at the time was the only source of business for the branch, was abandoned in 1894. The track removal date is from *Colorado & Southern Official Mileage* for Jan. 1, 1928, p. 71 (notation on map).
7. According to Board of Equalization reports train operations were reduced to a point near the Silver Belle Mine, 15.0 miles from Silverton, in 1894 and to the Yankee Girl Mine at 12.75 miles from Silverton in 1898. In 1901 the track was reopened to the Paymaster Mine ore track, 14.75 miles from Silverton and never again operated beyond that point.
8. Progress and problems in the construction of the switchback are mentioned in short news items which appeared intermittently in the *Cripple Creek Morning Journal* from January 31 through March 10, 1895.
9. This was a logging railroad but interstate in extent and partially classified as a common carrier, hence its inclusion in this report. Construction dates

and mileage data are from various sources which are not always in complete agreement.

10. The distance includes a loop and a spur track to the depot at Goldfield. The spur was later extended to a connection with the main track south of the loop, forming a continuous line via the depot. Thereafter GC mile posts were in reference to the F&CC depot at Victor rather than the initial point of construction. The mile-post distance between the Victor depot at Fourth Street and Diamond Avenue and the depot at the foot of Ninth Street in Goldfield was 1.21 miles.
11. *Colorado Sate Archives and Records Service,* Records of the State Board of Equalization; Denver, Lakewood & Golden R. R. Co. annual returns for 1896, 1900 and 1904.
12. Mileage is estimated. Progress in the lower part of Boulder Canon was delayed because of the necessity of correcting surveys, blasting away points of rocks to reduce curvature and delays in bridge construction. At one time around a thousand feet of completed track was reported to have been removed and later relaid on a corrected alignment.—*Boulder Daily Camera,* Nov. 11, 1897, p. 4; Nov. 12, 1897, p. 4; Nov. 16, 1897, p. 4 and Dec. 32, 1897, p. 1.
13. *Engineering News,* Sept. 8, 1898, p. 156
14. For an interesting account of the strategy in the construction of the trestle see *The Morning Times* (Cripple Creek), Jan. 1, 1898, p. 1.
15. *Boulder Daily Camera,* Feb. 21, 1898. According to *Railroad Gazette,* Feb. 25, 1898, p. 140, the line was completed by the end of 1897. M. C. Poor in "History of Denver, Boulder & Western Railroad Company," in *The Railway and Locomotive Historical Society Bulletin No. 65,* Oct. 1944, gives Jan. 15, 1898 as the date of completion to Sunset.
16. The remaining portion of the track between Boulder and Louisville, which had been out of service for through trains for several years, was rehabilitated and placed in operation following this gauge change.—*Boulder Daily Camera,* Jan. 10, 1898 and *Denver Times,* Dec. 31, 1898. Contrary to contemporary news items the track was never officially abandoned.
17. *Silverton Standard,* Aug. 5, 1899, p. 2 and Sept. 2, 1899, p. 2. According to *Three Little Lines,* Josie Moore Crum, 1960, p. 22, the property of the railroad was conveyed from the construction company to the railroad company on July 21, 1899.
18. *Colorado State Geological Survey,* Bul. No. 2 "Geology of the Grayback Mining District, Costilla County, Colorado", H. B. Patton, et al., p. 88.
19. *Colorado Springs Gazette,* Jan. 1, 1901, Part 3, p. 22. The 20-mile distance from Colorado Springs would place the railhead near Mt. Rosa wye, 0.8 mile east of Summit. *Railway Age,* March 14, 1901, p. 241 reports 18.0 miles of track laid in 1900 but the March 21, 1902 issue, p. 401, shows construction in 1901 beginning 2.0 miles east of St. Peters. The latter would be 16.6 miles from the Colorado Springs yard, assuming the reference was to St. Peters station and not the nearby mountain St. Peters Dome.
20. *State Coal Mine Inspector—Biennial Report,* 1901-1902.
21. According to an early track record the distance between Cameron and the Cripple Creek depot was 6.3 miles. However, 0.7 mile was over the track of the Second Electric Division (Low Line). Steam trains shared a joint depot with electric cars at Fourth Street and Warren Avenue in Cripple Creek until Nov. 1, 1905 at which time all passenger trains were rerouted to Victor, thence over MT tracks to the MT depot at Cripple Creek.

22. Lillie Junction was at a different location than the junction with the same name on the Golden Circle which by that time had been changed to Bull Hill Junction.
23. *Victor Daily Record,* Feb. 18, 1903, p. 1; Feb. 22, 1903, p. 1 and March 1, 1903, p. 1.
24. *Statistics of Railways of the United States,* Interstate Commerce Commission. The reduction is reported as 0.15 mile in the year ending June 30, 1902 and 0.35 mile in the year ending June 30, 1903. The exact location of the reduction is not shown but it is presumed to have been in the vicinity of Beach Hill.
25. The abandonment and removal of this trackage is not shown in any records examined for this report but logging and saw mill operations were reportedly discontinued in the Navajo River area about 1902.
26. This was the junction point of the steam line and the electric Low Line. The name change to Pisgah Junction was probably to avoid confusion with Victor Junction on the Midland Terminal near Victor.
27. Various short spurs built from the main tracks of the RG&PS are not included in this report because of inadequate data on ownership, mileages and dates of operation.
28. *Silverton Standard,* Aug. 20, 1904, p. 2 and Oct. 15, 1904, p. 2. The line was frequently referred to in news items as the "Eureka Northern" or the "Eureka Northerly Extension."
29. Track distances for the Trinidad Electric Railway and its successors are partly estimated from route descriptions and maps.
30. The Arkansas Valley *Railway* Company, organized in 1906, is not to be confused with the Arkansas Valley *Railroad* Company, the Kansas Pacific subsidiary which built the line between Kit Carson and La Junta in 1873-75.
31. *The Rio Grande Southern Story,* Josie Moore Crum, 1957, pp. 57, 113 and 405. According to *RGS Corporate History* the branch was constructed in 1908.
32. Branches other than those included in this report were built by the Gilpin (Tramway) Railroad but specific construction dates are not available. The following are shown on a sketch map prepared by the C&S Ry. Co. in 1905: Fullerton Mill Br., 0.81 mi.; Concrete Br. Switchback, 0.94 mi.; Pease Kansas Br., 0.68 mi.; Phoenix-Burroughs Br., 1.07 mi.; Quartz Hill Switchback, 2.09 mi. and Saratoga Br., 1.28 mi.
33. St. Vrains station was formerly 2.4 track miles west of its present location. Evidently it was relocated soon after construction of the line to Grant Mine.
34. For the first few months of operation Denver & Interurban cars were coupled to steam locomotives at Boulder and shuttled over the C&S main line pending the installation of transformers for its own track on Pearl Street. See *Boulder Daily Camera,* Aug. 31, 1908, p. 1; Sept. 18, 1908, p. 2 and Oct. 14, 1908, p. 1.
35. The usual gauge for Denver City Tramway tracks was 42 inches but the Globeville line was built standard gauge to accomodate D&I equipment. *Electric Railway Journal,* Vol. 34, Oct. 2, 1909 and *Mile High Trolleys,* Jones, Wagner and McKeaver, 1965, p. 22.
36. *Colorado Transcript,* Dec. 1, 1910, p. 4 and Jan. 26, 1911, p. 6.
37. Information is indefinite as to the exact date on which construction was completed. According to Vol. 103, *Interstate Commerce Commission Reports,* p. 232 (103 ICC 232) it was between June 12, 1908 and Nov. 28, 1910.

38. The specific date of abandonment is not available from sources examined for this report. The track appears on a map of the USGS Castle Rock Quadrangle surveyed in 1911 but according to correspondence from an official of the AT&SF Ry. Co. the track was not in place as of Nov. 1912.
39. The record is not specific but it is presumed to have been a part of the Banta Hill Extension.
40. Available records do not reveal a definite date for the abandonment of the Treasury Mountain railroad but the quarry closed in 1914 which precluded any further use. Annual reports of the *Colorado Tax Commission* indicate the tracks were not removed until 1944.

Part IV

1. Includes 0.45 miles previously reclassified as yard track sidings.
2. 1916 is the year in which the Rapson No. 2 Mine was closed. *State Inspector of Coal Mines,* Annual Report for 1916.
3. *175 ICC 748,* re: abandonment of track between Shelton Junction and Fenton.
4. All trackage south of Falcon was excluded from records and maps of C&S operated mileage beginning in 1913. The first official announcement of the abandonment was in the *Colorado & Southern Annual Report* (C&S A.R.) for the year ending Dec. 31, 1917, p. 16, which stated that the line had not been used for a number of years and that portions of the track had been removed.
5. C&S acquired trackage rights between Denver and Pueblo over the AT&SF in 1899 and transferred its through trains to that line. *212 ICC 769.* In Aug. 1900 the two companies entered into a long-term contract for use of AT&SF trackage between the two terminals. *C&S A.R., 1917,* p. 16. The agreement has been periodically renewed and is in effect as of the date of this writing.
6. *D&RG A. R.* for the year ending July 31, 1917; Ridgway in *Denver & Rio Grande: Development of Physical Property* and *99 ICC 816* are in agreement on 1917 as the year in which the track was abandoned. Also the trackage is excluded from records of operated mileage beginning with 1916. *Condensed Profile of the D&RGW R. R. System,* Jan. 1, 1964, Lines Abandoned section, shows 1924 as the last date of operation and 1925 as the year in which track was removed.
7. The trackage was included in annual reports of the *Colorado Tax Commission* until 1937.
8. Regular service on the Colorado Midland was discontinued Aug. 5, 1918 in compliance with a directive of the District Court of Colorado Springs. On Dec. 7 the Colorado Supreme Court over-ruled the lower court and held that jurisdiction over abandonments was vested in the Public Utilities Commission and not the District Court. After several hearings the PUC, by order dated Jan. 15, 1919, granted permission to dismantle the property. In the same order it confirmed the discontinuance of service which occurred the previous August. See Vol. 5, *Reports and Decisions of the Public Utilities Commission of the State of Colorado,* pp. 589-623 (5 PUC 589) or *Public Utilities Reports—Annotated,* 1919-C, pp. 592-620. For an account of events leading up to abandonment, attempts to revive service and the disposal of property, see *Colorado Midland,* Morris Cafky, 1965, pp. 177-194.
9. According to *Three Little Lines,* Josie Moore Crum, 1960, p. 22, an occassional train ran over the line after it was officially abandoned.

10. Operations over the main line were discontinued in May 1918 and service on the Cripple Creek District electric lines was terminated after a fire destroyed the car barns and much of the equipment in late 1919. A receiver appointed by the U. S. District Court restored operations over the steam lines in July 1919. In May 1920 main line service was reduced to a daily passenger train for tourists between Colorado Springs and Summit. All operations ceased again in Sept. 1920. The entire property was sold under decree of foreclosure in Oct. 1922 and on Feb. 20, 1923 the Colorado Public Utilities Commission (PUC) authorized the purchaser to abandon the system, except 3.5 miles in the Cripple Creek District which was transferred to the Midland Terminal. The transferred trackage included a section from the Last Dollar Mine to the Dante, Dexter and Gold Sovereign Mines and the Portland Mine Branch which ran from Portland Junction to the Portland No. 1 and No. 2 Mines and terminated at the Ajax Mine. For more detailed information on this abandonment see Vol. 6, *Reports and Decisions of the Public Utilities Commission of the State of Colorado,* pp. 389-97: Public Utilities Reports—Annotated, 1924-A, pp. 392-99 or *Poor's Manual,* 1921, 1922 and 1923. A more general and interesting account is given in *Rails Around Gold Hill,* Morris Cafky, 1955, pp. 182-86.
11. 82 ICC 785.
12. Abandonment of this isolated track was first authorized by ICC to take effect Sept. 24, 1923. *82 ICC 310.* After an appeal the decision was affirmed Feb. 11, 1924. Following a hearing on a petition by the State of Colorado the decision was again affirmed with abandonment to take effect March 24, 1924. *86 ICC 393.* A later amendment extended the abandonment date to Sept. 11, 1924. *94 ICC 657.*
13. The year of abandonment for these two sections of the Graneros Branch corresponds with D&RGW records. According to *99 ICC 816,* dated Oct. 28, 1925, abandonment was effective Nov. 27, 1925.
14. ICC authorized abandonment only of the section between Moffat and Crestone, declaring a lack of jurisdiction with respect to the portion between Crestone and Cottonwood. The Public Utilities Commission in a hearing a short time earlier granted abandonment of the entire line. *111 ICC 415* and *PUC Decision No. 994.*
15. *131 ICC 506* and *138 ICC 573.*
16. According to *The Moffat Road,* Bollinger and Bauer, 1962, p. 199, freight service through the tunnel was unofficially initiated on Feb. 14.
17. The mill was owned by the Portland Gold Mining Company but was commonly known as the Independence Mill, being adjacent to the Independence Mine. The original Portland Mill, dismantled after closing in 1918, was located near Portland Junction on the northwest slope of Battle Mountain.
18. *Colorado Springs Gazette,* April 30, 1932, p. 1 and May 1, 1932, pp. 1 and 6.
19. According to *The Denver Post,* May 13, 1934, pp. 1 and 8, physical connection was made by a D&SL crew on May 7 but D&RGW officials refused to recognize this as the completion date.
20. Informative discussions of early plans, construction of the line, financial aspects and trackage agreements between D&SL and D&RGW are contained in *The Moffat Road,* Bollinger and Bauer, 1962 and *Rebel of the Rockies,* Athearn, 1962.
21. *193 ICC 337* and *199 ICC 623.*
22. The track between Eureka and Animas Forks was removed in 1936 but there is a question as to the year in which actual abandonment occurred.

ICC considered the track abandoned and omitted it from the inventory in its valuation report of Feb. 25, 1927. This was done over the protest of the railroad company which contended that operations over the line were only temporarily suspended. *121 ICC 635*. The track is shown in place in an ICC finance docket dated July 30, 1932 with a statement that it had not been in use for more than ten years previous to that date.

23. Laying of the rails began at Las Animas Junction in August 1936 and from North Junction about Sept. 22. The two crews met at or near Two Buttes Creek in late Oct. but ballasting and bridge construction was not completed until early 1937. *Democrat-Herald* (Springfield), Aug. 26, 1936, p. 1; Sept 3, 1936, p. 1; Sept 17, 1936, p. 1; Sept. 24, 1936, p. 1; Oct. 8, 1936, p. 1; Oct. 22, 1936, p. 1; Jan. 28, 1937, p. 1 and Feb. 4, 1937, p. 1.
24. *Bent County Democrat* (Las Animas), Feb. 5, 1937, p. 1.
25. Abandonment was authorized by PUC Nov. 22, 1937 and confirmed by ICC Aug. 9, 1940. *240 ICC 725*.
26. *PUC Report,* 1936-37. It is also included in *PUC Report,* 1942-43. Trackage of the line is omitted from *Colo. Tax Commission* reports after 1937 but is included in *ICC Statistics of Railways* through 1941. By certificate dated Aug. 31, 1941, ICC authorized abandonment of all Silverton Northern lines ". . . as to interstate and foreign commerce." *252 ICC 807*.
27. *228 ICC 243*.
28. *PUC Report,* 1940-41, p. 22.
29. According to *D&RGW A. R.* for 1941, the California Gulch Branch was partially reconstructed and extended for the Resurrection Mining Company. No distance is given.
30. Not to be confused with another junction of the same name on the D&IM (formerly D&NW) at Arvada.
31. *Railway Age,* Jan. 15, 1951, p. 234; Feb. 26, 1951, p. 45 and Sept. 3, 1951, p. 47; also D&RGW A. R.'s for the years 1950 and 1951.
32. This railroad is not shown in reports of the *Colorado Tax Commission* after 1923 but its existence after that year is apparent. In Dec. 1928 PUC denied a petition to require the railroad to extend its line to a mine north of the end of its track. *7 PUC 1142*. Also the track is shown on the final map of the Wadge Mine prepared in 1951 for the Colorado State Coal Mine Inspection Division, Denver. The wye tracks connecting the Wolf Creek and other Wadge Mine trackage with the D&RGW main line were removed in 1953. *D&RGW Records,* AFE 3148, 1953.
33. The Associated Railroads include the AT&SF, CB&Q, CRI&P, C&S and D&RGW, each owning an equal share. Operations over the track are conducted in turn by each company for a specified number of years. The bridge across the Platte River was destroyed by a June 1965 flood, consequently access to the Denver end of the line has since been via the C&S tracks along the west bank of the river (the old Denver West Side Line).
34. Abandonment was approved by ICC Dec. 1, 1953 to be effective within forty days thereafter. *ICC Finance Docket 17889*. On Jan. 15, 1954 the railroad company declared the lines abandoned.

BIBLIOGRAPHY

Railroad Records and Reports

Atchison, Topeka & Santa Fe Railroad (Railway) Company—Annual Reports, 1873-1893, inclusive; 1905-1917, inclusive and 1927-1959, inclusive.

Chicago Burlington & Quincy Railroad Company—Annual Reports, 1880-1929, inclusive.

——— Corporate History of the CB&Q Railroad Company and Affiliated Companies, prepared by W. W. Baldwin, V. P., Chicago, 1921.

——— Documentary History, Vol. 3, Lines West of the Missouri River, compiled by W. W. Baldwin, V. P., Chicago, 1929.

Chicago Rock Island & Pacific Railway Company—Annual Reports, years ending April 1, 1888 and 1889 and Dec. 31, 1919.

——— "The Rock Island in Colorado." (This is part of a larger report covering other states), unpublished mimeographed report—nd.

Colorado & Southern Railway Company—Annual Reports, 1899-1966, inclusive.

——— Corporate History, prepared by T. S. Murray, Special Attorney, with Diagrammatic Chart by W. H. Hess, Valuation Engineer, January 1, 1916.

——— Genesis as of January 1899, compiled by Henry Michelson, Enigneering Department.

——— Genesis as of June 30, 1918, compiled in the Valuation Enigneer's Office, August 21, 1918.

——— Record of Major Main Track Abandonments from December 28, 1898 to March 8, 1962, compiled by Engineering Department.

Colorado Central Railroad—Report of the Board of Directors to the Stock holders, 1873.

Colorado Midland Railway (Railroad) Company—Minutes of Directors Meetings, 1897-1912, inclusive and May 31, 1917 to April 28, 1922, inclusive.

Cripple Creek Central Railway Company—Annual Reports, 1911-1928, inclusive.

Denver & Rio Grande Railroad (Railway) Company (Denver & Rio Grande Western after August 1921)—Annual Reports, 1872-1874, inclusive; 1880-1919, inclusive and 1921-1966, inclusive.

——— Corporate History as of June 30, 1919, compiled by Valuation Department, May 12, 1921.

——— Condensed Profiles, 1906-1909, inclusive; 1912, 1918, 1925-1927 inclusive; 1953 and 1964.

——— Official Rosters, 45 volumes, 1887-1908, inclusive, 1918 and 1923 (includes track records).

——— Detailed Statement of the Different Extensions of the D&RG R'y showing Distances, Elevations (other track data), dates when Track Laid and Open for Business and Total Miles Operated Each Year from Organization until December 31, 1881 (corrected to December 31, 1899), Office of Chief Engineer.

Golden Cycle Corporation—Annual Reports, 1936-1950, inclusive. (Contain yearly reports of the Midland Terminal Railway Company.)

Rio Grande Extension Company—Report of Engineering Department for 1881, Chief Engineer's Office, J. A. McMurtrie, Chief Engineer, December 31, 1881.

Rio Grande Junction Railway Company, Corporate History as of June 30, 1919, compiled by L. C. Keller, Valuation Accountant, August 20, 1921.

Rio Grande Southern Railway Company—Corporate History as of June 30, 1919, compiled by L. C. Keller, Valuation Accountant, August 20, 1921.

Union Pacific, Denver & Gulf Railway Company—Annual Reports, 1894-1898, inclusive. (These were reports of Frank Trumbull, Receiver, to U. S. Circuit Court, District of Colorado.)

Union Pacific Railroad (Railway) Company—Annual Reports, 1873-1887, inclusive; 1907-1911, inclusive and 1923-1966, inclusive.

———— "A Condensed Sketch of the Corporate History of the Companies Comprising the Union Pacific System" (mimeographed), 1950.

———— "Data Regarding Building of the Union Pacific Lines in Colorado," (mimeographed), Department of Public Relations, September 1959.

Reports of State and Federal Agencies

Colorado Public Utilities Commission—Annual Reports, 1913-1964.

———— Reports of Decisions, 1916-1930.

Colorado Railroad Commissioner, First Annual Report, 1885 and Biennial Report, 1891-92.

Colorado State Board of Equalization—Biennial Report, 1895-96, Annual Reports, 1902-1910.

Colorado State Coal Mine Inspector—Biennial Reports, 1884-1912.

Colorado State Inspector of Coal Mines—Annual Reports, 1913-1966.

Colorado State Railroad Commission—Biennial Reports, 1907-09, 1909-11 and 1911-13.

Colorado State Geological Survey—Bulletin No. 2, *Geology of the Grayback Mining District, Costilla County, Colo.,* Patton Smith, Butler and Hoskin, 1909.

Colorado State Geologist—*Report on the Development of the Mineral, Metallurgical, Agricultural, Pastoral and Other Resources of Colorado for the years 1881 and 1882* (Introduction of Railways, pp. 7-29, inclusive).

Colorado Tax Commission—Annual Reports, 1911-1966 inclusive.

United States Interstate Commerce Commission—Annual Reports of Transport Statistics in the United States, 1954-1961.

———— Finance Reports (issued intermittently), May 1920-January 1966.

———— Railroad Abandonments, 1920-1943.

———— Statistics of Railways in the United States, 1887-1953.

———— Valuation Reports (issued intermittently), July 1922-April 1938.

United States Geological Survey—Bulletin 381—Part II—Mineral Fuels, (Contributions of Economic Geology), 1910.

Newspapers and Periodicals

Alamosa Independent-Journal

Arapahoe Herald (Littleton)

Aspen Daily Times

Bent County Democrat (Las Animas)

Boulder County Herald

Boulder County News

Boulder Daily Camera

Boulder News and Courier

Camp and Plant (weekly employee publication, Colo. Fuel & Iron Co., 1902 and 1903. Contains information on CF&I-owned railroads)

Canon City Record

Center Post Dispatch

Chaffee County Times (Buena Vista)

Cheyenne (Wyo.) State Leader

Chronicle-News (Trinidad)

Colorado Banner (Boulder)

Colorado Chieftain (Pueblo)

Colorado Miner (Georgetown)

Colorado Springs Gazette

Colorado Springs Weekly Gazette

Colorado Springs Republic

Colorado Transcript (Golden)

Craig Empire

Cripple Creek Evening Star

Cripple Creek Times

Cripple Creek Times and Victor Daily Record

Daily Advertiser (Trinidad)

Democrat-Herald (Springfield)

Denver Post

Denver Republican

Denver Times

Denver Tribune

Durango Herald

Fairplay Flume

Fort Collins Courier

Fort Collins Express

Fremont County Record (Canon City)

Georgetown Courier

Gilpin County Miner (Central City)

Golden Weekly Globe

Grand Junction News

Greeley Daily Tribune

Greeley Tribune (Weekly)

Gunnison News-Champion

Gunnison News-Democrat

Gunnison Review

Hinsdale Phonograph (Lake City)

Holly Chieftain

Home Mirror (Longmont)

Jefferson County Republican (Golden)

La Junta Tribune

Lamar Register

La Plata Miner (Silverton)

Las Animas Leader

Leadville Daily Herald

Leadville Democrat

Leadville-Herald Democrat

Littleton Independent

Longmont Ledger

Loveland Reporter

Mesa County Mail (Fruita)

Moody's Steam Railroads (Moody's Railroads, Moody's Transportation) 1919-1957, inclusive

Morning Journal (Cripple Creek)

Morning Times (Cripple Creek)

Mountain Mail (Salida)

New Era (Walden)

Poor's Manual of Railroads (Poor's Railroads), 1870-1936, inclusive

Pueblo Chieftain

Pueblo Star Journal

Railroad Gazette

Railway Age

Railway Age-Gazette

Rocky Ford Enterprise

Rocky Ford Tribune

Rocky Mountain News (Denver)

Rocky Mountain Sun (Aspen)

Routt County Republican (Hayden)

San Juan (Silverton)

San Juan Herald (Silverton)

San Juan Prospector (Del Norte)

San Luis Valley News (Blanca)

Silver Standard (Silver Plume)

Silver World and Lake City Times (Lake City)

Silverton Democrat

Silverton Standard

Silverton Weekly Miner

Steamboat Pilot (Steamboat Springs)

Sunshine Courier (Boulder County)

Traffic World

Trinidad Monitor

Victor Daily Record

Victor Daily Times

Walsenburg Independent

Walsenburg World

Weekly Journal (Cripple Creek)

Weekly Miner (Cripple Creek)

Weekly Register Call (Central City)

Weld County Republican (Greeley)

Wellington Sun

Wet Mountain Tribune (Westcliffe)

Wyoming Tribune (Cheyenne)

Books and Articles

Anderson, George L.—*General William Palmer: A Decade of Colorado Railroad Building: 1870-1880,* Colorado College Publication, Colorado Springs, 1936.

———— *Kansas West,* Golden West Books, San Marino, California, 1963.

Athearn, Robert G.—*Rebel of the Rockies* (A History of the Denver and Rio Grande Western Railroad), Yale University Press, New Haven and London, 1962.

Baskin, O. L. (ed.)—*History of Clear Creek and Boulder Valleys, Colorado,* O. L. Baskin & Company, Chicago, 1880.

———— *History of the City of Denver, Arapahoe County, Colorado,* O. L. Baskin & Company, Chicago, 1880.

———— *History of the Arkansas Valley, Colorado,* O. L. Baskin & Company, Chicago, 1881.

Beebe, Lucius and Clegg, Charles—*Rio Grande, Mainline of the Rockies,* Howell-North, Berkeley, California, 1962.

Bollinger, Edward T.—*Rails That Climb* (The Story of the Moffat Road), The Rydel Press, Santa Fe, New Mexico, 1950.

———— and Bauer, Frederick—*The Moffat Road,* Sage Books, Denver, 1962.

Boner, Harold A.—*The Giant's Ladder* (David H. Moffat and his railroad), Kalmbach Publishing Co., Milwaukee, Wisconsin, 1962.

Boyles, B. L.—*Longmont's Baby Railroad,* Rocky Mountain Railroad Club, 1952.

Bradley, Glen Danford—*The Story of the Santa Fe,* The Gorham Press, Boston, 1920.

Brayer, Herbert O.—"History of Colorado Railroads," *Colorado and Its People,* Leroy R. Hafen (ed.), Vol. I, Lewis Publishing Company, Inc., New York, 1948.

———— *William Blackmore: Early Financing of the Denver & Rio Grande Railway and Ancillary Land Companies, 1871-1878,* Bradford Robinson, Denver, 1949.

Cafky, Morris—*Colorado Midland,* Rocky Mountain Railroad Club, Denver, 1965.

———— *Rails Around Gold Hill,* Rocky Mountain Railroad Club, Denver, 1955.

———— *Steam Tramways of Denver,* Rocky Mountain Railroad Club, 1950.

———— "The Railroad that Couldn't Make up its Mind," Trains Magazine, Vol. 26, No. 10, August 1966.

Crossen, Forest—*The Switzerland Trail of America,* Pruett Press, Inc., Boulder, Colorado, 1962.

Crofutt, George A.—*Crofutt's New Overland Tourist and Pacific Coast Guide,* Vol. I, 1878-79, The Overland Publishing Company, Chicago, 1879.

———— Crofutt's Grip-Sack Guide of Colorado, Vol. II, 1885, Reprinted and expanded by Rizzari, Ronzio and Ryland, Cubar Associates, Golden, Colorado, June 1966.

Crum, Josie Moore—*The Rio Grande Southern Story,* Railroadiana, Inc., Durango, Colorado, 1957.

———— *Three Little Lines,* Durango Herald-News, Durango, Colorado, 1960.

Davis, E. O.—*The First Five Years of the Railroad Era in Colorado,* Sage Books, Inc., Denver, 1948.

———— "The Circle Railroad," The Engineers Bulletin, June 1958.

Dunning, Harold M.—*Over Hill and Vale,* Johnson Publishing Company, Boulder, Colorado, 1956.

Electric Railway Journal—"Interurban Roads in Colorado," Vol. 34, No. 14, October 2, 1909, p. 509.

Fleming, Howard—*Narrow Gauge Railways in America.* Originally published 1875. Reproduced and Expanded by Hardy, Darrell and Thompson, Grahame H. Hardy, Oakland, California, 1949.

Glover, Vern, Jr.—"Narrow Gauge Logging Railroads in New Mexico and Colorado," New Mexico Railroader, Vol. 5, No. 3, March 1963.

Graves, Carl F.—"The Colorado Midland," The Railway and Locomotive Historical Society, Bulletin No. 36, 1936.

Griffith, Stanwood C.—"Denver Tramways," Electric Railroads, No. 30, Electric Railroaders' Association, Inc., December, 1961.

Hall, Frank—*A History of the State of Colorado,* 4 vols, Blakely Printing Company, Chicago, 1889-1895.

Hardesty, W. P.—"Colorado Springs and Cripple Creek District Railway," Engineering News, May 1, 1902.

——— "The Railways of the Cripple Creek District," Engineering News, September 8, 1898.

Harvey, Mr. and Mrs. James R.—"The Quarries of the Castle Rock Area," The Colorado Magazine, Vol. 23, No. 2, Denver, May 1946.

Hayes, William Edward—*Iron Road to Empire: (The history of 100 years of the progress and achievements of the Rock Island Lines).* H. Wolff Book Manufacturing Company, Inc., 1953.

Holmich, Ed and Kelley, Mike—"Carpenter: Ghost Town," The Colorado Magazine, Vol. 39, No. 4, October, 1962.

Helmers, Dow—*Historical Alpine Tunnel,* Sage Books, Denver, 1963.

Hilton, George W. and Due, John F.—*The Electric Interurban Railways in America,* Stanford University Press, Stanford, California, 1960.

Hollenback, Frank R.—*The Argentine Central,* Sage Books, Denver, 1959.

——— *The Gilpin Tram,* Sage Books, Denver, 1958.

——— *The Laramie Plains Line,* Sage Books, Denver, 1960.

——— and Russell, William Jr.—*Pikes Peak by Rail,* Sage Books, Denver, 1962.

Hunt, Louie—*The Silverton Train,* Louie Hunt, Leucadia, California, 1955.

Jackson, William S.—"Railroad Conflicts in Colorado in the 'Eighties.' " Speech to annual meeting of the Colorado State Historical Society, December 11, 1945, The Colorado Magazine, Vol. 23, No. 1, Denver, 1946.

Jones, William C.; Wagner, F. Hol, Jr., and McKeever, Gene C.—*Mile High Trolleys,* Intermountain Chapter, National Railway Historical Society, Inc., Golden, Colorado, 1965.

Kindig, R. H., Haley, E. J., and Poor, M. C.—*Pictorial Supplement to Denver, South Park & Pacific,* Rocky Mountain Railroad Club, Denver, 1959.

Krakel, Dean F.—*South Platte (A history of old Weld County, Colorado, 1739-1900),* Powder River Publishers, Laramie, Wyoming, 1954.

LeMassena, R. A. et al.—*Colorado Mountain Railroads.* 6 volumes, The Smoking Stack Press, Golden, Colorado, 1963-1968.

Lipsey, John J.—"J. J. Hagerman, Builder of the Colorado Midland," The Westerners Brand Book, Denver, 1954.

Longmont Times—"Annals of Longmont." A series of articles covering the economic, social and political development of the Longmont area from the establishment of the town through 1888. Clippings in Western History Research Library, University of Colorado (n.d.).

National Electric Railway News Digest (The), Interurban, Special No. 5, "The Denver & Interurban Railroad," October, 1947.

National Land & Improvement Company—Annual Reports, 1873-1910, inclusive. Copies in Western Historical Collections, University of Colorado Library.

Ormes, Manly D. and Elinor R.—*The Book of Colorado Springs,* The Denton Press, Colorado Springs, 1933.

Ormes, Robert M.—*Railroads and the Rockies* (A Record of Lines In and Near Colorado), Sage Books, Denver, 1963.

Overton, Richard C.—*Burlington Route* (A History of the Burlington Lines). Alfred A. Knopf, New York, 1965.

—————— *Gulf to Rockies* (The Heritage of the Fort Worth and Denver—Colorado and Southern Railways, 1861-1898), University of Texas Press, Austin, 1953.

—————— "The Colorado & Southern Railway: Its Heritage and Its History, 1898-1948," The Colorado Magazine, July, 1949.

"Place Names in Colorado," The Colorado Magazine, Vol. 17-20, inclusive, 1940-1943.

Poor, M. C.—"Brief History of the Aregntine Central Ry. Co." The Railway & Locomotive Historical Society Bulletin, No. 64, May 1944.

—————— "History of Denver, Boulder & Western Railroad Company," The Railway and Locomotive Historical Society Bulletin, No. 65, October 1944.

—————— *The Denver, South Park and Pacific,* Rocky Mountain Railroad Club, Denver, 1949.

Public Utilities Reports-Annotated (containing decisions of the Public Service Commissions and of State and Federal Courts), Public Utilities Reports, Rochester, New York, 1915-1933, inclusive.

Rizzari, Francis B.—"The Railways of the Crystal River Valley," Denver Westerners Monthly Roundup, April 1964.

Ryland, Charles S.—*Colorado Eastern Railroad,* Rocky Mountain Railroad Club, 1951.

Sanford, Albert B.—"The Old South Park Railroad," The Colorado Magazine, Vol. V, No. 4, August, 1928.

Smiley, Jerome C. et al.—*Semi-Centennial History of the State of Colorado,* Vol. I, The Lewis Publishing Company, Chicago and New York, 1913.

Shoemaker, Len—*Roaring Fork Valley,* Sage Books, Denver, 1958.

Stephens, Kent—"The Colorado Railroad," The New Mexico Railroader, Vol. 7, No. 10, October, 1965 (issued January, 1966).

Stone, Wilber Fisk (ed.)—*History of Colorado,* Volume I, S. J. Clark Publishing Company, Chicago, 1918.

Trottman, Nelson—*History of the Union Pacific* (A Financial and Economic Survey), A. M. Kelley, New York, 1966.

Union Pacific Coal Company—*History of Union Pacific Coal Mines,* 1868-1940, Colonial Press, Omaha, 1940.

Waters, L. L.—*Steel Trails to Santa Fe*, University of Kansas Press, Lawrence, Kansas, 1950.

Wolcott, Frank H.—"Monarch of Grand County," The Westerners Brand Book, Denver, 1954.

Unpublished Manuscripts

Bergner, Merton N.—"The Development of Fruita and the Lower Valley of the Colorado River from 1884 to 1937." M.A. thesis—University of Colorado, 1937.

Berthoud, E. L. "History of Jefferson County," typewritten copy in Pioneer Museum, Golden, Colorado, n.d.

Culhane, Albert E.—"A History of the Settlement of La Plata County, Colorado." M.A. thesis, University of Colorado, 1934.

Gaynor, Lois Marguerite—"History of Colorado Fuel and Iron Company and Constituent Companies." M.A. thesis, University of Colorado, 1936.

Jefferies, Marguerite (ed.)—*History of Golden,* Vol. 4, Railroad Items. Information taken from early newspapers. Typewritten copy in Pioneer Museum, Golden, Colorado, n.d.

Logan, Paul Stewart—"The History of the Denver & Rio Grande Railway, 1871-1881." M.A. thesis, University of Colorado, 1949.

Logan, Roger Lee—"The Economic Reasons for the abandonment of Railroads and Portions of Railroads in Colorado." M.S. thesis, University of Colorado, 1949.

Mock, Samuel Donald—"Railroad Development in the Colorado Region to 1880." Ph.D. dissertation, University of Nebraska, 1938.

Rait, Mary—"Development of Grand Junction and the Colorado River Valley to Palisade from 1881 to 1931." M.A. thesis, University of Colorado, 1931.

Ridgway, Arthur—"Denver & Rio Grande—Development of Physical Property in Chronological Narrative," January 1921. (Copy in D&RGW Archives in the Library of the Historical Society of Colorado, Denver.)

——— "History of Transportation in Colorado." (n.d.) (Microfilm of typewritten copy in Documents Department, Norlin Library, University of Colorado.)

Rinker, Catherine—"The History of Cripple Creek, Colorado." M.A. thesis, University of Colorado, 1934.

Traxler, Ralph N., Jr.—"Some Phases of the History of the Colorado Central Railroad, 1865-1885." M.A. thesis, University of Colorado, 1948.

Van Hook, Joseph Orlando—"Settlement and Economic Development of the Arkansas Valley from Pueblo to the Colorado-Kansas Line, 1860-1900." Ph.D. dissertation, University of Colorado, 1933.

Collections and Papers

Charles A. Wolcott Collection—Western History Department, Norlin Library, University of Colorado, Boulder.

Colorado Springs & Cripple Creek Railway Company Papers—Western Historical Collections, Norlin Library, University of Colorado, Boulder.

Colorado State Board of Equalization, Annual Reports of Railroads—Colorado State Archives and Records Service, Denver.

Denver, Northwestern & Pacific, Letters and Reports of the Chief Engineer—State Historical Society of Colorado, Denver.

E. L. Berthoud Collection—State Historical Society of Colorado, Denver.

Henry M. Teller Papers—Western Historical Collections, Norlin Library, University of Colorado, Boulder.

Leonard H. Eicholtz Diaries—Western History Research Center, Coe Memorial Library, University of Wyoming, Laramie.

Rio Grande Southern Papers—Colorado Railroad Museum Library, Golden.

Union Pacific (Union Pacific Denver & Gulf) Division Engineer Letter Books—Colorado Railroad Museum Library, Golden.

INDEX

Railroads and Affiliated Companies

Amalgamated Development Corporation, 1917
American Power & Coal Company, 1916, 1925
Argentine & Grays Peak, 1905, 1918
Argentine Central (AC), 1905, 1906, 1918
Arkansas Valley (AV) (Kansas Pacific subsidiary), 1873, 1875, 1877, 1906 (fn)
Arkansas Valley (AV), 1906, 1907, 1931
Aspen & Western (A&W), 1888, 1892
Aspen Short Line, 1888
Associated Railroads, 1891, 1953
Atchison, Topeka & Santa Fe (AT&SF; Santa Fe), 1873, 1875, 1876, 1878, 1879, 1880, 1887, 1889, 1899, 1901, 1902, 1906, 1907, 1908, 1910, 1912, 1916, 1917, 1926, 1927, 1931, 1937, 1938, 1940, 1947, 1953 (fn), 1966.

Beaver, Penrose & Northern (BP&N), 1909, 1919
Blue Seal Coal Company, 1917, 1921
Book Cliff (BC), 1899, 1925
Boston Coal & Fuel Company, 1901
Boulder Coal & Fire Clay Company, 1893
Burlington & Colorado Railroad, 1881
Burlington & Missouri River, 1889
Busk Tunnel Railway, 1893, 1899

Calumet Fuel Company, 1901, 1926
Canon City & Cripple Creek (CC&CC), 1899, 1915
Canon City & San Juan, 1879
Canon Coal Railway Company, 1872
Canon de Agua Railroad Company, 1889, 1900

Cedar Hill Coal & Coke Company, 1911
Central Pacific, 1870 (fn)
Cheyenne & Burlington Railroad, 1887
Cheyenne & Northern Railway Company, 1890
Chicago, Burlington & Quincy (CB&Q; Burlington), 1881, 1882, 1887, 1889, 1890, 1891, 1892, 1893, 1896, 1900, 1904, 1905, 1906, 1907, 1908, 1912, 1917, 1918, 1919, 1925, 1927, 1936, 1939, 1946, 1948, 1951, 1953 (fn)
Chicago, Kansas & Nebraska, 1888
Chicago, Rock Island & Colorado 1888
Chicago, Rock Island & Pacific (CRI&P; Rock Island), 1888, 1896, 1901, 1916, 1941, 1950, 1953 (fn), 1961
Chicosa Canon Railway Company, 1888, 1890
Colorado & Nebraska Railroad, 1887
Colorado & New Mexico Railroad Company, 1873, 1875
Colorado & Northwestern (C&NW), 1897, 1898, 1899, 1904, 1905.
Colorado & Southeastern (C&SE), 1899, 1904, 1907, 1937, 1944, 1952
Colorado & Southwestern, 1924, 1948
Colorado & Southern (C&S), 1870, 1874, 1881, 1884, 1885, 1887, 1896, 1898, 1899, 1900, 1901, 1902, 1903, 1904, 1905, 1906, 1907, 1908, 1909, 1910, 1911, 1912, 1914, 1915, 1916, 1917, 1918, 1919, 1922, 1924, 1925, 1926, 1927, 1928, 1929, 1931, 1932, 1933, 1934, 1936, 1937, 1938, 1939, 1940, 1941, 1942, 1943, 1947, 1948, 1949, 1950, 1951, 1952, 1953 (fn), 1954, 1955, 1958, 1960, 1962.

295

Colorado & Wyoming
  (Railroad) (CB&Q
  subsidiary), 1887
Colorado & Wyoming
  (Railway) (C&W), 1888,
  1901, 1902, 1903, 1906,
  1913, 1930, 1931, 1932,
  1933, 1938, 1940, 1952.
Colorado Central (CC), 1868,
  1870, 1872, 1873, 1874,
  1877, 1878, 1879, 1880,
  1881, 1884, 1886, 1887,
  1888, 1889, 1890, 1891,
  1898, 1902
Colorado Central Rail Road
  Company (Wyoming),
  1877, 1890
Colorado Eastern (CE), 1886,
  1905, 1915
Colorado-Kansas, 1910, 1911,
  1912
Colorado Midland (CM;
  Midland), 1886, 1887,
  1888, 1890, 1893, 1899,
  1906, 1919
Colorado Northern, 1881
Colorado Railroad Company,
  1903, 1906, 1907, 1908,
  1909, 1911, 1929
Colorado Railroad, Inc., 1910,
  1957
Colorado Railway Light
  & Power Company, 1904
Colorado Springs & Cripple
  Creek District (CS&CCD;
  The Short Line), 1897,
  1900, 1901, 1902, 1903,
  1904, 1905, 1908, 1923
Colorado Springs & Interurban
  (CS&I), 1890, 1932
Colorado Springs & Manitou
  Railway Company, 1890
Colorado Springs & Suburban,
  1890
Colorado Springs Rapid Transit
  (CSRT), 1890, 1893
Colorado, Wyoming & Eastern,
  1911
Colorado, Wyoming & Great
  Northern, 1894
Cripple Creek & Colorado
  Springs (CC&CS), 1894,
  1896, 1915, 1917, 1920
Cripple Creek District Railway,
  1897

Crystal River (CR), 1888,
  1892, 1893, 1898, 1899,
  1900, 1906, 1909, 1941
Crystal River & San Juan
  (CR&SJ), 1906, 1910, 1941

Denver & Boulder Valley
  (D&BV), 1870, 1871, 1873,
  1881
Denver & Intermountain
  (D&IM), 1891, 1910, 1941,
  1949 (fn), 1950, 1953
Denver & Interurban (D&I),
  1907, 1908, 1911, 1916,
  1918, 1921, 1922, 1926
Denver & Middle Park
  (D&MP), 1884, 1890, 1898
Denver & Montana, 1900
Denver & New Orleans
  (D&NO), 1881, 1882,
  1887, 1917
Denver & Northwestern
  (D&NW), 1901, 1902,
  1903, 1904, 1950
Denver & Rio Grande
  (D&RG; Rio Grande)
  1871, 1872, 1874, 1876,
  1877, 1878, 1879, 1880,
  1881, 1882, 1883, 1885,
  1886, 1887, 1888, 1889,
  1890, 1891, 1893, 1895,
  1896, 1898, 1899, 1900,
  1901, 1902, 1903, 1904,
  1905, 1906, 1907, 1908,
  1909, 1910, 1911, 1912,
  1913, 1914, 1917, 1919,
  1922
Denver & Rio Grande Western
  (D&RGW; Rio Grande)
  1871, 1882 (fn),
  1890, 1903, 1916, 1922,
  1923, 1924, 1925, 1926,
  1927, 1929, 1930, 1932,
  1933, 1934, 1935, 1937,
  1938, 1939, 1940, 1941,
  1942, 1943, 1944, 1945,
  1946, 1947, 1948, 1949,
  1950, 1951, 1952, 1953,
  1954, 1956, 1958, 1961,
  1962, 1963, 1966
Denver & Rio Grande Western
  (Utah), 1882, 1890

Denver & Salt Lake (D&SL;
  The Moffat Road), 1903,
  1913, 1915, 1916, 1917,
  1923, 1925, 1928, 1934,
  1935, 1947, 1951
Denver & Salt Lake Western
  (D&SLW; Dotsero Cutoff),
  1934, 1947
Denver & Santa Fe, 1887
Denver & Scranton, 1886
Denver & South Platte,
  1907, 1908, 1926
Denver & Southwestern
  Railway Company (holding
  company), 1899
Denver Boulder & Western
  (DB&W), 1897, 1916, 1919
Denver City Tramway
  Company, 1908
Denver, Clear Creek & Western,
  1889
Denver Circle (DC; Circle
  Railroad), 1880 (fn), 1882,
  1883, 1884, 1886, 1887,
  1898
Denver, Golden & Morrison,
  1910, 1953,
Denver, Lakewood & Golden
  (DL&G), 1891, 1892, 1894,
  1896, 1949
Denver, Laramie & Northern,
  1909, 1917
Denver, Laramie & North-
  western (DL&NW), 1909,
  1910, 1913, 1917
Denver, Leadville & Gunnison
  (DL&G; South Park), 1874,
  1894, 1895, 1896, 1897,
  1898, 1899, 1902, 1908,
  1909, 1911, 1934
Denver, Longmont & North-
  western, 1881
Denver, Marshall & Boulder
  (DM&B), 1881, 1885, 1886,
  1888, 1889, 1890
Denver, Northwestern & Pacific
  (DNW&P; The Moffat
  Road), 1903, 1904, 1905,
  1906, 1907, 1908, 1913
Denver Pacific (DP), 1868,
  1869, 1870, 1874, 1880,
  1908
Denver Railroad, Land & Coal
  Company, 1886

Denver, South Park & Hill Top,
  1896, 1899
Denver, South Park & Pacific
  (DSP&P, South Park), 1874,
  1878, 1879, 1880, 1881,
  1882, 1883, 1884, 1885,
  1887, 1888, 1894, 1908,
  1909, 1911, 1934,
Denver, Texas & Fort Worth
  (DT&FW), 1887, 1888,
  1889, 1890, 1899
Denver, Texas & Gulf (DT&G),
  1881, 1887, 1890
Denver Tramway Company
  (System), 1892, 1949, 1950
Denver, Utah & Pacific
  (DU&P), 1881, 1885, 1887,
  1889, 1890
Denver, Western & Pacific
  (DW&P), 1881, 1885, 1889
Dodge City & Cimarron Valley,
  1926, 1937
Dolores, Paradox & Grand
  Junction, 1924
Durango Railway & Realty
  Company, 1895, 1904, 1920

East Denver Belt Line, 1913
Eldorado Springs Railway, 1907
Elk Creek Coal Company,
  1917, 1921
El Paso Rapid Transit
  Company, 1890
Eureka Northern, 1904 (fn)
Eureka Northerly Extension,
  1904 (fn)

Florence & Cripple Creek
  (F&CC), 1894, 1896, 1898,
  1899, 1902, 1904, 1915
Fort Collins Development
  Railway Company, 1903,
  1905, 1906,
Fort Worth & Denver City,
  1887, 1888

Georgetown & Grays Peak,
  1905, 1918
Georgetown, Breckenridge &
  Leadville, 1884, 1890
Gilpin Railroad (Gilpin Tram),
  1887, 1907, 1914, 1917
Gilpin Tramway (Gilpin
  Tram), 1887, 1888, 1898,
  1905

Golden & Ralston (Knox Railroad), 1878, 1880
Golden, Boulder & Caribou (GB&C), 1877, 1878, 1879, 1885, 1886, 1901
Golden Circle (GC), 1896, 1897, 1898, 1899, 1901 (fn), 1915, 1920
Golden City & South Platte, 1879, 1895
Grand Junction & Grand River Valley, 1909, 1910, 1935
Grand River Valley, 1909, 1935
Great Western (GW), 1902, 1903, 1904, 1905, 1906, 1907, 1917, 1919, 1920, 1939, 1947, 1957
Greeley, Salt Lake & Pacific (GSL&P), 1881, 1882, 1883, 1887, 1890, 1894, 1897
Greeley Terminal Railway Company, 1910, 1917

Hill Top Mining Company, 1896
Holly & Swink (H&S), 1906, 1907
Huerfano Fuel Company, 1907

Kansas-Colorado, 1910, 1911
Kansas Pacific (KP), 1870, 1873, 1877, 1906 (fn)
Knox Railroad, 1878

La Plata, 1890, 1900
Laramie, Hahns Peak & Pacific, 1911
Laramie, North Park & Western, 1911
Leadville Mineral Belt, 1898, 1900
Little Book Cliff, 1889, 1890
London, South Park & Leadville, 1882, 1890

Manitou & Pikes Peak, 1890
Midland Terminal (MT), 1893, 1894, 1895, 1896, 1899, 1917, 1919, 1920, 1923 (fn), 1930, 1948
Missouri Pacific (MP, Mo-Pac), 1887
Moffat Tunnel Commission, 1928

Noland Land & Transfer Company, 1890, 1902, 1915
Northern Colorado & Eastern, 1911
Northwestern Terminal, 1905, 1909, 1913, 1947, 1950

Pueblo & Arkansas Valley Railroad Company, 1875, 1879, 1880

Pueblo & State Line Railway, 1887

Rio Grande & Pagosa Springs (RG&PS), 1895, 1896, 1897, 1900, 1901, 1902, 1903, 1904, 1911, 1913, 1914
Rio Grande Gunnison Railway, 1891
Rio Grande Junction, 1890, 1947
Rio Grande, Pagosa & Northern, 1899, 1900, 1935
Rio Grande, Pueblo & Southern, 1902
Rio Grande Railroad Company, 1900, 1902, 1904, 1907
Rio Grande Sangre de Cristo Railroad Company, 1901
Rio Grande Southern (RGS), 1890, 1891, 1892, 1894, 1900, 1901, 1906, 1908, 1924, 1926, 1952
Rio Grande Western (RGW), 1890, 1899
Road Canon Railroad Company, 1890
Rocky Mountain Fuel Company, 1896
Rocky Mountain (RM), 1907, 1917
Routt-Pinnacle Coal Company, 1915, 1916

San Cristobal Railway, 1933
San Luis Central, 1913
San Luis Southern, 1910
San Luis Valley Southern, 1910
Silverton Gladstone & Northerly (SG&N), 1899, 1937
Silverton Northern (SN), 1893, 1896, 1899, 1904, 1905, 1936, 1937, 1942

Silverton Railroad (SR), 1887, 1888, 1889, 1892, 1893, 1894, 1896, 1906, 1922
South Park & Leadville Short Line, 1882, 1900
Southern Colorado Power & Railway Company, 1904, 1908
Southern San Luis Valley, 1910, 1957, 1959
Stone Mountain Railroad & Quarry Company, 1890, 1915

Treasury Mountain, 1910, 1914
Trinchera Estate, 1899
Trinidad & Denver Railroad Company, 1887
Trinidad Electric Railway, 1904, 1908
Trinidad Electric Transmision Railway & Gas Company, 1904, 1923

Uintah, 1904, 1939
Union Pacific (UP), 1867, 1869, 1870, 1872, 1873, 1877, 1880, 1881, 1885, 1888, 1889, 1890, 1899, 1900, 1903, 1907, 1908, 1909, 1910, 1911, 1913, 1915, 1917, 1918, 1921, 1924, 1926, 1927, 1939, 1940, 1942, 1943, 1946, 1947, 1949, 1950, 1960, 1964, 1965
Union Pacific, Denver & Gulf (UPD&G), 1870, 1881, 1884, 1885, 1887, 1890, 1891, 1892, 1893, 1894, 1895, 1896, 1897, 1898, 1899

Victor Fuel Company, 1899, 1904

Walsenburg & Western, 1907
Wolf Creek, 1916, 1951

Locations: Cities, Towns, Stations, Mines and Other Places

Aberdeen Junction, 1889

Aberdeen Quarry, 1889
Acequia, 1879, 1887 (fn)
Acme Junction, 1892, 1895, 1899, 1902, 1952
Acme Mines, 1892
Adit Tunnel, 1919
Adobe, 1947
Aguilar, 1892, 1895, 1940, 1952
Ajax Mine, 1901, 1923 (fn)
Alamo, 1923, 1942
Alamo, No. 2 Mine, 1942, 1953
Alamosa, 1878, 1880, 1881, 1890, 1899, 1900, 1901, 1902, 1930, 1951, 1958
Albany, 1889, 1892, 1904
Allen Mine, 1952
Allen Bond Mine, 1892 (spur), 1893, 1902 (spur)
Alliance, Nebraska, 1900
Allison (C&NW-C&S), 1898, 1905, 1919
Allison (D&RGW), 1962
Alma, 1882, 1937
Alpine, 1882
Alpine Tunnel, 1881, 1882, 1910, 1911
Altman, 1902
Amarillo, Texas, 1937
Anaconda, 1895, 1902, 1904
Anchor Mine, 1907
Anderson's Mine, 1876, 1877
Animas City, 1895, 1920
Animas Forks, 1904, 1936
Anthracite, 1882, 1947
Anthracite Coal Mine, 1882
Antonito, 1880, 1901, 1941
Apex, 1910
Ara, 1960,
Arapahoe, 1872, 1873
Argo Junction, 1885
Arkansas Junction, 1888, 1906, 1919
Arkansas Station, 1880
Arkins, 1887, 1926, 1937
Arrow, 1904, 1905
Arrowhead, 1904
Arvada, 1901, 1902, 1903, 1949 (fn), 1950
Arvada Junction, 1950
Aspen, 1886, 1887, 1888, 1919, 1926
Aspen Junction, 1887
Atomic Energy Commission (A.E.C.) Plant, 1952, 1961

299

Austin Bluffs, 1890 (fn)
Avalanche, 1893

Badger, 1903
Baker Mine, 1889, 1896 (spur)
Bakerville, 1884, 1898
Baldwin, 1883, 1911, 1946
Banta Hill, 1905
Barnes, 1904, 1937, 1938
Barnes Junction, 1904, 1937, 1952, 1954
Barnum, 1892, 1949
Barnum Junction, 1892, 1949
Basalt, 1887
Baum Mine, 1907, 1958
Baum Mine Junction, 1907, 1958
Beach Hill, 1890, 1902 (fn), 1915
Beacon Mine, 1902, 1903
Bear Canon Mine, 1917
Bear Canon Mine No. 3, 1915
Bear Canon Mine No. 6, 1939, 1955
Bear Creek Junction, 1874, 1878
Beaver, 1909, 1919
Belcher Stone Quarries, 1880 (fn)
Belleview College, 1911
Bellevue Junction, 1881, 1906, 1918
Belt, 1950,
Berwind, 1890
Beshoar Junction, 1888, 1927
Bessemer, 1887, 1907
Bessemer Junction, 1904
Big Bend, 1906
Big Five Junction, 1899
Big Four, 1907, 1922
Black Hollow, 1906
Black Hollow Junction, 1906
Black Hawk, 1872, 1878, 1887, 1898, 1917, 1931, 1941
Blanca, 1910
Blanco, 1902, 1903, 1904, 1911, 1913
Blende, 1902, 1937
Blind Tom Mine, 1937
Blue Bird Mine, 1903
Blue Bird Station, 1903
Blue Ribbon Mine, 1906
Boettcher, 1965
Bon Air Mines, 1900
Bon Carbo, 1917, 1950

Bond, 1934
Boone, 1901, 1902
Boreas Pass, 1880, 1881, 1882
Boulder, 1870, 1872 (fn), 1873, 1877, 1878, 1881, 1886, 1894, 1897, 1898, 1905, 1907, 1908, 1916, 1918, 1919, 1926, 1932, 1947, 1960
Boulder Valley Junction, 1917, 1919
Bowles Park, 1908
Bragdon, 1901
Briggsdale, 1910, 1965
Brighton, 1870, 1964
Bristol, 1906, 1908
Broadmoor, 1890 (fn)
Brodhead Junction, 1902
Brodhead Mine, 1896
Broomfield, 1881, 1889
Brush, 1900
Buchtel, 1906, 1907
Buckeye, 1924, 1965
Buda, 1902, 1903
Buena Vista, 1880, 1884, 1887, 1904, 1924
Buffalo Hill, 1881, 1884, 1886
Bulkley Junction, 1907, 1947
Bulkley Mine, 1907, 1947
Bull Hill, 1899, 1917
Bull Hill Junction, 1898, 1917, 1901 (fn)
Bunell, 1921
Burns Junction, 1881, 1889
Burro Bridge, 1887, 1888
Busk, 1893, 1899
Busk-Ivanhoe Tunnel, 1893, 1899

Cable Junction, 1896
Caddoa, 1940
Calcite, 1903, 1932
Calumet, 1881, 1923
Calumet No. 2 Mine, 1958, 1962
C&S Junction, 1958
C&W Quarry, 1898
Cameron, 1894, 1901, 1923
Cannon Junction, 1883
Cannon Mine, 1883, 1890
Canon City, 1874, 1879, 1880, 1887, 1888, 1890, 1899, 1915, 1947
Canon Mine, 1891
Capers, 1924, 1954

Capitol Mine, 1908, 1936 (spur)
Carbondale, 1888, 1892, 1893, 1941
Carbon Junction, 1905, 1923
Cardiff, 1887
Carpenter, 1890, 1925
Carr, 1908
Cascade, 1880
Castle Rock, 1880, 1881, 1889, 1902, 1924
Castleton, 1883, 1894, 1896, 1897, 1914, 1943, 1946
Cedar Creek, 1948, 1952
Center, 1913
Central City, 1878, 1931
Chama, New Mexico, 1880, 1881
Chambers, 1903, 1904
Chandler Junction, 1881, 1898, 1907, 1911, 1914, 1944
Chandler Mine, 1890, 1944
Chappell, 1888, 1892
Chatfield, 1939, 1942, 1950
Cheyenne Wells, 1870
Cheyenne, Wyoming, 1868, 1869, 1870, 1873, 1877, 1878, 1889, 1908, 1911
Chicosa Junction, 1888, 1937
Chromo, 1896, 1897, 1900
Chrysolite Junction, 1944
Church's Brick Yard, 1941
Cimarron, 1882
Cisco, Utah, 1890
CK&N Mine, 1904
Clayton Junction, 1921, 1943
Clayton Mine, 1921, 1943
Clear Creek Junction (C&S), 1949
Clear Creek Junction (D&NW-D&I), 1904, 1950
Clelland, 1880, 1887, 1947
Cleora, 1890, 1911
Clifton Belle Mine, 1898
Climax, 1937, 1943
Cloverly, 1910
Coal Basin, 1900
Coal Branch Junction, 1880
Coal Creek (D&RG), 1872
Coal Creek (DNW&P), 1903, 1904
Coal Creek Mine No. 2, 1880, 1924
Coal Junction, 1876, 1877

Coalmont, 1911, 1963
Coalton, 1936, 1947
Cox & Wood Mine, 1899
Cohen Spur, 1910, 1937
Cokedale, 1906, 1908, 1917
Colorado Central Junction, 1888
Colorado City, 1886, 1887, 1890, 1919
Colorado City Junction, 1901
Colorado Iron & Coal Company Mine, 1888
Colorado Springs, 1871, 1872, 1880, 1882, 1886, 1888, 1890, 1899, 1900, 1901, 1917, 1919, 1923, 1932, 1939, 1948
Columbine Mine, 1919, 1946
Como, 1879, 1880, 1881, 1883, 1937
Conchita Junction, 1888
Concrete Mine, 1887 (fn)
Connors, 1936
Corona, 1904, 1935
Cottonwood, 1901, 1926
Craig, 1913, 1963
Crane's Park, 1880, 1881
Crested Butte, 1881, 1882, 1893, 1907, 1929, 1947, 1954
Crestone, 1926
Crevasse, 1890
Cripple Creek, 1893, 1894, 1895, 1897, 1900, 1101, 1903, 1915, 1917, 1923, 1948
Cripple Creek Sampler, 1899, 1917
Crown Mine Spur, 1932, 1936
Cuatro, 1903, 1913
Cuatro Junction, 1906, 1913
Cuatro Mine, 1903
Cuchara Junction, 1876, 1887, 1888, 1889, 1890, 1911, 1917, 1932, 1937
Cucharus, 1876
Culbertson, 1898, 1919
Culbertson Mill, 1898, 1919
Curtis Coal Mine (AT&SF), 1899, 1916
Curtis Mine (D&SL), 1915, 1923
Cut-Off Junction, 1874

D&I Junction, 1908, 1922
D&RG Junction, 1907, 1944
Dante Mine, 1923
Danville Coal Mine, 1902, 1916
Delagua, 1899, 1904, 1952
Del Norte, 1881, 1901, 1902
Delta, 1882, 1902, 1906
Dent, 1911
Denver, 1868, 1870, 1871,
    1895, 1897, 1900, 1901,
    1874, 1878, 1879, 1881,
    1882, 1884, 1885, 1886,
    1887, 1888, 1889, 1890,
    1891, 1895, 1900, 1902,
    1903, 1905, 1908, 1909,
    1911, 1913, 1915, 1916,
    1921, 1934, 1938, 1941,
    1942, 1950, 1952, 1953
Denver Federal Center (Spur),
    1941
Denver Junction, 1880
Denver Stockyards, 1913
Denver Union Terminal, 1878,
    1909
Denver University, 1886
Dew Drop Tunnel, 1899, 1919
Dexter Mine, 1904, 1923
Diamond, 1907
Dick, 1870, 1871
Dickey, 1883, 1937
Dillon, 1882, 1883, 1923
Divide, 1893, 1919, 1947
Dixon, 1906, 1925 (Spur),
    1926 (spur)
Dolores, 1891, 1922
Dotsero, 1934
Douglas, 1881, 1902
Dow Chemical Company, 1952
Dragon, Utah, 1904
Dry Creek, 1878
Duke, 1920, 1939
DuPont Junction, 1909, 1937
DuPont Powder Plant, 1908
DuPont Powder Works, 1909,
    1937
Durango, 1881, 1890, 1891,
    1895, 1899, 1901, 1905,
    1920, 1923, 1942, 1952
Dyer Station, 1901, 1902, 1903

Eagle Junction, 1902
Eagle Mine, 1939
Eagle Sampler, 1902
Eaton, 1905, 1907
Echley, 1881, 1882

Economic Mill, 1902, 1908
Economic Junction, 1902
    (spur)
Edith, 1895, 1896, 1901, 1902,
    1913, 1914
Eilers, 1880, 1888, 1890, 1902,
    1925, 1940
Eldora, 1904, 1919
Eldorado Springs, 1907, 1908,
    1926
Electric Mine, 1907
Elizabeth, 1881, 1882
Elk Creek Mine, 1917, 1921
Elm, 1917
El Moro, 1876
El Moro Mines, 1877
El Paso Ore Reduction
    Company Plant
El Paso Mine, 1902, 1904,
    1917, 1948
Elsmere, 1888, 1896, 1941,
    1961
Energy, 1962
Engleville, 1877, 1889, 1929
Engleville Junction, 1887,
    1889, 1929
Englewood, 1889, 1907, 1926
Enterprise Mine, 1892, 1900
Erie, 1871, 1873, 1881, 1889,
    1903, 1910, 1919, 1946
Espanola, New Mexico, 1880
Eureka, 1896, 1904, 1936,
    1942
Eureka Mine, 1917, 1940
Evans, 1869, 1870, 1881
Evergreen Cemetery (Colo.
    Spgs), 1890 (fn)
Eversman, 1907, 1912
Excelsior Mine, 1892, 1896

Fairplay, 1881
Fairview, 1903, 1905
Falcon, 1917, 1936
Farmington, New Mexico, 1905
Fenton, 1917, 1931
Firestone, 1910
Firestone Junction, 1921, 1942
Firestone Mine, 1921, 1942
Fitzsimons Army Hospital,
    1921
Flaugh, 1904, 1911
Florence, 1872, 1881, 1887,
    1888, 1894, 1899, 1905,
    1907, 1911, 1914, 1915,
    1924

Floresta, 1893, 1929
Floresta Junction, 1893
Floyd Hill, 1873, 1877
Forbes, 1899, 1900, 1904, 1928, 1948
Forbes Junction, 1888, 1895, 1897, 1937
Forbes Mine, 1888, 1897, 1899, 1928
Forks Creek, 1872, 1873, 1941
Fort Collins, 1877, 1881, 1882, 1889, 1898, 1902, 1903, 1906, 1911, 1924, 1926
Fort Logan, 1889, 1962
Fort Morgan, 1882
Fort St. Vrain, 1909, 1910
Fort Worth, Texas, 1881, 1888, 1895
Fountain, 1882, 1898
Four Mile Canon, 1882, 1883
Fox Mine, 1879, 1885, 1901, 1924
Fox Patterson Mine, 1901
Franceville, 1882, 1898
Franceville Junction, 1882, 1898
Franklin Junction (CE), 1905, 1915
Franklin Junction (RGS), 1901, 1926
Fremont Junction, 1893, 1942
Fremont Mine, 1893, 1898, 1914, 1942
Fremont Pass, 1880
Frontenac Mine, 1888, 1905
Fruita, 1910, 1935

Galeton, 1943
Garfield Quarry, 1878
Garland City, 1877, 1878
Garland Junction, 1958
Garos, 1881, 1910, 1937
Gato, 1962
Georgetown, 1877, 1884
Georgetown Loop, 1884
Gillette, 1894
Gladstone, 1899, 1937
Gladstone Mine, 1896, 1906
Gladwin, 1903
Glencoe, 1884, 1898
Glenwood Springs, 1886, 1887, 1888, 1889
Globeville, 1908, 1921
Golden, 1868, 1870, 1872, 1878, 1879, 1884, 1887
(fn), 1890, 1891, 1894, 1895, 1896, 1910, 1941, 1942, 1950, 1953
Golden Junction, 1872, 1873, 1878, 1879
Goldfield, 1896, 1897, 1898, 1899, 1902, 1903
Gold Sovereign Mine, 1904, 1923
Goodland, Kansas, 1888
Graham Park Junction, 1900, 1913, 1917, 1941
Granada, 1873, 1875
Granby, 1905, 1907, 1917
Grand Junction, 1882, 1889, 1890, 1899, 1904, 1906, 1909, 1910, 1922, 1925, 1935
Graneros, 1917, 1924
Grant Junction, 1910, 1947
Grant Mine, 1907, 1910
Grape Creek Canon, 1880
Grape Creek Junction, 1880, 1889
Grassy, 1894
Gray Creek, 1892, 1925 (branch)
Graymont, 1884, 1898
Great Western Sugar Factory (Loveland), 1901
Greeley, 1872 (fn), 1873, 1874, 1881, 1882, 1909, 1910, 1917
Greeley Junction, 1910
Green Mountain Mine, 1905, 1936
Gulf Junction, 1882, 1890, 1917
Gunnison, 1881, 1882, 1883, 1889, 1911, 1948, 1954

Hagerman Tunnel, 1887, 1893, 1899
Hancock, 1881, 1910, 1924
Harris, 1916
Hastings, 1889, 1890, 1899, 1904
Hasty, 1907, 1908
Hathaway, 1917
Hathaway Quarry, 1880, 1924
Hawley, 1907, 1966
Hayden, 1963
Hazard, Wyoming, 1877
Hebron, 1964
Hecla Junction, 1881, 1923

Henry Adney Mine, 1904, 1917
Hesperus, 1892, 1906
Hesperus Mine, 1892
Hezron Junction, 1903, 1932
Hezron, 1903, 1932
Hidden Treasure Mill, 1887
High Line Crossing No. 1, 1903
High Line Crossing No. 2, 1903
Hill Top Junction, 1896, 1937
Hitchens, 1962
Holly, 1906, 1908
Holyoke, 1887
Hooper, 1930, 1950, 1951, 1958
Hoosier Pass, 1901, 1902, 1905, 1923
Horace, Kansas, 1887
Hot Springs, 1893, 1898
Hot Springs Mines, 1881
Hot Sulphur Springs, 1905, 1906
Howard, 1903, 1932
Howard's Quarry, 1903
Howardsville, 1905, 1936
Howes Springs, 1897, 1898
Hughes, 1870
Hungerford, 1910
Ibex, 1898, 1917, 1944
Ibex Junction, 1898
Idaho Springs, 1939, 1941
Ideal Mine, 1909, 1935 (spur)
Idealite Company Plant, 1961
Iliff, 1881
Imperial Mine, 1927
Independence, 1898, 1901, 1903
Independence Mill, 1930
Independence Mine, 1895
Ingleside Quarry, 1906, 1929, 1931
International Fuel Company, 1916
Ironton, 1888, 1889, 1892, 1894
Irvington, 1892, 1904, 1906, 1908, 1951
Isabella Mine, 1898, 1899
Ivanhoe, 1893, 1899

Jansen, 1901, 1906, 1908, 1938
Jarosa, 1910, 1957
Jersey Junction, 1870, 1874
Jewell Mine, 1911
Jewell-Creston Mine, 1911, 1943

Jewell Park, 1883
Joe Dandy Mine, 1903
Johnson, 1908
Johnstown, 1902, 1904, 1905, 1919
Joker Tunnel, 1894 (fn), 1906, 1922
Julesburg, 1867, 1872, 1873, 1880, 1881

Kansas City, Missouri, 1870, 1887
Kansas Pacific Junction, 1870
Kebler No. 2 Mine, 1907, 1923, 1953, 1958
Kebler Pass, 1893
Keenesburg, 1925
Keesee, 1906, 1907
Kenosha Pass, 1879
Kenwood, 1887, 1947
Keystone, 1883, 1912, 1937
King Mine, 1880, 1884 (spur), 1899 (spur)
Kit Carson, 1870, 1873, 1877, 1906 (fn)
Kokomo, 1880, 1881, 1883, 1884, 1895, 1937
Kornman, 1906
Kremmling, 1906, 1907
Kubler Mine, 1896, 1943

La Bella Junction, 1920
Labran, 1872, 1874
Lafayette, 1888, 1891, 1893, 1896, 1905, 1906, 1951
La Junta, 1875, 1878, 1906 (fn)
Lake City, 1889, 1933
Lake Junction, 1889, 1933
Lakeside, 1901, 1904, 1950
Lamar, 1906, 1908
La Plata Junction, 1890, 1900
La Plata County Fair Grounds, 1904
La Plata Mine, 1890, 1900
Laramie, Wyoming, 1911
Larimer, 1924
La Salle, 1881
La Salle Junction, 1910, 1911
Las Animas, 1873, 1907, 1908, 1937
Las Animas Junction, 1937, 1940
Lascar, 1917, 1924, 1932
Last Dollar Mine, 1917, 1923

La Veta, 1876, 1877, 1890, 1899, 1907
La Veta Pass, 1899
Lay's Junction, 1906, 1908
Leadville, 1880, 1881, 1884, 1887, 1888, 1890, 1898, 1906, 1913, 1917, 1919, 1923, 1937, 1940, 1943, 1944
Leadville Junction, 1887, 1890, 1940
Leavick, 1896, 1937
Lechner Mine, 1880, 1883
Left Hand Canon, 1881
Lehigh Junction, 1883, 1890
Lehigh Mine (D&RG), 1883, 1890
Lehigh Mine (UP), 1903, 1910
Leyden, 1903
Leyden Gulch, 1878
Leyden Junction, 1902, 1903
Leyden Mines, 1901, 1903, 1950
Liberty, 1905, 1906
Lillie Junction (GC), 1898, 1901 (fn)
Lillie Junction (CS&CCD), 1901
Lillie Mine, 1898
Limon, 1888
Lincoln Mine, 1949
Little Book Cliff Mines, 1890
Littleton, 1907, 1908, 1926
L.M.B. Junction, 1898, 1937
Loma Junction, 1888, 1890, 1966
London Junction, 1882, 1900
London Mine, 1882, 1900
Longmont, 1872 (fn), 1873, 1874, 1877, 1881, 1885, 1889, 1906, 1919,
Longmont Sugar Factory (fn), 1907
Longsdale, 1906, 1950
Long's Junction, 1888, 1906, 1908, 1924, 1938, 1940
Lord's, 1905
Los Angeles Station, 1904
Louisville, 1888, 1892, 1898 (fn), 1904, 1905, 1907, 1908, 1921, 1927, 1951
Louisville Junction, 1896, 1908, 1922, 1926
Louviers, 1908

Loveland, 1887, 1901, 1902, 1907
Lowery Quarry, 1904, 1914 (spur)
Ludlow, 1888, 1889, 1890, 1892, 1938, 1954, 1955
Lumberton, New Mexico, 1895, 1911, 1914
Lyons, 1885, 1887, 1889

Mack, 1904, 1939
Macune, 1880, 1884, 1908, 1910
Madge Quarry, 1881, 1902
Maitland, 1896, 1904
Majestic Mine, 1900, 1928
Malaby's Spur, 1909
Maloy, 1920, 1939
Malta, 1880, 1890, 1925
Manitou, 1880, 1888, 1890, 1893, 1932, 1939
Manitou Junction, 1882, 1896, 1917
Marble, 1906, 1910, 1914, 1921
Maroon Creek, 1887, 1888
Marshall, 1878, 1879, 1886, 1901, 1907, 1908, 1924, 1932
Marshall Coal Banks, 1877, 1878
Marshall Junction, 1886, 1888, 1908
Marshall Pass, 1881
Martinsen, 1888, 1890
Mary McKinney Mine, 1917, 1948
Matchless Mine, 1904, 1928
Mathews, 1965
May Day, 1906
May Day Mine, 1906, 1926 (branch)
Mayne, 1937
Mayne Junction, 1941
Maysville, 1881
May Valley, 1906
Mears Junction, 1881, 1950
Midland, 1893, 1894
Midway, 1897, 1899, 1902, 1905, 1915, 1917
Military Junction, 1889, 1962, 1964
Milliken, 1904, 1910, 1947, 1957

305

Milner, 1915, 1917, 1921, 1948
Mining Exposition Building, 1882, 1883
Minnequa, 1881, 1887, 1890, 1902, 1911, 1917
Minnequa Junction, 1902, 1904, 1917
Mitchell, 1881
Moffat, 1901, 1926
Moffat Station (Denver), 1909
Moffat Tunnel, 1928, 1935
Monarch (D&RG), 1883, 1956
Monarch (RM), 1907, 1917
Monarch Mine, 1908, 1922
Monson, 1941, 1949
Monte Vista, 1900, 1901, 1913
Montrose, 1882, 1897, 1906, 1948, 1952, 1953
Moon Anchor Station, 1903
Morningside, 1941, 1953
Morrison, 1874, 1878, 1933
Mortimer, 1899
Moyer, 1883
Moyer Mine, 1888
Mt. Harris, 1916, 1951
Mt. Rosa Wye (fn), 1900
Muldoon, 1881, 1892
Munroe Mine, 1917, 1940
Murphy Coal Mine, 1872, 1878, 1880
Mustang, 1924, 1954
McClelland, 1906, 1918
McClintock, 1957, 1959
McFerran Mine, 1888, 1896
McGregor Mine, 1915, 1947
McKissick, 1908
McNally Mine, 1907
McNeal Mine, 1915, 1947
McPhee, 1924, 1948

Nathrop, 1880, 1884, 1885, 1904
National, 1939
Nevada Gulch, 1887, 1888
Nevadaville, 1887
Navajo River, 1895, 1896, 1898
New Baker Mine, 1904
New Castle, 1888, 1890, 1919
New Centennial Mine, 1936, 1948
Newcomb, 1928, 1935
Newdale, 1907, 1966
New Hungerford, 1910

New Market, 1898, 1919
New Mitchell Mine, 1893, 1927 (spur)
New Pacific Junction, 1927, 1937
New Pacific Mine, 1927, 1937
New York Mill, 1887
Night Hawk, 1902, 1915
No. 4 Jct., 1896, 1902, 1903
Nob Hill, 1890 (fn)
Noland, 1887, 1915, 1918
North Creede, 1891, 1902
North Junction, 1937
North Moyer, 1941
Northern Colorado Power Company, 1907

Oak Creek Junction, 1881, 1905
Oak Creek Mines, 1905
Oakdale Junction, 1935
O'Brian's Quarry, 1882, 1902, 1917
Officer Junction, 1907, 1919
Ogden, Utah, 1890
Ojo, 1912, 1938
Old Baldwin Mine, 1883, 1894
Old Gold Mine, 1904
Old Line Junction, 1887, 1890
Old Rouse, 1888, 1904
Oliver Mine, 1930
Omaha, Nebraska, 1881
Orcutt, 1926, 1946
Orestod, 1934
Orient, 1881, 1942
Oro Junction, 1883, 1902, 1963
Oro Junta, 1899, 1915
Osage Coal Company, 1949, 1962
Otis Mine, 1891
Ouray, 1887, 1950, 1952
Ouray Junction, 1887, 1952
Overland Junction, 1902, 1943
Overland Park, 1883, 1902, 1943

Pagosa Springs, 1900, 1904, 1935
Pagosa Junction, 1899, 1935
Pando, 1890
Pandora, 1891, 1952
Paramount Mine, 1928
Parkdale Junction, 1908
Parkdale Mine, 1906, 1917 (spur)
Parlin, 1911, 1934

Pawnee, 1900
Paymaster Mine, 1894, 1906
Pease Kansas Mine, 1898
Pels, New Mexico, 1908
Pennsyvlania (Penn) Gulch, 1883, 1894
Pennsylvania Mill, 1898, 1919
Penrose, 1908, 1919
Perrins, 1901, 1926
Peterson Field, 1941, 1961
Pictou, 1888, 1896, 1927
Piedmont, 1904, 1906
Piedmont Mine, 1902, 1930
Pikes Peak, 1890
Pisgah Junction, 1903
Placer (D&RG), 1881, 1899
Placer (DSP&P), 1883
Placita, 1899, 1906, 1941
Pluto Mine, 1906
Point Sublime, 1900
Poncha Junction, 1880, 1881, 1954
Poncha Pass, 1881
Porter Coal Mines, 1890, 1891
Portland, 1927, 1947
Portland Junction, 1902, 1923
Portland Mill, 1930, 1948
Portland Mine(s), 1894, 1895, 1901, 1923 (fn)
Power Plant (Hayden), 1963
Price, 1898, 1902
Primero, 1901
Primero Junction, 1901, 1933
Primrose Mine, 1899, 1927
Pritchett, 1926
Promontory, Utah, 1870 (fn)
Prospect, 1949
Prospect Lake, 1890 (fn)
Prowers, 1940
Pryer, 1941
Pueblo, 1872, 1873, 1876, 1880, 1881, 1882, 1887, 1888, 1890, 1901, 1902, 1907, 1909, 1910, 1911, 1917, 1924, 1927, 1957
Pullman, 1870, 1942
Purcell, 1910, 1943
Puritan, 1908
Puritan Mine, 1908, 1939

Quartz, 1910, 1911, 1934

Ralston, 1884, 1888, 1890, 1898
Rapson Mine (C&S), 1907, 1962

Rapson No. 2 Mine (CRI&P), 1901, 1916
Raton Pass, 1876, 1878
Raven Hill Station, 1903
Red Cliff, 1881, 1882
Red Rock, 1892
Redstone 1898, 1899, 1900, 1906
Reliance Junction, 1912, 1938
Remington Arms Plant, 1941 (spur)
Rex, 1929
Rico, 1891, 1892, 1900
Ridgway, 1890, 1891, 1952, 1953
Ridgway Junction, 1890
Rifle, 1889, 1900
Rifle Creek, 1889, 1890
Ripple, 1926, 1946
Rock Creek, 1882, 1886, 1887
Rockvale, 1880, 1947
Rockwood, 1881, 1882
Rocky, 1952
Rocky Flats, 1952, 1961
Rocky Ford, 1875, 1876, 1906, 1907, 1908, 1917, 1931
Rocky Mountain Arsenal, 1942
Roggen, 1925
Rollins Pass, 1904, 1928, 1935
Roswell, 1888, 1901, 1890 (fn)
Rouse, 1888, 1949
Rouse Coal Mines, 1888
Rouse Junction, 1888, 1937
Routt-Pinnacle Mine, 1916, 1925
Roydale, 1942
Royal Gorge, 1879, 1880
Ruby Quarry, 1910, 1953 (spur)
Rugby, 1899, 1962
Rugby (Torrid) Mine, 1927, 1950
Russell, 1881

Sable, 1921
Salida, 1880, 1881, 1890, 1911, 1925, 1956
Salt Lake City, Utah, 1882, 1903, 1934
Sand Creek Junction, 1909
Sandown Junction, 1950
San Juan Smelter, 1881, 1942
Santa Clara, 1888
Santa Clara Junction, 1888, 1904

307

Santa Fe Quarry, 1889, 1912
Sapinero, 1948, 1954
Satanta, Kansas, 1926
Schwanders, 1884, 1908
Scranton, 1886, 1915
Sedalia, 1883
Semper, 1908, 1926, 1927
Sewell, 1892
Shamrock Junction, 1915, 1939
Shamrock Mine, 1915
Sheehan, 1925
Shelbina, 1898
Shelton Junction, 1906, 1917 (fn), 1931
Sheridan Junction, 1874, 1933, 1938, 1939, 1950
Sidney Tunnel, 1905, 1906
Silica, 1909, 1941
Silver Belle Mine, 1894 (fn)
Silver Plume, 1884, 1898, 1903, 1905, 1918, 1939
Silverton, 1882, 1887, 1893, 1896, 1899, 1922, 1937, 1942
Silverton Smelter, 1882
Silverton Smelter Junction, 1882
Simpson Mine, 1891, 1896
Simms Street, 1953
Sloan, 1925
Snowden, 1888, 1906
Soda Lakes, 1878
Somerset, 1902, 1906, 1930
Sonora, 1917, 1924
Sonora Junction, 1917, 1924
Sopris, 1902, 1904, 1906, 1930, 1938, 1940
Sopris Junction, 1888
Sopris Mine, 1888, 1940 (spur)
South Arkansas, 1880
South Denver, 1936
South Denver Junction, 1887
South Fork, 1881, 1883
South Junction, 1937
South Platte, 1902, 1916, 1937, 1942
South Pueblo, 1872
Southern Junction, 1902, 1911
Southwestern Mine, 1903
Springfield, 1926, 1937
Spring Gulch, 1887
Standard Mine, 1905, 1939 (spur)
Starkville, 1904, 1923
State Mine, 1918, 1943

State Mine Junction, 1918, 1927, 1943
Steamboat Springs, 1908, 1913, 1916, 1962
St. Elmo, 1880, 1881
Sterling, 1887, 1890
Sterling Mine, 1921, 1965 (spur)
Sterling Mine Junction, 1921
St. Louis, Missouri, 1887
Stockyard Junction, 1913
Stone City, 1912, 1957
Stout, 1881
St. Peters Dome, 1900 (fn)
Strasburg, 1870
Stratton Park, 1890 (fn)
Straub, 1887
Strauss Quarry, 1910, 1914
Strong, 1904, 1907
Strong Junction, 1920
St. Vrain Canon, 1881
St. Vrains, 1907, 1909, 1939, 1940, 1949, 1964
Sugar Factory (Grand Junction), 1899, 1922
Sugar Junction, 1913
Summit, 1900, 1901, 1923, (fn)
Sunlight Mine, 1887
Sunnyside Mine No. 1, 1906
Sunnyside Mine No. 2, 1906, 1907, 1912, 1922
Sunset, 1883, 1894, 1898, 1904, 1919
Superior, 1885, 1886, 1932, 1936, 1947
Swink, 1875, 1906, 1907

Tampa, 1925
Taylor, 1920, 1930
Telluride, 1890
Tennessee Pass, 1881, 1890
Tercio, 1902, 1903, 1906, 1952
Texas Creek, 1879, 1880, 1900, 1937
Thompson Creek, 1888, 1892
Thompson Mine (A&W;CR), 1888, 1892
Thompson Mine (DT&FW; C&W), 1888, 1940 (spur)
Thor Mine, 1904, 1948
Timpas Creek, 1875, 1877
Tindale, 1894, 1896

Tolland, 1904
Toller Mine, 1911, 1915
Torrid (Rugby) Mine, 1927, 1950
Tower, 1887, 1889, 1890, 1915, 1918
Tower Junction, 1887, 1889, 1890, 1918
Trinchera Mine, 1881, 1899
Trinidad, 1873, 1876, 1878, 1887, 1888, 1889, 1892, 1893, 1895, 1901, 1904, 1906, 1923, 1937, 1938
Trinidad Rolling Mill, 1893, 1895
Tropic Junction, 1907, 1935
Tropic Mine, 1907, 1935
Trout Creek, 1884, 1908
Trout Creek Pass, 1879, 1880, 1887
Tucker Mine, 1907
Turkey Creek, 1911, 1912
Two Buttes Creek, 1937 (fn)

Union, 1880, 1881, 1900
Union Station (Denver), 1921
Utah Junction, 1889, 1903, 1905, 1908, 1909, 1913, 1917, 1921, 1926
Ute Junction, 1892, 1908, 1909
Ute Mine, 1892, 1908

Vance Junction, 1890, 1891, 1952
Vasquez, 1928, 1935
Vasquez, New Mexico, 1890
Vaughn Mine, 1904
Vesta Junction, 1899, 1915
Veta Pass, 1877, 1881, 1899
Victor, 1894, 1895, 1896, 1897, 1900, 1901, 1902, 1903, 1915, 1917, 1920, 1923
Victor Junction, 1895, 1903, 1948
Vidler Tunnel, 1906
Villa Grove, 1881, 1890, 1942
Vindicator Junction, 1901, 1923
Vindicator Mine, 1917
Vista Grande, 1899, 1915, 1917
Vulcan Mine, 1905

Wadge Coal Mine, 1916
Wagon Creek Junction, 1899

Wagon Wheel Gap, 1883, 1891
Walden, 1911
Waldheim Mine, 1893, 1896
Waldorf, 1906
Wallstreet, 1898
Walsenburg, 1888, 1892, 1893, 1895, 1907, 1911, 1917, 1924, 1937
Walsenburg Junction, 1895, 1911
Wann Brick Yard, 1917
Ward, 1898, 1899, 1919
Washington Mine, 1940
Watertown, 1902, 1909, 1937, 1941
Watson, Utah, 1904, 1939
Wattenberg, 1919, 1947
Waveland, 1907, 1908
Waverly, 1905, 1954
Webb, 1906, 1908, 1922
Webster, 1878, 1879
Weir, 1872 (fn)
Wellington, 1903, 1905, 1906, 1911, 1954
Welty, 1903
Westcliffe, 1881, 1889, 1900, 1901, 1937
West Las Animas, 1873, 1875
Westminster, 1911
Westminster University, 1911, 1916
Weston, 1901, 1902, 1952
Wheeler, 1881, 1882
Wilds, 1904, 1926, 1937
Wiley, 1906
Wilfley's Mill, 1895, 1937
Wilson Junction, 1906, 1908
Windsor, 1905, 1907
Wolftone Junction, 1913, 1941
Wolftone Mine, 1900, 1941
Wyman, 1910

Yankee Girl Mine, 1894
Yarmony, 1907, 1908
Yoxall, 1964

Zink Junction, 1902, 1937
Zuni, 1949, 1958